The Gospel Interpreting Cultural Traditions for Reconciliation

A Theological Reflection on *Mbuki* Blood Pact in Central African Republic

Plaisance Rivoli M'bara

ACADEMIC

© 2025 Plaisance Rivoli M'bara

Published 2025 by Langham Academic
An imprint of Langham Publishing
www.langhampublishing.org

Langham Publishing and its imprints are a ministry of Langham Partnership

Langham Partnership
PO Box 296, Carlisle, Cumbria, CA3 9WZ, UK
www.langham.org

ISBNs:
978-1-78641-049-8 Print
978-1-78641-263-8 ePub
978-1-78641-264-5 PDF
DOI: https://doi.org/10.69811/9781786410498

Plaisance Rivoli M'bara has asserted his right under the Copyright, Designs and Patents Act, 1988 to be identified as the Author of this work.

All rights reserved. No part of this publication may be reproduced, stored in a retrieval system or transmitted, in any form or by any means, electronic, mechanical, photocopying, recording or otherwise, without the prior written permission of the publisher or the Copyright Licensing Agency.

Requests to reuse content from Langham Publishing are processed through PLSclear. Please visit www.plsclear.com to complete your request.

Scriptures taken from the Sango Bible. Copyright © 2010 The Bible Society in Central African Republic.

Scripture quotations marked (NIV) are taken from the Holy Bible, New International Version®, NIV®. Copyright © 1973, 1978, 1984, 2011 by Biblica, Inc.™ Used by permission of Zondervan.

British Library Cataloguing-in-Publication Data
A catalogue record for this book is available from the British Library

ISBN: 978-1-78641-049-8

Cover & Book Design: projectluz.com

Langham Partnership actively supports theological dialogue and an author's right to publish but does not necessarily endorse the views and opinions set forth here or in works referenced within this publication, nor can we guarantee technical and grammatical correctness. Langham Partnership does not accept any responsibility or liability to persons or property as a consequence of the reading, use or interpretation of its published content.

A creative part of the process of Christian conversion is the use of indigenous ideas that have been re-examined in the light of the gospel of Jesus Christ as fundamentally mediated by the Bible. Dr. M'bara has demonstrated how the traditional idea of *Mbuki* (or *Mbèlé*), understood through the lens of Scripture, contributes to the national reconciliation narrative in the Central African Republic. A bold effort that should inspire other projects.

Rudolf K. Gaisie, PhD
Senior Research Fellow,
Akrofi-Christaller Institute of Theology, Mission and Culture, Akropong, Ghana

Peace and reconciliation in the Central African Republic occupy an important place in discussions around the world. What was missing is this precious theological contribution from Dr. Plaisance Rivoli M'bara. The study is based on *Mbuki*, the blood pact that a significant portion of the Central African community seems to ignore. For him, in its new form, *Mbuki* brings lasting peace, reconciliation, unity, cohesion, and prosperity to a country undermined by deadly conflicts.

This book, far from aiming at the Christianization of culture, helps scholars to understand how to interpret culture through the gospel. I recommend it to scholars in the field of peace and reconciliation in Africa, and especially to those who focus on African theology in their quest to interpret culture in the light of the gospel. The absence of this precious resource in African theological libraries would represent an enormous lack.

William Mbuluku, PhD
Lecturer in New Testament,
Faculté de Théologie Evangélique de Bangui, Yaoundé, Cameroon

Contents

Chapter 1 1
   Understanding the CAR Conflict, Key Problem, and Mbuki *Practice of Reconciliation*
      1. Introduction 1
      2. Key Problem 5
      3. Intellectual Frameworks 7
      4. Literary Sources on *Mbuki* and Field Study 13
      5. Conclusion 24

Chapter 2 25
   Fambul Tok: *An Example of a Cultural Tradition for Reconciliation in Sierra Leone*
      1. Introduction 25
      2. *Fambul Tok* and the Reconciliation Ritual 30
      3. The Results of the *Fambul Tok* Ritual 38
      4. Conclusion 39

Chapter 3 41
   Understanding the Social, Political, Economic, and Religious Contexts of CAR
      1. Introduction 41
      2. Overview of CAR 41
      3. Social Organization of CAR 44
      4. Economic Situation 45
      5. Religious Worldview 47
      6. Conclusion 52

Chapter 4 53
   Overview of Institutionalized Violence in CAR
      1. Introduction 53
      2. Insurgencies in the Colonial Period 53
      3. Background to the Conflict 57
      4. Conclusion 59

Chapter 5 61
   Parties Involved in the 2013 Armed Conflict
      1. Introduction 61
      2. The Séléka 62

    3. The Anti-Balaka 65
    4. The Armed Forces 68
    5. Conclusion 70

Chapter 6 71
Possible Factors Underpinning the Conflict
    1. Introduction 71
    2. Socio-Ethnic Cleavages 72
    3. Economic Interests 72
    4. Subregional Armed Conflicts 76
    5. Theories of Interreligious Conflict 77
    6. Conclusion 79

Chapter 7 81
Peace and Reconciliation Processes and Actors
    1. Introduction 81
    2. The Interfaith Platform 81
    3. Peacekeeping Missions 83
    4. The Non-Governmental Organizations (NGOs) 86
    5. The Sidelining of Indigenous Leaders 87
    6. Conclusion 90

Chapter 8 91
The Political Settlements of the Conflict
    1. Introduction 91
    2. Peace Agreements 91
    3. The Prospect of Transitional Justice 94
    4. Assessing Peacebuilding Policies 96
    5. Conclusion 97

Chapter 9 99
The Mbuki *Blood Pact for Reconciliation*
    1. Introduction 99
    2. Conceptual Understanding of *Mbuki* 100
    3. Significance of *Mbuki* 109
        3.1 *Mbuki*: An Alternative to Social Ties 110
        3.2 *Mbuki* for Mutual Assistance 114
        3.3 *Mbuki* for Socio-Economic Purposes 117
    4. Widespread Practice of *Mbuki* in Traditional Society 119
    5. *Mbuki* and the Culture of Peace 120
    6. The Obligations of *Mbuki* 126
    7. Conclusion 129

Chapter 10 131
   Scripture Interpretation and Theology of Reconciliation in
   Light of Mbuki
      1. Introduction 131
      2. Scripture Interpretation 132
      3. Theology of Reconciliation in Light of *Mbuki*............................135
          3.1 Reconciliation Starts with Forgiveness 137
          3.2 Reconciliation: A Mission for CAR Churches........................142
          3.3 The Imperative of Social Justice..153
          3.4 Dealing With Evil Structures in Conflict 164
          3.5 Embracing Victims of Trauma..173
      4. Conclusion..178

Chapter 11 181
   Conclusion and Recommendations
      1. Introduction 181
      2. Significance of the Study..185
      3. Rationale for Key Recommendations 185
          3.1 Recommendations to the Government 186
          3.2 Recommendations to Traditional Leaders 188
          3.3 Recommendations to Armed Groups.....................................189
          3.4 Recommendations to Christians 190
          3.5 Recommendations to CAR Muslims 192
      4. Implications for Christian Mission and Scholarship 193
      5. Conclusion..195

Appendix 1 197
   Interview Questions

Appendix 2 211
   Focus Group Discussions

Bibliography...213

CHAPTER 1

Understanding the CAR Conflict, Key Problem, and *Mbuki* Practice of Reconciliation

1. Introduction

Over the past decades, Central African Republic (CAR) has experienced multiple violent conflicts, as has been the case in some of Africa's French-speaking countries. The 2013 coup led by predominantly Muslim rebels, known as "the Séléka conflict," which brought to power Michel Djotodia, the first Muslim President was "accompanied by widespread community-level violence."[1] Due to the serious consequences of the crisis, national authorities and the international community continue to seek ways to end the conflict and achieve peace. The issue of peace and reconciliation in sub-Saharan Africa in general, and in French-speaking Africa in particular, has become a global concern. This concern engages scholars in analysing the dynamics of conflicts by focusing on the structural causes that sustain them, while others are interested in the processes of resolution. Consequently, each study develops specific perspectives for scholarly analysis and approaches to peacebuilding.

---

1. Brown and Zahar, "Social Cohesion as Peacebuilding," 10–24.

In general, people living in conflict and post-conflict contexts are more or less committed to peacebuilding and reconciliation.² According to Michael James Brown and Marie-Joëlle Zahar, in CAR, social cohesion is the main approach to peacebuilding but Centrafricans³ do not apply the ideal of social cohesion to building peace.⁴ To ascertain the relevance of traditional concepts and initiatives for peace, John S. Mbiti points out that, "traditional concepts could shed light on understanding and implementing peace in our times."⁵ To do so, people in some African countries use traditional initiatives to address violence and conflicts in their context as effective tools to deal with truth, justice, forgiveness, reconciliation, and peace. This was the case of *Ubuntu* in South Africa, *Gacaca* in Rwanda, *Mato Oput* in Uganda, and *Palava Hut* in Liberia, to mention but a few.⁶ Phil Clark argues that, as an indigenous process, the Rwandan *Gacaca* "represents a holistic approach to transitional justice, aiming to rebuild individual and communal lives and to contribute to reconstruction in both the short and long term."⁷ Michael Battle, analysing the theology of *Ubuntu*, points out that a traditional process of reconciliation can help "to study possibilities for transferring this process to other areas of conflict."⁸ This also means discovering the possibilities for dealing with reconciliation in CAR and beyond.

Academics and non-academics as well as media have interpreted the CAR situation in various ways: a "phantom state,"⁹ a "state of crises"¹⁰ and a state that lacks viability¹¹, a "religious war,"¹² or a country "on the verge of

---

2. In her 2006 doctoral dissertation on the comparison of reconciliation paradigms that the Christian tradition and African tradition use as contribution to achieve "social reconciliation" in the South African context, Claudia Nolte-Schamm stressed that, "Reconciliation is a word that is widely used in South Africa." See Nolte-Schamm, "A Comparison Between Christian," 8.

3. I borrow the term "Centrafrican" from Jacqueline Woodfork to designate the population of CAR, different from the Central Africans that represent the populations of the sub-region of Central Africa. See Woodfork, *Culture and Customs*, 1.

4. Brown and Zahar, "Social Cohesion as Peacebuilding," 10.
5. John S. Mbiti, "Relating Peace in African Religion," 110.
6. United Nations, *Rapport du Projet Mapping*, 310.
7. Clark, *The Gacaca Courts*, 32.
8. Battle, "A Theology of Community," 181.
9. International Crisis Group, "Central African Republic," 1–40.
10. Nash, "Political Unsettlement and Continuing."
11. Mehler, "Rebels and Parties: The Impact," 115–139.
12. Ochab, "The Religious War."

genocide."[13] Their arguments stemmed from their perception of the political crisis, which regional and international organisations have tried in vain to settle.[14] Since the 1990s, socio-political crises have destroyed the country's structures, caused violence against people and loss of property. The parties have organized peace conferences at which they have signed various peace agreements. At the *Accord Politique de Paix et de Réconciliation* (APPR-RCA), a peace talk held in Khartoum in February 2019, representatives of the fourteen rebel groups and those of the government signed another peace deal under the auspices of the head of the African Union Peace Commission (AUPC) and the United Nations (UN).

In addition to the International Criminal Court (ICC) operating in the country and a Special Criminal Court (SCC), which was decided at the 2015 Forum National de Bangui (FNB), the Truth, Justice, Reparation and Repatriation Commission (in French, CVJRR) was set up to examine the extent to which atrocities were committed. Today, the expectations of Centrafricans for justice are high. They cannot achieve reconciliation without truth, justice, forgiveness, and reparation for the atrocities that have left millions of victims, orphans, widows, and humanitarian needs.

As mentioned above, countries such as South Africa, Rwanda and others have made efforts to resolve their conflicts, to reconcile former enemies, and to heal their wounds, although in reality, many problems related to truth, justice and/or effective peace remained unresolved. Conversely, in CAR, efforts at reconciliation could be helped further when "local initiatives" are consciously employed.[15] This book investigates the extent to which the practice of *Mbuki* (blood pact) in traditional societies could provide foundations for the formation of the theology of reconciliation and the achievement of peace and reconciliation.

The theology of reconciliation can be defined as the Christian process of restoring the relationships broken by sin between human beings and God, and between human beings and others. In The Cape Town Commitment is the call of believers into action to preserve peace and reconciliation. It states,

---

13. Prince, "Is the Central African Republic?"
14. Zahar and Mechoulan, "Peace by Pieces?," 1.
15. Idris, "Supporting Reconciliation," 2.

> Reconciliation to God is inseparable from reconciliation to one another. Christ, who is our peace, *made* peace through the cross, and *preached* peace to the divided world of Jew and Gentile. The unity of the people of God is both a fact ('he made the two one') and a mandate ('make every effort to preserve the unity of the Spirit in the bond of peace').[16]

Robert Schreiter argues that "vertical reconciliation" relates to God reconciling humanity to himself and "horizontal reconciliation" relates to people's efforts to reconcile with each other.[17] He goes on to say that vertical reconciliation makes horizontal reconciliation possible and effective. The Forum for World Evangelization on the theme, "Reconciliation as the mission of God" states that, ". . . God's mission of reconciliation is holistic, including relationships with God, self, others, and creation."[18] Since the fall of humanity because of sin, relationships of human beings with others have been broken. The Cape Town Commitment expresses this clearly as the consequence of the loss of human identity and commitment to preserving God's creation. On the latter point, the over-exploitation of mineral resources by armed men and the unethical mining contracts concluded by the CAR authorities with foreign companies, to name but a few, affect God's creation and the resources that he grants to people in the country. The Commitment laments that human beings fail to be "stewards of the rich and abundance of God's good creation."[19] In other words, they fail to align with God's principles "to exercise godly dominion in using it [the creation] for the sake of human welfare and needs, for example in farming, fishing, mining . . ."[20] Their actions, therefore, cause "the widespread abuse and destruction of earth's resources," resulting in climate change and other degradation. This leads to famine, poverty, and the migration of abused people as well as ethnic violence or conflicts on land/terriroty. Thus, reconciliation becomes the urgent need and the surest way to restore broken relationships, and the Church charged with this mandate. This

---

16. The Third Lausanne Congress, "Building the Peace of Christ," 64–65.
17. Schreiter, "Peacemaking and Reconciliation," 639.
18. Lausanne Committee for World Evangelisn, "Reconciliation as the Mission of God," 11.
19. The Third Lausanne Congress, "Building the Peace of Christ," 73–74.
20. The Third Lausanne Congress, "Building the Peace of Christ," 74.

begins with the restoration of broken relationships with God, with oneself as a "redeemed identity," and with others as a "new humanity in Christ."[21]

This book aims at developing a theology of reconciliation from an African Christian perspective as an "emerging theology" of reconciliation. Therefore, I explore stories and traditional values that stem from the *Mbuki* ritual to understand how the gospel interprets that tradition[22] in order to provide insights into proposing alternatives to reconciliation. The theological perspective of reconciliation that I propose in this book is a contribution to other scholarly analyses on the issue.

2. Key Problem

In CAR, there is a gap between understanding and implementing reconciliation. The key problem that the book explores is the lack of indigenous initiatives and leadership for reconciliation. The arguments that follow help to illustrate this. Brown and Zahar explain that, in CAR, social cohesion efforts focus more on "de-escalating violence rather than building bonds of trust."[23] This situation seems to lead people to have a view that does not heal relationships between victims and offenders. Some victims seek revenge, while others reject any connection with their former offenders. In other words, there is mistrust between victims and offenders.

Individuals who perceive the cost of restoring a community are more likely to act towards reconciliation. Conversely, those who do not perceive it are not or are less likely to take part in restoring harmony with others, as shown in the following illustration. In a report broadcast on Deutsche Welle on 21 January 2022, Jean-Firmin Koena highlighted "la difficile cohabitation entre les anciens rebelles et leurs victimes" (the difficult coexistence between former rebels and their victims).[24] He reported that the local people of Alindao and Bambari, two strongholds of the "Union pour la Paix en Centrafrique" (UPC) rebel leader Ali Darassa, disagreed that the government trains and incorporates Darassa's defectors into the national army. According to those who

---

21. The Third Lausanne Congress, "Building the Peace of Christ," 66.

22. In this book, I use the terms "tradition" and "indigenous" interchangeably to describe what is related to primal societies, not modern or contemporary.

23. Brown and Zahar, "Social Cohesion as Peacebuilding," 11.

24. Koena, "Centrafrique: la Difficile Cohabitation."

opposed the initiative of the government, the former rebels raped, burned villages, and killed innocent people; it was unthinkable that the government authorities stationed them in Bambari until they were disarmed. Koena went on to say that the civilian population saw this as an act of impunity granted to them to encourage the others to lay down their arms. This could lead to some victims taking justice into their own hands.[25]

The victims of the conflict in Alindao and Bambari, as Koena mentioned, did not appreciate the fact that the government did not automatically arrest the armed rebels who perpetrated violence in their localities. Their resentment was understandable, given the atrocities and trauma they have gone through; and of course, people in other parts of the country are still going through. This group of people represented those who did not promote any coexistence with the former rebels nor the peace process, which obviously required their patience. Koena also noted that, while Darassa and his faction were opposed to the peace process for the sake of reconciliation, Hassan Bouba Ali, second in command of the UPC, was open to it. As a result, the Touadéra administration appointed him Minister of Livestock.[26]

Another illustration helps to understand the key problem of the study. In March 2019, during a radio broadcast on traditional justice and conflict resolution, Honoré Douba raised the very issue of the neglect of indigenous practices and the side-lining of traditional leaders in conflict resolution and reconciliation in CAR. He asserted, "Oui, je vous dis, quand quelque chose se fait en dehors de notre culture, c'est-à-dire quand on n'invoque pas l'esprit des ancêtres rien ne marchera, même sur le plan national." It translates, "Yes, I told you that when something is not in line with our culture, I mean, when we do not rely on the spirit of our ancestors, nothing will be good, even for the whole country."[27] Douba noted that since the beginning of the conflict, none of the neighbourhood chiefs (*chefs de quartiers*), the sultans and the lamido (Fulani leaders) have been invited to participate in the reconciliation processes.[28] This view reinforces the problem of the lack of involvement of indigenous leadership to reconciliation. Jacqueline Woodfork, in her book

---

25. Koena, "Centrafrique: la Difficile Cohabitation."
26. Koena, "Centrafrique: la Difficile Cohabitation."
27. Douba, "L'importance du Jugement."
28. Douba, "L'importance du Jugement."

on customs and culture of CAR, has already pointed out that the political leaders have diminished the authority of the traditional leaders.[29] The latter are set aside to manage the conflict. As a result, many victims have lost their rights to justice that can foster unity and effective reconciliation.

In light of the key problem, I raised a question to guide the reflection: "To what extent can the insights into the traditional *Mbuki* ritual bring about an emerging theology of reconciliation in CAR?" The Sierra Leonean *Fambul Tok* reconciliation initiave is explored in the next chapter as the background study to understand the significant contribution it brought to reconciliation in this context. I also discuss the fundamental factors that caused the 2013 conflict in CAR, the characteristics of *Mbuki* ritual, the engagement of the gospel with *Mbuki* culture for reconciliation, and the contribution of the reflection to a theology of reconciliation. The following section explores the intellectual framework that guides the reflection.

3. Intellectual Frameworks

The theme of peace and reconciliation is central to the book.[30] Although the reflection falls within the field of peace and reconciliation studies, the primary fields from which I propose to draw possible intellectual frameworks are related to the primal worldview and spirituality, gospel and culture, personhood and kinship, and peace and reconciliation. These can also be explored in Theology and religious studies, Intercultural studies, African studies, and Peace and Reconciliation studies. However, the intellectual frameworks that I propose integrate the above themes with the practice of *Mbuki* as an emerging theology of reconciliation in order to formulate an alternative approach to reconciliation in CAR.

Although primal religions in many parts of the world "exhibit many of the same categories and have many shared features", as Andrew F. Walls has

---

29. Woodfork, *Culture and Customs*, 130.

30. The Cape Town Commitment reflected on the issue at hand and called on believers to actions to promote peace. Its theological convictions particularly fall under the section "Building the peace of Christ in our divided and broken world." See The Third Lausanne Congress, "Building the Peace of Christ."

pointed out, some scholars have contested the use of the term "primal."[31] Other scholars such as Harold Turner, John V. Taylor, John B. Taylor, and Kwame Bediako accepted the term "primal" and acknowledged the relevance of the African primal worldview and epistemology to the vibrancy of African Christianity and scholarship.[32] They regarded Turner's Six Features helpful to assess the phenomenological framework of the primal religions and their affinities with the "Christian tradition."[33] They also posited that when Christians engaged in dialogue with other religions, they discovered what they shared as a primal inheritance.[34] Before assuming that *Mbuki* brings into play an understanding of reconciliation, the study highlights the primal religious characteristics that Turner discussed in his six-feature analysis. Indeed, in his second, third and fourth features, Turner describes that man has a deep sense of weakness, he has the conviction that he is not alone in the universe, and that "man can enter into relationship with the benevolent spirit-world and so share in its powers and blessings and receive protection from evil forces by these transcendent helpers."[35]

In his contribution to the subject, Balcomb discusses Charles Taylor's characterizations of the "porous" and "buffered" selves and the relevance of these concepts to the African context. He argues that in Taylor's *A Secular*

---

31. Walls, "The Background to the Project," 1. In his article "Primal or Indigenous: A Critical Assessment of an Ongoing Debate on African Religion", Anthony Balcomb examines how "non-practitioners" view "African Religion" and assesses the debate among scholars on the understanding of primal/indigenous religions. He observes that in modern society, there is a "resurgence" of indigenous religions despite their criticism or rejection by non-practitioners in the Western missionary and colonial era. While early Christian missionaries saw African Religion as non-existent, early missionaries and early Christian converts saw it as evil, and the mainly African Independent Churches (AICs), as inadequate. However, African Christians who celebrate the phenomenal success of Christian mission see African Religion as a preparation for the Christian gospel, and "scholars of religion who reject the *praeparatio* thesis, assert the integrity of African Religion as an end itself, and advocate for inclusion of African Religion as part of the many world religions." See Balcomb, "Primal or Indigenous," 2–3. Balcomb also argues that John S. Mbiti, Bolaji Idowu, and Kwame Bediako claim that African Religion is a "primal religion." See Balcomb, "Primal or Indigenous," 6. This point is significant for understanding the vibrancy of African Christianity, which borrows the beliefs and practices of traditional religions to adapt to the Christian faith. However, in Balcomb's critical assessment of the opponents of the term primal, the voices of the indigenous are not examined.

32. Taylor, *The Primal Vision*, 18; Turner, "The Primal Religions," 27; Walls, "The Background to the Project," 1–2; Bediako, *Christianity in Africa*, 91–108.

33. Turner, "The Primal Religions," 32.

34. Taylor, *Primal World-Views*, 2.

35. Turner, "The Primal Religions," 32.

Age, the "porous self" governs the "enchanted world,"[36] while the "buffered self" describes "the norm in the disenchanted, secular world."[37] He asserts that those who function in the enchanted universe are vulnerable to everything that surrounds them; they are vulnerable to their environment, which is the opposite in the disenchanted world. Therefore, people's vulnerability to humans and spiritual forces that surround them leads them to seek communal relationships with others.[38] This analysis is in line with Turner's third feature according to which range of spiritual powers surround man's universe, making him vulnerable. Balcomb points out that the principle of *Ubuntu* ("A person is a person through other people") is significant to understand the characteristic of communal life in the enchanted world that is not limited to "interactive identity and philanthropic African humanism."[39]

The spirit of community that predominated in Zandé society through the experience of *Mbuki*, as will be explored later, could explain the reality of an enchanted universe. The spirit of community, solidarity and togetherness characterize African humanity and guide moral principles that concern the well-being of a community. Such a view forms part of the framework that can define the reconciliation process in a post-conflict context. In this book, I have chosen to use the term "primal" rather than "enchanted." At times, I use "indigenous" interchangeably with "primal."

To explain the practice of peace and reconciliation in the traditional African societies, I have drawn on the works by David Shenk and Thomas Christensen. These scholars have attempted to understand the significance of

---

36. In literature, some scholars mainly use the term "enchanted" rather than "primal" to define people's religious worldview in a particular context. Charles Taylor's book, *A Secular Age*, contributes to discussion on the issue of the "enchanted" and "disenchanted" worlds. He points out that it is difficult for many Westerners in contemporary times to believe in God, whereas a few centuries ago, in the 1500s for example, they did so easily. To understand the reasons for this change, he argues that at that time there was no need to disbelieve because people lived in a God-centred environment, God-centred societies, and an enchanted universe; while in the modern society, they are the most secularised in the world. See Taylor, *A Secular Age*, 25. However, he acknowledges that the use of the term "enchanted" in this context is not appropriate. The word enchanted "is perhaps not the best expression [because] it seems to evoke light and fairies . . . The enchanted world in this sense is the world of spirits, demons, and moral forces which our ancestors lived in." See Taylor, *A Secular Age*, 25–26. Turner defines this feature as part of the primal worldview.

37. Balcomb, "The Porous Self," 234.

38. Balcomb, "The Porous Self," 238–239.

39. Balcomb, "The Porous Self," 239.

trees, indigenous practices, and elements of nature as well as their relevance to peace, justice, and reconciliation in the African context. Both recognized, not only the adoption of physical objects of nature and animals in the search for reconciliation, but also the use of men as mediators.[40] Indeed, the processes of reconciliation varied according to the conflicts.[41] Shenk revealed that when harmony between people was broken, animal sacrifices were made to restore peace. Those involved in the conflict shared sacrificial food to solidify the peace covenant.[42] Both also describe a cosmological, epistemological, and sociological understanding of reconciliation when they point out that, in the traditional African context, to reconcile with a clan member is to reconcile with the whole clan, the ancestors and the spirits. In considering these arguments, the book interrogates how the *Mbuki* ritual practice can inform the quest of reconciliation in CAR.

To explore the gospel and culture in relation to peace and reconciliation, the works of Richard Niebuhr, Kwame Bediako, and Allison Howell, among key scholars, guide the study.[43] All three, regard culture as referring to people and their achievements, while the gospel refers to the person of Jesus Christ. Niebuhr defines culture as the expression of people in terms of "language, habits, ideas, beliefs, customs, social organisations, inherited artefacts, technical processes, and values."[44] Since culture is about "human achievements," one cannot talk about people without referring to their culture. Some consider culture as something wrong to reject. This view, for example, predominated responses of French colonial authorities and missionaries who regarded the traditional practices of inhabitants of Oubangui Chari (the colonial name of CAR) as superstitious.[45] The view also relates to the attitude of those among Christians who hate or reject everything about Islam or Muslims and vice versa, as evil. These attitudes are one cause of the socio-religious exclusion that has exacerbated violence. However, in addressing the issue, Bediako

---

40. Shenk, *Justice, Reconciliation*, 64–68.
41. Christensen, "Rites of Reconciliation," 197.
42. Shenk, *Justice, Reconciliation*, 64–68.
43. Niebuhr, *Christ and Culture*; Bediako, "Scripture as the Hermeneutic," 2–11; Bediako, "Gospel and Culture," 8–17; Howell, "Researching Gospel and Culture," 22–28 and Howell, *The Religious Itinerary*.
44. Niebuhr, *Christ and Culture*, 33.
45. Woodfork, *Culture and Customs*, 25. See also Christensen, "Rites of Reconciliation," 173.

distinguished between the "corrupt elements" of culture and the "positive dimensions" of culture. He states,

> Cultures . . . include such dimensions as languages, arts, crafts, eating habits, patterns of social relationships; how men, women and children relate, how they ought to relate, and how they see each other. Political organisation, notions of leadership, authority, power and rule are also dimensions of culture. Religious and moral values, things deemed acceptable and unacceptable, are elements of culture. They affect how particular persons and their social groupings understand themselves, how they understand the world, how they think or relate to the natural or physical environment; how they relate to the departed, and how they deal with ancestors. These are all dimensions of culture.[46]

Bediako's statement shows that culture is not only a set of traditions or artefacts, but also a sense of identity. According to him, it goes beyond fixed entities and encompasses the "sense of tradition, history, identity and continuity."[47] Bediako claims that human beings make culture alive, because "Culture is, essentially, an attribute of persons."[48] Culture is expressed in human habits, signs, symbols, rituals, songs, proverbs, or dances, as expressions of human life. The function of the gospel through Scripture is to interpret culture and tradition. This is possible when (African) Christians begin to discern within their "own cultures and traditions, the strands that point the way to Jesus, that show that Jesus is Lord, and to distinguish these from the strands that lead away from Jesus and deny him."[49]

Howell adds to the discussion that, "If the gospel is to be the interpreter of culture," then it is essential that scholars take into account "the story behind events and rites, and understanding the meanings behind those rites and artefacts as a key part of the process of research."[50] Her investigation on Kasena tradition and spirituality, more importantly, the *Kukula* river shrine, to understand the reasons for conversion and the impact of the religious

---

46. Bediako, "Gospel and Culture," 8.
47. Bediako, 8.
48. Bediako, 8.
49. Bediako, 12.
50. Howell, "Researching Gospel and Culture Issues," 22.

itinerary on the Kasem people in northern Ghana is a tangible case of research on gospel and culture.[51] This method of the gospel interpreting culture provides a framework for this research in seeking to explore the meanings behind *Mbuki* and to highlight how it may relate to the gospel of reconciliation and peace in CAR.

Bediako refutes the simplistic understanding of the gospel as a set of spiritual principles, moral laws, or a message of prosperity. He observes that the gospel is about the person of Christ, what he did during his life on earth and even after his death.[52] He sums up his arguments by saying that, "In the gospel and culture engagement, our concern is to seek ways in which the gospel may be relevant to our cultures."[53] Based on the above, engaging the gospel with culture consists in engaging Christ with people by considering their values, structures, and achievements.

In "Christ the Transformer of Culture," Richard H. Niebuhr sees the possibility of turning the elements of culture to Christ.[54] When the gospel engages with culture, the transformation occurs because human beings and the structures of their culture turn towards God. Walls emphasizes this as follows: "Conversion is not the substitution of something new for something old . . . nor the addition of something new to something old . . . Conversion is the turning, the re-orientation, of every aspect of humanity – culture-specific humanity – to God."[55] The point is how does the Scripture interpret cultural tradition. For Bediako, to do so, people allow Scripture to shed light on their story and determine who they are. He states that Scripture interprets tradition by becoming the controlling experience alongside people's story, so that the two work towards a fusion. In doing so, people can recognize themselves in the Scripture, which also becomes increasingly recognizable as their story and narrative.[56] Howell's statement below helps to understand the process that guides the engagement of Scripture or the gospel and cultural traditions:

---

51. Howell, *The Religious Itinerary*, 30–145.
52. Bediako, "Gospel and Culture," 8.
53. Bediako, "Scripture as the Hermeneutic of Culture," 2.
54. Niebuhr, *Christ and Culture*, 190–208.
55. Walls, *The Missionary Movement*, 28.
56. Bediako, "Scripture as the Hermeneutic of Culture," 6.

> In gospel and culture research, once we have learnt people's action and opinion about an issue or a problem and the cultural meanings behind each aspect, symbol, rite and ritual, we are able to understand more about their theology. We can then move into the most crucial stage of the process, where Scripture becomes the hermeneutic or interpreter of that issue, event or problem and its associated cultural meanings.[57]

In his analysis on gospel interpreting cultural traditions, Bediako uses both the terms "gospel" and "Scripture" synonymously as the "hermeneutic of culture and tradition." He indicates that Jesus permeates throughout Scripture and he is the gospel. Therefore, the synonymous use of the terms "gospel" and "Scripture" in this book refers to the same reality because they do not contradict each other.

4. Literary Sources on *Mbuki* and Field Study

E. E. Evans-Pritchard studies the Azandé people's practice of blood brotherhood.[58] He defines blood brotherhood as "a pact or alliance formed between two persons by a ritual act in which each swallows the blood of the other."[59] Those who exchange the blood of each other addressed each other as *bakurëmi* ("my blood-brother") or *nakurëmi* ("my blood-sister," referring to the wife of a blood brother). The extended family and the entire clan of the blood brothers also become members of the kinship.[60] Evans-Pritchard also notes that blood brotherhood protects someone from danger in a foreign area; it guarantees mutual assistance and exchange of gifts. However, blood pacts did not include relatives and the chieftaincy did not allow a ruler to conclude blood pact with villagers, because it "would militate against the fairness of their judgement and paralyse their execution."[61]

Writing on reconciliation in the light of blood pact in CAR, Father Nazaire Diatta argues that the practice was not limited to the Azandé; they involved

---

57. Howell, "Researching Gospel and Culture," 13.
58. Evans-Pritchard, "Zande Blood-Brotherhood," 369–401.
59. Evans-Pritchard, 269.
60. Evans-Pritchard, 370–371.
61. Evans-Pritchard, 374.

many ethnic groups. Those involved in blood pact were aware of the consequences of breaking the rules.[62] It is what Jean-Paul Ngoupandé points out when he argues that, in the past, tribal clashes could not last and always ended in blood pacts. Therefore, nobody could break a pact by resorting to conflict and escape disastrous consequences.[63] Although his article provides the study with relevant information on the extent of blood pact practices in the CAR context and its link to the understanding of reconciliation in a Christian environment, Diatta did not research the traditional context in which this culture emerged. This book attempts to research the context of such a culture and examines what has changed to make it disappear. The theology of reconciliation pursued in this book derives from the analysis of the Sango Bible, both Old and New Testaments, as well as from the scriptural interpretation of the ritual.

To explore the experiences and expectations of people in terms of peace and reconciliation, I used a qualitative approach. During the field research, I collected primary data through archival documents in the archives in Bangui and France, as well as through research interviews. Unfortunately, the research in the archives in Bangui was not fruitful. The main reason was that the armed men, who took power after the 2013-coup, looted and destroyed major archival materials of the National Archives located in the compound of the presidential palace and related to the research. Another centre where I expected to find archival materials was the Musée Barthélemy Boganda (Barthélemy Boganda Museum) that rebels also pillaged. Thus, my fieldwork in CAR focused more on collecting data through interviews, participant observations, and exploration of secondary sources.

Research at the Archives Nationales d'Outre-Mer (ANOM) in Aix-en-Provence, France, from 20 February to 19 March 2022 showed that, while archival sources on French colonial policy were dominant, details on history, cultures, and traditions of Oubangui Chari were scarce. A few reports mentioned the assassination of Karnu, the numerous dissidences following colonial violence, and the influence of colonial authorities on the traditional leadership. The data also reported the French perception of the emergence of Barthélemy Boganda's political party as a threat to colonial actions in the

---

62. Diatta, "Le Concept de la Réconciliation," 66.
63. Ngoupandé, *Chronique de la Crise*, 133.

colony. The scarcity of sources on the *Mbuki* ritual practice was evidence of the decline or lack of interest in CAR's cultural and traditional values. However, although most of the data I collected focused more on the colonial rulers' relations of domination in Oubangui Chari, it was useful in understanding how these policies laid the foundation for conflicts in CAR.

In addition, the qualitative approach used the "action-oriented research process, in which researchers are activists dedicated to social transformation."[64] The action research aimed at testing out whether or not *Mbuki* blood pact has the potential to promote peace and reconciliation in an armed conflict context. Apart from that, I collected data from sources such as books and articles from the library of Alliance Française de Bangui (AFB) and that of the Bangui School of Theology (FATEB). I also collected information from newspapers, signboards, radio programmes, and internet (YouTube and website) interviews.

John V. King highlights the challenges of field research in areas of armed conflict. He argues that challenges and dilemmas a researcher might encounter "particularly in the difficult, unstable, and dangerous contexts . . . can at the minimum threaten the validity of one's data and at maximum threaten the personal security and well-being of the respondents, their families, the researcher, and members of her or his research team."[65] King further stresses that, in such a context, the researcher should work at avoiding "unanticipated ethical, social, and political challenges in the field."[66] In CAR, the conflict has created mistrust and suspicion between Christian and Muslim communities, which can turn violent. For this reason, the purposive sampling that I used to collect data during research in the field sought to avoid such situations. To do so, I purposively selected participants and geographical areas through purposive sampling to get information or to collect data while avoiding being exposed and/or exposing respondents to insecurity.

The research used semi-structured interviews to allow the respondents, both in individual interviews and focus groups, to express their views on each topic. The interview questions for individuals were formulated in three parts: Part A comprised the "General Background to all the Groups", Part B was

---

64. Chilisa, *Indigenous Research Methodologies*, 191.
65. King, "Demystifying Field Research," 8.
66. King, 8.

about the "Conflict, Peace and Reconciliation Questions" and Part C covered the "Questions to Specific Groups." In this division, nine sets of questionnaires served as open-ended questions to the nine categories of people for individual interviews (See appendix 1). In addition, I formulated another questionnaire comprising fifteen open-ended questions for group discussions (See appendix 2). This aimed at drawing, both Christian and Muslim viewpoints on the possible contribution of *Mbuki* to fostering reconciliation in the country.

Before using them on the field, I submitted the questionnaires to peer-reviewers who provided observation and comments. I formulated the interview questions in French and Sango according to the expected respondents' understanding and translated them into English for analysis. In addition, during the research in the field, I hired a research assistant in Bossangoa and another in Bouar to help guide me into safe areas, to identify potential interviewees, and to interpret communications in local languages.

The general questions for all groups as well as questions related to conflict, peace, and reconciliation sought to draw people's views on the 2013 conflict and on the characteristics of *Mbuki*, especially concerning reconciliation. These questions aimed at understanding among others, the root causes of violence, the motives of rebels to keep committing exactions, the coexistence between Christians and Muslims before and after the clash. They also examined the reasons for failure in peace processes, the failure of regional and international peace actors to resolve the conflict, and the possible contribution of indigenous processes to peace and reconciliation. I expected all nine categories of people to answer the general questions according to their understanding and experiences.

The first set of "questions to specific groups" concerned ordinary Christians. These questions helped understand the role of the Bible teachings according to the believers interviewed and the relevance of the indigenous initiatives to peace and reconciliation. It was meant to understand how Christians regarded the Bible as relevant to respond to the ongoing conflict. It also examined the extent to which some churches affiliated with the mainline denominations such as Roman Catholic, Baptist/Evangelical, Pentecostal/Charismatic and the AICs assisted internally displaced people. The second set of questions targeted church ministers and sought to find out whether or not their biblical sermons covered the themes of peace and reconciliation. It also concerned their use of stories, proverbs, and the like, to convey the messages of peace and reconciliation, their assistance to internally displaced people, and commitment to promoting conflict resolution and social cohesion.

Two sets of questions that followed targeted respectively the Youth and Women. In these sets of questions, my aim was to understand whether or not cultural or traditional values were key to the search for peace and reconciliation in CAR. I also discussed how the members of each group could contribute to achieving peace in their context. Specifically, questions about Youth focused on which values of the past the young people have lost concerning peace and reconciliation and how they could promote them.

The specific questions concerning the CAR Muslims comprised questions about the relevance of Qur'an to conflict resolution and the search for peace. They also sought to find out whether the teachings of Qur'an in mosques helped address the issue of conflicts in CAR and how Muslims assisted internally displaced people. According to the data collected, the views of Muslims and Christians on the issues explored during the fieldwork served to enrich the understanding of both groups who, sometimes, came to the same conclusion. For example, Christians and Muslims interviewed shared the view that the current armed conflict was not religious but rather fuelled by military-political actors.

To the government workers, the specific questions sought to understand how traditional values could help promote patriotism and national unity in the context of armed conflict but also, how the work sector of the interviewee contributed to this achievement. I also explored the work of the UN institutions and Non-Governmental Organisations (NGOs) involved in the search for peace and reconciliation. This helped find out the changes that occurred, since the UN peacekeeping force, MINUSCA, and NGOs were involved in searching and mainting peace and reconciliation, and the satisfaction of the civilian population vis-à-vis achieved results.

The last categories of the specific questions concerned the Interfaith Platform and Indigenous Leaders. Through questions to the members of the Interfaith Platform, I aimed at understanding the outcomes of efforts made to achieving reconciliation as well as the positive results and challenges they encountered in the process. The last questions explored the involvement of traditional leaders in the conflict resolution and their opinions about the peace processes carried out so far.

In these categories, the voice of Séléka and Anti Balaka rebel groups is missing because any interview with the armed groups was impossible. As mentioned earlier, the relationships of mistrust and suspicion between Christians and Muslims during the conflict made any interview with the above-mentioned groups difficult. With the exception of journalists and international UN actors, any academic research with the militiamen was unsuccessful and could expose the researchers to mortal danger, since the latter were often accused of collecting information on behalf of the government officials or security forces. However, some militiamen were aware of the *Mbuki* blood pact that linked their forefathers or ethnic groups in the past. This is the case of the *Mbuki* existing between the Mbomu people and their Vakaga blood brothers who planned to organize an attack against them (see chapter 9, section 5).

Initially, I planned to carry out the field research in two phases. Phase one concerned individual interviews. This phase targeted the localities of Bangui, Bossangoa and Bouar. Phase two was held as focus group discussions in Bouar and Bangui. The reason for these choices was that people's perceptions concerning peace and reconciliation varied from one locality to another. In Bangui, the relationships between Christians and Muslims affecting peace and reconciliation were ambivalent. In Bossangoa, some members of the Christian community were opposed to the return of the Muslim population to the locality, while in Bouar quiet harmonious relationships existed between the two communities, despite some clashes observed in some areas.

According to Linda Tuhiwai Smith, in researching traditional contexts, scholars are identified as "insiders" and/or "outsiders."[67] During the field research, for both individual interviews and focus groups, I acted as an insider but also as an outsider in the researched communities. As an insider, I had identified myself as a member of affected communities to understand the traumatic experiences that people have gone through, to feel their difficulties, and to think about solutions to be brought. However, as an outsider, I strived to maintain the objectivity of my research to take a critical look at the issues discussed. Details about the fieldwork are described in the following paragraphs.

---

67. Smith, *Decolonizing Methodologies*, 5.

I carried out phase one of field research in Bossangoa from October to November 2020. During this period, I conducted interviews with twenty-five people, specifically non-Muslims. When the conflict broke out in 2013, the Anti-Balaka militiamen expelled the Muslim community from that locality. Furthermore, former President Bozizé led the "Coalition des Patriotes pour le Changement" (CPC), which merged Anti-Balaka and Séléka fighters to stage an attempted coup two weeks after I left the locality. Hostilities ended around February 2021 in the capital, while in remote areas fighting has still been going on between the CPC-rebel groups and armed forces. In April of the same year, I undertook individual interviews and focus group discussions in the locality of Bouar during phase one of fieldwork. I combined both individual interviews and focus group because of the delay caused by the CPC's coup and the threat of the COVID-19 pandemic. Below are the summary tables of the interviews.

Table 1: Summary table of idividual interviews

Category of Interviewees	Number of people interviewed		
	Bangui	Bossangoa	Bouar
Individual interviews	39	25	34
Total	98		

Table 2: Summary table of focus groups

Category of Interviewees	Number of focus groups		
	Bangui	Bossangoa	Bouar
Focus groups	10	No focus group	12
Total	22		

I did not reach the number of interviewees initially planned (180 people) due to the context of insecurity, both in the capital and the provinces. During the field research period, the security situation in Bangui was very precarious, with outbreaks of violence, robberies, and all forms of crime. Gunshots were also heard every night in the neighbourhoods. In the provinces, insecurity continued to grow. The armed men often attacked the population, causing desolation in the communities but also fighting between armed forces and the Russian and Rwandan soldiers.

Some church leaders were not willing to embark their congregations on sensitive issues like these. On other occasions, I postponed or cancelled interviews altogether. New clashes frequently interrupted my trips and field research, affecting the entire work I carried out. In Bangui, the one-to-one interviews with targeted people were more difficult than expected. Most of the church leaders I contacted for interviews in their specific congregations preferred filling out questionnaires or making their congregants fill them out rather than granting me direct interviews.[68] Using this approach would not benefit the research because the face-to-face interviews enabled me to control and guide the discussions. Despite the challenges, I covered one hundred and twenty interviews during the fieldwork, as shown above, using the action research approach.

Bagele Chilisa describes action research as "a process of doing, reflecting on the action, drawing conclusions, and then reflecting again on the process."[69] This method requires the participants sharing viewpoints on an issue through a conversational attitude in which a respondent may react to the ideas of others in constructive interaction.[70] Bob Dick also notes that action research has an objective, which consists in provoking a change in people's community.[71] Concerning this study, action research aimed at helping affected people to reflect on the conflict in order to come to a collective response and to take the appropriate decision(s) for their wellbeing.[72] Indeed, as stated earlier, action research was scheduled as phase two of my fieldwork. Initially, I planned to carry it out in Bangui and Nola. However, due to security constraints in reaching Nola, I undertook the field research in Bouar.

Chilisa further observes that, to make a focus group discussion effective, the research participants provide information on the issues of discussion. During the field research, participants reflected on the issue of peace and reconciliation. More specifically, they discussed the contribution of *Mbuki*

---

68. Some church leaders were not willing to embark their congregations on sensitive issues like these. On other occasions, I postponed or cancelled interviews altogether.
69. Chilisa, *Indigenous Research*, 192.
70. Chilisa, 180.
71. Dick, "Postgraduate Program Using Action Research," 162.
72. Chilisa, *Indigenous Research*, 192.

to achieving peace and reconciliation. Chilisa goes on to say that, in action research, the researcher uses semi-structured questions and "Most focus groups consist of between 6 and 12 people."[73] In the process of research on the field, the context on the ground determined the number of participants for the focus group. In Bouar, twelve participants made up the focus group, while in Bangui they were ten. I was unable to conduct a focus group in Bossangoa, as militiamen drove the Muslim community out of the locality.

However, during my stay in Bouar, accompanied by a research assistant, I discussed the merits of a focus group with the chief of the Hausa neighbourhood as well as some Muslims and Christians who had agreed to participate in the discussion. Thus, an appointment was made for Friday 9 April 2021. Among those gathered for the discussions were six Muslims and six Christians. The objective of the meeting was for me to act as both a researcher and a participant in the researched context. Therefore, together with the respondents, we reflected on questions to understand what reconciliation and peace were, how other people's perspectives differed from that of everyone in the group. We also reflected on why rebels continued to commit atrocities against civilians, and how traditional initiatives were essential to the search for peace. We further sought to understand together whether *Mbuki* could contribute to reconciliation. The participants' sharing helped to enrich the reflection.

In Bangui, the focus group discussion was held on Friday 9 July 2021 in the Gobongo neighbourhood, next to the area mosque. The meeting took place after much hesitation and mistrust on the part of those I contacted. Imam Balla Traoré, accompanied by the mature faithful Muslims of Gobongo as well as Christians from this area had responded to the meeting. Ten participants in all gathered for the discussions including five Muslims and five Christians. As in Bouar, the participants' accounts of atrocities and gross violations, the responsibilities of armed groups, the failure of peace processes, the contribution of traditional initiatives to peace, and other issues raised enriched the discussions.

King notes that researchers in the field are aware that "technologies are a boon and a great asset in gathering, managing, and communicating data

---

73. Chilisa, *Indigenous Research*, 180.

easily from the field and dealing with it in post-field settings."⁷⁴ He goes on to argue that the recording of "local folklore, songs, dances, [and] poetry that provide insight into values, history, practices, and beliefs of the community" may contribute to research in traditional contexts.⁷⁵ His assertion suggests that technologies allow the digitisation of research with the introduction of computers and the internet. In other words, multimedia plays a significant role in research in traditional contexts in the sense that, pictures, audio-visual and sound recordings facilitate the analysis of data and provide insights into research and knowledge. This has guided the research I undertook to take photographs as well as audio-visual recordings that served as tools for analysis.

Thus, during the research in the field, I used a digital audio recording device and camera for interviews. I also used the audio recording device to record individual interviews and focus group discussions. Both individual interviews and focus group discussions were conducted with the full and signed permission of the participants. The device was also used to record "Dialogue des cultures et des religions," broadcasting interviews from Radio Ndeke Luka's website.⁷⁶ Other recordings included TV video interviews concerning the conflict in CAR, particularly on Afrique Média website.⁷⁷ I also took photographs and short-recorded videos during the focus groups with the permission of the participants. The digital camera also served to take pictures of signboards advertising peace and reconciliation.

However, conducting field research in an insecure context like in CAR was highly challenging. During the process, several expected participants were not willing to share their opinions about the conflict. It was obvious that the fear of stigma, social exclusion and abandonment by the community made it difficult to speak out. Some did not speak out for fear of retaliation if they disclosed the truth about what happened. Others were afraid to disclose the truth about crimes and violence they went through, as their perpetrators were in power or still controlled their communities. In addition, pending

---

74. King, "Demystifying Field Research," 12.

75. Chilisa, *Indigenous Research*, 210.

76. Nina Verdiane Niabodé was the author of the broadcasting interviews whom I met and whith whom I discussed.

77. Afrique Media, "Pourquoi la France?"

interviews were cancelled because key respondents I selected did not make themselves available for interviews.

I explained earlier that the recorded interviews constituted a large part of my field research. I carried out the interviews in Sango or in French language.[78] Thus, to analyse the recorded data, I transcribed the information into French before translating into English. I also translated the data I collected from books, articles, newspapers, and audio-visual recordings into English. I am not competent in understanding nor speaking Gbaya Bossangoa and Gbaya Kara, the local dialects of Bossangoa and Bouar. I, therefore, benefited from the assistance of an indigene as a research assistant in each locality to help interpret or translate communications from mother tongues into Sango during interviews. The research assistant also assisted me in transcribing the words and expressions from the vernacular languages into Sango or French to facilitate the translation into English. During the process, I ensured that this phase be properly done to complete the transcriptions on time. More importantly, to ensure the confidentiality concerning the collected data, each research assistant agreed and signed a statement of confidentiality as a declaration of commitment. During the process also, I followed the ethical principles and had permission from interviewees before taking photographs and recording audio.

Furthermore, I ensured to disclose only the identity of potential interviewees who had given their consent. To encourage them to participate in the research, I indicated to them my commitment to keep all information confidential. Therefore, during the process, I gained positive experiences and encountered challenges that I briefly listed as follows:

1. Some elderly people showed their enthusiasm to share their views on the *Mbuki* ritual in the search for reconciliation;
2. The person-to-person interviews made the discussions dynamic and enriching, as I rephrased misunderstood questions to clarify them for the participants;

---

78. Sango and French are respectively the national and official languages spoken in CAR. The Sango language is a *lingua franca* spoken beyond the borders of the country, while the French language "is the medium of communication of government and education" since the colonial period. See Woodfork, *Culture and Customs*, 5–8.

3. The difficulty of contacting primal religious people in the localities where I conducted field research. In CAR, there has been loss of cultural and traditional practices to such an extent that, even in some remote villages, it was difficult to find people with the knowledge of these practices. Also, remote areas were risky and inaccessible due to road conditions and insecurity;
4. In cities, and especially in Bangui, it was very difficult to keep appointments with potential respondents. Some postponed appointments and others cancelled them due to their unavailability or refusal to respond. Others did not agree to the interview request they had received;
5. Some church ministers did not give their consent for granting face-to-face interviews, including their congregants, on sensitive issues of the conflict. They did not permit official interviews with members of their congregations;
6. Resentment over the sad events has prevented some people from speaking out freely;
7. Mistrust, suspicion, rumours and fear of stigmatisation, fear of repression by those involved in the violence, and fear of abandonment by family or friends, prevented some people from disclosing what they had experienced; and
8. The new coup triggered by the CPC rebellion and violence that followed after December 2020 affected the field research both in Bangui and in the rural areas.

5. Conclusion

Chapter 1 of this book introduces the 2013-armed conflict, its key problem, the intellectual framework, and the methods applied for research. It allows understanding that the CAR *Mbuki* may offer possible tool to initiate national reconciliation even though the government and peacebuilding organizations set it aside. The next chapter deals with Sierra Leone reconciliation process through *Fambul Tok* as a background study to inform the CAR *Mbuki* practice for sustainable peace and reconciliation.

CHAPTER 2

Fambul Tok: An Example of a Cultural Tradition for Reconciliation in Sierra Leone

1. Introduction

Before exploring the context of the 2013 conflict, the drivers, the political settelements, and the actors involved in the peace processes in CAR, it is important to raise the question, "Why incorporate Sierra Leone's *Fambul Tok* to the current study, and what contribution can it bring to the issue being addressed while there is no connection between Sierra Leone's and CAR's conflicts?" This chapter seeks to show that traditional approaches to peace and reconciliation, like *Fambul Tok*, are being used to provoke national healing and reconciliation in the contemporary African post-conflict context. It is therefore a background study to CAR's context. It emphasizes the traditional practice of reconciliation and community healing, its meaning, and the context in which it was used. It also seeks to understand whether this practice has changed, and whether it is possible to apply it to the modern context. One cannot understand the relevance of the *Fambul Tok* practice for post-conflict reconciliation in Sierra Leone without an overview of the civil war that tore the country apart for over a decade.

Sierra Leone existed long before the slave traders arrived and brought people to work in plantations in the New World Colonies.¹ The name "Sierra Leone" came from the Portuguese *Serra Lyoa* ("Lion Mountains") and was given by the navigator Pedro da Cindra, who discovered the region in 1462.² Between the seventeenth and eighteeenth centuries, the region on the African coast served as a centre for the slave trade. In 1787, when the British abolished the Transatlantic Trade, the slave traders freed some captives in Freetown. The country became a British colony in West Africa in 1895 and gained independence in 1961. However, several coups took place in the following years,³ as well as a civil war that broke out and lasted about eleven years, from 23 March 1991 to 18 January 2002.⁴

Se Young Jang points out that the root cause of Sierra Leone's war can be traced back to the late eighteenth century, when the British created "a two class-society" in the country and "thereby [sowed] the seed for the later popular discontents."⁵ The colonial authorities divided the society into the Crown Colony (composed of Krio) and the protectorate (composed of the other ethnic groups) with disparities that caused grievances between the two groups and led to war. Furthermore, through the policy of indirect rule, "the colonial government [appointed or maintained] autocratic chiefs who served the interests of the British and themselves."⁶ As a result, clashes frequently arose between families and ethnic groups over chieftaincy and the benefits that it brought. This continued until independence.

Post-independence resentment towards the chiefs increased because they "were directly appointed by the central government," and thus neglected their own people, who were "alienated by [the] decision-making process in their own communities."⁷ In addition, corruption, mismanagement, unemployment, politicisation of the army, and other social ills characterized Sierra Leone and provoked further grievances. In 1991, the Revolutionary United Front (RUF) plunged the country into conflict. The first assault led by Foday

---

1. Lovejoy and Schwarz, "Sierra Leone in the Eighteenth," 1–28.
2. Oyètádé and Luke, "Sierra Leone: Krio," 123.
3. Cole, "All in the 'Fambul': A Case Study."
4. Alie, "Reconciliation and Traditional Justice," 129.
5. Jang, "The Causes of," 3.
6. Jang, 4.
7. Jang, 4.

Sankoh, originated from the northern and western Temne tribe, invaded the Kailahun district of Mende, the majority ethnic group in the eastern and southern regions. The second assault came four days later and, on 28 March 1991, the third attack conquered Zimmi in Pujehun district.[8] The rebels were made up of men trained in Libya such as Sierra Leonean dissident soldiers, Liberian and Burkinabe mercenaries. They claimed that their aim was to oust President Joseph Saidu Momoh and to restore the proletariat "in all the decision-making processes."[9]

Against this backdrop of political unrest, to express their grievances against the government over the poor conditions of the army, a group of young Sierra Leonean officers attacked Freetown and seized power, establishing the National Provisional Ruling Council (NPRC) led by Captain Valentine Strasser. The military regime "appealed to traditional hunters, some of whom had formed themselves into a civil defence at the start of the war, to help them prosecute the rebels since they knew their terrain very well."[10] Susan Shepler explains that the latter, known as *Kamajohs*, were a group of "traditional secret hunting societies."[11] Sierra Leoneans held a presidential election that resulted in victory to Ahmed Tejan Kabbah. Once in power, Kabbah led peace-talks with the rebels in Abidjan, Côte d'Ivoire, which resulted in the "Abidjan Peace Agreement" signed on 30 November 1996.[12]

After a short-lived peace, Johnny Paul Koroma launched another coup on 25 March 1997 under the Armed Forces Revolutionary Council (AFRC). Koroma's regime ended in 1998 as loyal soldiers drove the AFRC out of the country and restored Kabbah's regime.[13] In January 1999, the AFRC and RUF united and infiltrated Freetown where they fought the national army. On 7 July 1999, to end the conflict, the government, civil society, and international community held peace talks in Togo, known as the "Lomé Peace Accord." On 18 January 2002, the war ended.[14] Sierra Leone's conflict, which began

---

8. Alie, "Reconciliation and Traditional Justice," 135.
9. Alie, 123.
10. Alie, 124.
11. Shepler, "The Rites of the Child," 197.
12. Alie, "Reconciliation and Traditional Justice," 125.
13. Alie, 125.
14. Alie, 125.

in 1991, resulted in the death of thousands of people with many victims of mutilation, rape, and loss of property.[15]

Joe Alie highlights the internationalization of the conflict and the involvement of foreign troops for economic resources. He states,

> The civil crisis became heavily internationalized due to the involvement of neighbouring 'rogue states', many of whose interests were purely economic—namely, access to Sierra Leone's resources, particularly its diamonds. It has been argued, and with justification, that without the support of foreign states the war would probably not have become so protracted and bloody. Burkina Faso, Côte d'Ivoire, Liberia and Libya were notorious for fuelling the conflict. Libya provided bases and military training for the insurgents, while Burkina Faso provided many fighters to bolster the rebel ranks.[16]

Contrary to Alie, Jang argues that the economic factor cannot explain the onset of war in Sierra Leone. Jang points out that it is possible to trace back to the political and economic grievances of the colonial period that laid the foundation for the conflict. This situation created disparities between the populations.[17] He concludes that it was a mistake to consider Sierra Leone's diamond as the driver force behind the war. Indeed, while diamond-mining provided the RUF with "an invaluable funding source to sustain its warfare,"[18] the structural problems that caused grievances among the population led to the crisis.

Jang also argues that five factors could explain the outbreak of the civil war in Sierra Leone. The first factor was "maladministration." The government of Momoh was "corrupt, tribalistic and lacking a popular mandate."[19] The mal-governance and political dictatorship, the over-centralization of power, as well as the neglect of rural areas led to disastrous effects. Second, the "poor

---

15. Kaldor and Vincent, "Evaluation of UNDP," 1–40.
16. Alie, "Reconciliation and Traditional Justice," 127.
17. Jang, "The Causes of," 3.
18. Jang, 3. Alie adds that the internationalization of the conflict also led to mercenaries from other countries looting Sierra Leone's resources. See Alie, "Reconciliation and Traditional Justice," 127.
19. Alie, "Reconciliation and Traditional Justice," 126.

economic policies" in the 1970s and 1980s, the inflation rate of goods and the increasing socio-economic problems related to "life expectancy, primary school enrolment, child mortality rates and death rates" constituted the major problems. Third, the politicization of state institutions due to corruption of the judiciary and traditional courts "led to abuse of power by judges, lawyers and local court officials."[20] Fourth, the lack of adequate educational programmes led to the alienation of young people who felt their only choice was to turn to rebellious recruitments, and fifth, the declined security system caused by the politicization of the security forces and corruption. This context led to a climate of violence even before the civil war outbreak.[21]

Another feature of the civil war in Sierra Leone was the use of child soldiers.[22] In Sierra Leone, when RUF gunmen abducted boys and girls, they cut them off from their family and community ties, forced some to kill family members, encouraged cohesion and solidarity among them, and pushed some boys into leadership positions.[23] This is evidence that, in the context of armed conflict in many African countries, young boys and girls are manipulated. Thus, in this context or thereafter, child soldiers became cruel, violent, and brutal, displaying anti-social behaviour that needed to be addressed in communities to enable their forgiveness and reintegration.[24]

It is essential to understand that, in addition to social, economic, and political structural problems that facilitated the conflict, material factors such as the existence of mountains and large forests contributed to the intensification of the war. Considering its impacts, Sierra Leoneans, both individuals and communities, attempted to address the conflict in order to achieve community healing through reconciliation. They have been carrying out this reconciliation initiative through *Fambul Tok*, digging out from their primal heritage.

---

20. Alie, "Reconciliation and Traditional Justice," 126.
21. Alie, 127.
22. Susan Shepler states that, "blood diamond, amputation as a weapon of war and child soldiers" were the main features of the war in Sierra Leone. See Shepler, "Sierra Leone, Child Soldiers," 242.
23. Denov, *Child Soldiers*, 103–106.
24. Goins, *Forgiveness and Reintegration*, 1–4.

2. *Fambul Tok* and the Reconciliation Ritual

Before describing *Fambul Tok*, it is important to mention that six months after the end of the eleven year war, Sierra Leoneans launched the Truth and Reconciliation Commission (TRC-SL). The objectives of the Commission were to (1) to create a historical record of the crimes committed, (2) to respond to impunity, (3) to address the needs of the victims, and (4) to promote healing and reconciliation.[25] The Commission attempted to address the atrocities committed during the war, punish the perpetrators, and provide relief to the victims. Alie indicates that,

> The commission involved traditional, civil society and religious elders in its truth-seeking and reconciliation sessions (including traditional rites of forgiveness), especially in the provincial areas. It did not encourage local rituals of cursing but it did, in concert with the local elders, establish monuments or memorials, particularly at mass grave sites in the districts, and supported traditional reconciliation ceremonies such as the pouring of libations and cleansing rituals.[26]

The TRC-SL valued elements of culture and tradition such as "mediation, purification, token appeasement and willingness to show remorse" as being consistent with the objectives of the Commission during its hearings.[27] It also recognized that ethnic groups used their traditional belief systems to promote truth-telling and reconciliation, swearing, cleansing and seeking forgiveness as contributing to restoring harmony in communities.[28] The Commission worked from mid-2002 to 2004, covering about twelve districts, and collecting over eight thousand accounts of horrors against the victims.[29] Despite the establishment of the TRC-SL by the Sierra Leonean Parliament to hear and address human rights violations, to respond to the needs of victims and to prevent recurrence of abuses, Alie notes that,

---

25. TRC, "Truth and Reconciliation Commission Act 2000," 3.
26. Alie, "Reconciliation and Traditional Justice," 130.
27. Sierra Leone Truth and Reconciliation Commission, Vol. 3b, Chap. 7, Section 36, pp. 440.
28. Sierra Leone Truth, Vol. 3b, Chap. 7, Section 33, pp. 439.
29. Alie, "Reconciliation and Traditional Justice," 130.

the TRC and local communities considered vague expressions of regret sufficient as long as former combatants displayed humility towards the community during the hearings. The commission performed general reconciliation ceremonies where the perpetrators accepted their wrongdoings and asked for forgiveness, and the victims were also encouraged to accept and to gradually work towards forgiveness and reconciliation.[30]

This approach was undoubtedly problematic as it sacrificed the rights of victims by giving credit to "vague expressions of regret" from perpetrators. While victims were encouraged to work towards reconciliation with their perpetrators, it is not clear whether this process included reparation or not. However, for a reconciliation initiative to be effective, it is essential that reparation follows, as it has been done at the community level in Sierra Leone. Elders were also involved in the process in remote areas. They worked towards a lasting peace in their communities by practicing "traditional rites of forgiveness" as well as "pouring of libations and cleansing rituals."[31] It is doubtful that the TRC-SL has fully succeeded in the process because hearings of truthful confessions of former fighters in some districts did not occur due the time constraints.[32] In Alie's opinion, if the government were to implement the Commission's recommendations, "they would without doubt act as catalyst for the social and legal reform required to address impunity and establish a culture of respect of human rights in Sierra Leone."[33]

Apart from the Truth Commission, the Special Court in Sierra Leone (SCSL) was set up to prosecute criminals who violated the 1999 Lomé Peace Agreement. It sent prosecutors to rural communities to listen to people's grievances and balanced local customs with international standards to set legal standards for the treatment of children and women after the conflict.[34] In March 2003, the Special Court arrested Foday Sanko and Issa Sesay of the RUF, Sam Hinga Norman, the leader of Kamajor militia, the priest Aliu

---

30. Alie, "Reconciliation and Traditional Justice," 131.
31. Alie," 131.
32. Alie, 131.
33. Alie, 130.
34. Raghu, "From Retribution to Restoration."

Kundorwa, and other key actors.³⁵ In their attempt to deliver justice and lead the nation towards reconciliation, Courtney Cole claims that the TRC-SL and the SCSL in their areas of jurisdiction have done little to engage and influence ordinary Sierra Leoneans.³⁶

John Caulker indicates that, "The international community spent $300 million on a Special Court in Sierra Leone, which is prosecuting nine men considered most responsible for causing the war."³⁷ He further opines that, rather than spending a huge amount of money to prosecute a few people, the government could use it to improve the living conditions of the victims of the war. Elisabeth Hoffman also notes that, despite the huge amount of money used in the process, the TRC-SL and SCSL have failed to change the daily lives of Sierra Leoneans who are still struggling with the aftermath of the conflict.³⁸ While the TRC-SL recognized the effectiveness of traditional beliefs for conflict resolution and reconciliation at the community level, it "has not felt entirely comfortable relying on traditional structures to help foster reconciliation," because some traditional leaders were reportedly involved in the conflict.³⁹

It is also important to briefly point out that, among the indigenous methods of reconciliation, there was the practice of justice based on the Kpaa Mende tradition according to which "justice and reconciliation are generally inseparable."⁴⁰ This tradition promoted truth-seeking through restorative and retributive justice, depending on the case, and led to reconciliation. The conditions for granting restorative justice to an offender were his or her apology for the wrongs he or she had committed, his or her sincere remorse and agreement to help the victim deal with the problem caused, as payment or reparation.⁴¹

This initiative aimed at addressing the consequences of the conflict and achieving community healing in order to reconcile people with their community. Women also held key positions in the process. Alie argued that those

---

35. Alie, "Reconciliation and Traditional Justice," 132.
36. Cole, "All in the Fambul Tok," 1.
37. Caulker, "Introducing Fambul Tok."
38. Hoffman, "Reconciliation in Sierra Leone," 131.
39. Sierra Leone Truth, Vol. 3b, Chap. 7, Section 25, 438.
40. Alie, "Reconciliation and Traditional Justice," 133.
41. Alie, 136.

who made up the panel showed a "Belief in the supernatural (God, priests and priestesses, and ancestors)" and the deities who "play a crucial role in the judicial process. The mechanisms also involved rituals such as cleansing ceremonies, songs and dance."[42] In addition, other key actors in the process comprised traditional authorities, local courts, tribal elders, community and religious leaders. Although this indigenous justice was not necessarily linked to the civil war, the culture is preserved despite the influence of colonialism and modernism.[43]

As the initiator of the *Fambul Tok* project, Caulker stated, "Fambul Tok is Krio for family talk. It's an old tradition, which is as old as Sierra Leone itself. So, it's a way of resolving disputes as a community, as a family."[44] Although this culture was part of Sierra Leone's primal heritage, it is difficult to trace its pre-colonial practice. Shekou M. Sesay asserts that traditional practices such as the *Fambul Tok*, under the leadership of paramount chiefs, were in decline under the influence of the British colonizers and long before the civil war broke out although the influence of the chiefs remains important, especially "in matters of traditional culture and justice."[45] Apart from this observation, it should be noted that the government did not implement *Fambul Tok* as part of the traditional justice system, alongside the TRC-SL and SCSL; to the contrary, a national human rights NGO initiated *Fambul Tok*.

Since the TRC-SL and SCSL paid little attention to the most affected villagers by the conflict, the community-based approach, *Fambul Tok* "stepped into the breach" to promote "village-level reconciliation ceremonies around a bonfire."[46] The practice of *Fambul Tok* follows more or less the same pattern for healing and reconciliation in villages.[47] The various cases brought before the elders and the community, and for which reconciliation is sought relate to torture, looting, and kidnapping, destruction of houses and properties, and amputation or killing of loved ones. The initiative promotes forgiveness and

---

42. Alie, "Reconciliation and Traditional Justice," 133.
43. Alie, 133.
44. Caulker, "Transcribed from Ch 10 Clip,"
45. Sesay, "Encyclopaedia Britannica Online." Accessed 18 June 2022, https://www.britannica.com/place/Sierra-Leone/Government-and-society.
46. Hoffman, "Community Healing," 6
47. Hoffman, 6.

reconciliation. From a short video on the reconciliation process of *Fambul Tok*, I transcribed the following episode.

The video commences with traditional music and voices speaking in a Sierra Leonean language. It is a dark night setting with only a fire burning and people appear to be standing or seating around.[48]

> *Esther:*
> Two months into the war, the rebels entered this village. They beat us and raped us. About 15 men. I was 12 years old at the time. About 15 men raped me, but there was a man among them I knew. He was my uncle. As little as I was, he had the mind to rape me. That man, I still see him around. And whenever I see him, I feel afraid. That man, he is among us tonight. And I would like to bring him forward so that all of you can see.
>
> *Sounds of other voices talking in their language.*
>
> *Esther:*
> "This is the man. He is the man!"
>
> *Voice of an old man:*
> "We will now listen to this man to hear why he did this."
>
> *The uncle:*
> To begin, I apologize. It was not only my intention to do it. They hit me and said if I didn't join them, I would be killed. So, I joined them. I asked Esther to forgive me. I said, *"We are from the same family, from the same village."* I really begged her to forgive me. From now on, I will do whatever she wants. Anything she asks for me, I will do it for her. Please forgive me.
>
> *The old man comes closer to Esther and her uncle and speaks to Esther in Sierra Leonean language.*
>
> *Esther:*
> "I forgive him. I forgive him."

---

48. Marchant, "'Fambul Tok' Reveals."

The uncle:
"You really forgive me?"

Esther:
"Yes, I forgive him."

Esther and her uncle held their hands and performed a ritual dance to the sound of traditional music. The crowd joined them, beating hands and drums in a rhythm of the music.[49]

As indicated in the transcription above, a woman, Esther, over thirty years old narrated the story of her rape by fifteen men. She detailed the trauma she went through since the incident occurred. This phase marks the first step of healing from trauma and is indispensable for recovering one's own identity.[50] Once she brought her rapist uncle forward, she confronted him to know the truth about his action. Here *Fambul Tok* comprises establishing the truth.[51] In the video, Esther's uncle explained the reason he raped her as a way to attest the truthfulness of his story. *Fambul Tok* also facilitates dialogue between victims and offenders. In the transcribed video, Esther's uncle asked for forgiveness.

In her analysis of Sierra Leone's conflict, Stephanie Goins reports that a person "who was victimized and then forced to be a perpetrator certainly deserves forgiveness."[52] This plea is reflected in the statement below,

> We were victims. We did not want to do want we did but we were forced. We deserve to be forgiven and taken back into the community. Our circumstances do not make us guilty, because we were all victims. Otherwise, you have to hold the victims guilty rather than perpetrators.[53]

Another respondent said, "The girls that were taken forcibly by the rebels – the community recognizes them to be prostitutes."[54] Esther may have recovered through the *Fambul Tok* reconciliation process. However, this has not been the case for all the women/girls who have been raped. Many of them

---

49. Documentary Educational Resources, "Fambul Tok – PREVIEW."
50. Goins, *Forgiveness and Reintegration*, 178.
51. Clark, *The Gacaca Courts*, 33.
52. Goins, *Forgiveness and Reintegration*, 178.
53. Goins, 178.
54. Goins, 179.

remained burdened by trauma, shame, stigma, sexually transmitted diseases, and unplanned births. From this analysis, it is important to note that some communities and traditions condemn victimized people as perpetrators, as one respondent points out in the quote above. In case a person was victimized and was involved in violence or rape, it is essential for the community to forgive him or her for being forced to commit the act. The community has forgiven Esther's uncle because he declared he was forced to rape the woman.

In shame and guilt cultures, "shame [is] felt by the victim of rape, but in some cases the rapist feels shameful and/or guilty."[55] Generally, communities of "collective cultures" despise rapists or victims of rape because rape affects not only the perpetrator and/or the victim, but also the whole family and community. In this case, forgiveness is essential. However, the effective way to solve such a problem is repentance and restitution. In other words, marriage will restore honour to the girl and her family.[56]

Discussing the issue of forgiveness in the context of transitional justice, Clark argues that some critics see forgiveness as a concept more related to a religious perspective to which many people do not adhere.[57] Others assume that when perpetrators are forgiven, "they will not receive the punishment they deserve or that may be necessary to discourage future criminality" and still others claim that forgiveness leads to forgetting the crimes committed so that the victims give up.[58] However, in Sierra Leone, although she did not base her study on *Fambul Tok*, Goins showed that many people saw forgiveness as the best way to reintegrate perpetrators, particularly former child soldiers, into communities, reconciling them with their home.[59]

Brian Castle points out that the South African Truth and Reconciliation Commission (SATRC) led by Tutu and TRC-SL led by Bishop Joseph Humper were also the "organs of forgiveness and reconciliation used in pursuit of political end," namely national unity and reconstruction.[60] However, Sandra Fancello and André Mary argue that some politicians responsible for crimes in Africa try to escape the consequences of their actions and seek forgiveness

---

55. Goins, *Forgiveness and Reintegration*, 176.
56. Goins, 176.
57. Clark, *The Gacaca Courts*, 42.
58. Clark, 42.
59. Goins, *Forgiveness and Reintegration*, 108–113.
60. Castle, *Reconciling One and All*, 63.

through peace and reconciliation fora.[61] This strategy usually leads to "cheap reconciliation,"[62] which does not make them accountable to the victims. In the case of CAR for example, on 27 January 2020, the former president Bozizé solemnly asked the Centrafricans for forgiveness for the wrongs committed against them because of his leadership.[63] Soon after, he joined the CPC group, launched the attempted coup during which many people died, undermining his request for forgiveness.

Fambul Tok is a process of reconciliation, which allows resentment and revenge to be released, and relationships to be rebuilt in a peaceful manner. It goes far beyond political forgiveness at peace fora and conferences. In exploring the Christian vision for reconciliation and justice, Emmanuel Katongole and Chris Rice argue that, "Reconciliation has become a popular notion in our time, finding its way into the potential rhetoric and public policy of many governments."[64] This helps us to understand that the forgiveness that some African politicians seek during peace and reconciliation fora generally ignores the agony of people and sets aside the expectations of the victims.[65] However, in *Fambul Tok*, victims are encouraged to forgive perpetrators, who are expected to repair their wrongdoings.

In the above transcript of video, Esther's rapist went on to say, "From now on, I will do whatever she wants. Anything she asks of me, I will do it for her." The rapist's decision to do whatever Esther would ask is called "reparation." In transitional justice, reparation is part of the restorative justice. Goins argues that human beings long for justice because when "the needs of justice" are met, they can justify forgiveness.[66] In Esther's case, justice was to be achieved through coming restitution and/or reparation that the rapist promised in front of the crowd, as the video highlighted. Discussing the contribution of transitional justice to peace processes, Carl Stauffer points out that restorative justice is accomplished in three ways: (1) justice rooted in relational bonding, not just legal criminal justice, (2) Justice achieved through restitution, reparations,

---

61. Fancello and Mary, "Institutions du Pardon et Politiques," 1.
62. Bonhoeffer, *The Cost of Discipleship*, 45.
63. TV5 Monde, "Centrafrique : l'ex-président François."
64. Katongole and Rice, *Reconciling All Things*, 25.
65. Fancello and André, "Institutions du Pardon," 1.
66. Goins, *Forgiveness and Reintegration*, 43.

not just the interpretation of criminal law, and (3) justice achieved through restoration, rehabilitation, and healing, not punishment.[67]

The attitude of Esther's rapist shows that he was willing to be accountable by promising to "repair" his mistake. In the *Fambul Tok* culture, Sierra Leoneans strategize about reparation in a reconciliation process. In this regard, Caulker says, "For instance, the community will come with recommendations that offenders who are responsible for burning down their houses should work with the victims to help rebuild these houses."[68] Even though reparations may not equal the value of lost lives and goods, such initiatives can bring healing and relief to victims, and can restore relationships between them and offenders. It is only in this perspective that Sierra Leoneans understand the deepest meaning of life. Hoffman says, "When asked what justice would look like, to them it wasn't about separating and punishing offenders, but rather mending the broken bonds of community, making the communities—and therefore the people in them—whole again."[69]

3. The Results of the *Fambul Tok* Ritual

Fambul Tok has great potential and is an outstanding model of how a community can engage in post-conflict healing. The initiative has become an organization for Human Rights, known as "Fambul Tok International," which continues to play key roles in the communities. The initiators continue to carry out activities through consultations on reconciliation, pilot activities, training of parties, organisation of the reconciliation initiatives, and follow-up.

In another transcribed video interview, documentarian and photographer Sara Terry says, "It's really time for all of us [Westerners] to stop talking about saving Africa and to find ways to be learning from Africa . . . because in the media, Africa is [said to be] a place of disaster, war, famine, conflict . . . I am so stunned by the fact that Africa has answers that invite our humility."[70] In the same video, Libby Hoffman contends that, "The process of reconciliation

---

67. Stauffer, "Finding Justice Amidst," 10.
68. Caulker, "Introducing Fambul Tok."
69. Hoffman, "Community Healing," 9.
70. Fambul Tok Project, "Fambul Tok Filmmaker Interview - Complete."

happening in Sierra Leone has universal lessons that the world needs to learn from and that proves to be incredibly true."[71]

4. Conclusion

The expectations of Sierra Leoneans in the aftermath of the civil war, which tore the country apart, was great. The *Fambul Tok* initiative helped them meet this expectation by emphasizing forgiveness between both the perpetrators and the victims of the war. For the former, it is a way for the victim or his or her family and the community to re-accept the offender. To authenticate the need for forgiveness, the perpetrator agrees to repair the wrong he or she has committed, while for the victim, forgiveness means re-accepting the perpetrator and restoring the broken relationship. *Fambul Tok* is therefore an initiative for community-based forgiveness, reparation, and reconciliation.[72]

In light of this study, it is understood that the *Fambul Tok* initiative offers a biblically-based process of reconciliation because it allows victims and their perpetrators to offer forgiveness and to receive reparation. In accordance with Ephesians 2:11–18, they destroy the wall of hostility and unite with one another, establishing peace. They also emphasize the truth about what happened and reparation of the wrong as a means to achieve justice. God's intention for reconciliation includes the restoration of relationships with God, with one another, and with the material creation, as stated at the Lausanne Forum for Evagelization in light of Colossians 1:15–20, God reconciling all things in heaven and on earth to himself.[73] We can affirm that *Fambul Tok* also promotes reconciliation with God's creation when, during the ritual ceremony, the community demands that the offendor repair what he/she has destroyed. For example, when it is established that the offendor set fire to the victim's field, the elders of the community demand that the offendor help to repair with the victim what he/she has done by setting the fire to the crops. Therefore, if interpreted scripturally, *Fambul Tok* shows that Jesus Christ is for Sierra Leoneans the "New *Fambul Tok*" (new family talk) since the gospel

---

71. Fambul Tok Project, "Fambul Tok Filmmaker Interview."

72. The TRC-SL also process emphasized forgiveness, reconciliation and national healing. However, promoters of *Fambul Tok* felt that the TRC-SL and the SCSL proved to be insufficient initiatives to deal with the conflict issues.

73. Lausanne Committee for World Evangelisn, "Reconciliation as the Mission of God," 15.

of Christ is the "good news" or the "word of God" that forgives, heals, and transforms broken relationships.

This initiative is a perfect example and Centrafricans can apply such a method to *Mbuki* to meet the expectations of reconciliation in their context. The study provides a basis for addressing the problem being identified, namely the lack of use of traditional methods and the sidelining of traditional leaders from the national reconciliation process. Since the country has a variety of traditional concepts and practices, analysing them can lead to a better understanding of how societies in the past sought truth, delivered justice, and promoted forgiveness and reconciliation. The relevance of *Mbuki*, therefore, cannot be understood without situating the context in which the conflict broke out and examining what has been done so far.

CHAPTER 3

Understanding the Social, Political, Economic, and Religious Contexts of CAR

1. Introduction

This chapter is a brief overview of the social, political, economic, and religious organization of CAR. It seeks to explain that the country has a variety of what makes the existence of its inhabitants. To this end, the diversity of its social formation, its political, economic, and religious worldview needs to be scholarly explored to understand what is needed to foster reconciliation in light of the *Mbuki* belief.

2. Overview of CAR

Louisa Lombard claims that people often do not notice CAR when viewing the map of Africa, even though it lies in the centre of the continent.[1] The name of the country in Sango *Ködörösêse tî Bêafrîka*, for short *Bêafrîka*, means the country in the heart of Africa.[2] It is a landlocked territory of about six hundred and twenty-three thousand square kilometres. As shown in figure 1 below, CAR is bordered to the north by Chad and to the east by Sudan

---

1. Lombard, *State of Rebellion*, Kindle, loc. 233.
2. Bissengué and Indo, *Barthélemy Boganda*, Kindle, loc. 107.

and South Sudan. The DR Congo is to the south, the Republic of Congo to the southwest, and Cameroon to the west.³ The CAR's population is about five million.⁴ The country's geographical location has both advantages and disadvantages for its population and its development. For example, being surrounded by neighbouring countries, CAR has an opportunity to share with and receive from others. As a disadvantage, security threats due to frequent interferences by external powers from the neighbouring countries affect the country and its domestic affairs.

Vegetation also plays a role in the daily life of the population. It consists of savannah and forests with semi-desert in the northern part of the country. The CAR's large forest lies to the south-east and south-west and occupies 15 percent of the total territory. Savannah areas cover the centre, east and west, and the far north is the driest region. The north is drier and warmer with a short rainy season from June to September, while the south is humid and the dry season is shorter, raining from May to October.⁵ Centrafricans use the savannah areas for agriculture, hunting, and other activities, while the forest provides wood, rubber, caterpillars, coco leaves, and other products. The use of savannah and forests has been a source of conflicts.⁶

In the colonial period, France regarded the lands of Oubangui Chari as "vacant and without owners."⁷ Therefore, they transferred the fertile parts of some regions to twenty-seven concessionary companies for exploitation.⁸ In addition, the colonial administration conceded the lands of Bouar, in western CAR, to the Fulbe pastoralists (originating from northern Cameroon) to graze their herds. The Fulbe spoiled the lands that the Gbaya used for agriculture. As a result, the Gbaya farmers expressed their *ressentiment* when they triggered

---

3. Dongombe, *L'Oubangui-Chari et son Evangélisation*, Kindle, loc. 220. The DRC also claims to be in the centre of Africa.

4. Geneva Centre for Security Sector Governance, "Central African Republic Background Note." Last update 01 October 2019. Accessed 29 April 2020, https://issat.dcaf.ch/Learn/Resource-Library/Country-Profiles/Central-African-Republic-Background-Note.

5. Woodfork, *Culture and Customs*, 3.

6. Woodfork, 3.

7. Castelino, "Central African Republic," 1835. See also Baxter, *France in Centrafrique*, Kindle. loc. 340.

8. Bissengué and Indo, *Barthélémy Boganda*, Kindle loc. 363.

Understanding the Social, Political, Economic, and Religious Contexts of CAR   43

a revolt against the Fulbe and the colonial rulers.⁹ Francis Fukuyama points out that when people's rights and identities are disregarded, the humiliated group expresses its resentment to regain its dignity.¹⁰

Figure 1: Map of Africa showing the location of CAR[11]

A July 2015 report described how the Séléka rebels continued to loot forest resources. Alice Harrison pointed out that some European companies have

---

9. Trinidad Deiros, "Central African Republic: The Invention of a Religious Conflict." *Opinion Papers*, Vol. 67, 1–14. Last updated 16 June 2014. Accessed 10 March 2020, http://www.ieee.es/en/Galerias/fichero/docs_opinion/2014/DIEEEO67-2014_RCA_InvencionConflictoReligioso_T.Deiros_ENGLISH.pdf.

10. Fukuyama, *Identity: The Demand*, 16–17.

11. https://en.m.wikipedia.org/wiki/File:Central_African_Republic_in_Africa_(-mini_map_-rivers).svg, TUBS, CC BY-SA 3.0 <https://creativecommons.org/licenses/by-sa/3.0>, via Wikimedia Commons.

been funding the Séléka rebels in order to benefit from the "illegal timber trade."[12] Being in a landlocked country, the Centrafricans face a great challenge that affects "trade, agriculture, and transportation."[13] Some use rivers with dugout canoes to facilitate transport and provide resources on the most important rivers such as Oubangui, Chari, Sangha, Mbomou, Ouham, Pendé, to mention a few.[14]

3. Social Organization of CAR

Although in traditional CAR societies clashes often broke out, people settled disputes peacefully in order to live in harmony and solidarity with each other. Initiation rites also forged the socialization of people and enabled them to form social bonds in that "those who go through initiation together are a family of a sort and individuals identify themselves as a member of their initiation group throughout their lives."[15] Also, in CAR, ethnic groups and villages constitute the widest circles of societal organization. Within each ethnic group, there are different subgroups with dialects and customs; and within the subgroups, different clans "whose extended families trace their lineage to a common male ancestor,"[16] and from which the extended families derived.

In the social organization, common languages and cultural practices also bind people together. The languages, customs, and cultures are not static and can change due to "internal and external factors, including lineage, location, lifestyle . . . intermarriage and assimilation" which bring changes in the socialization of people.[17] Thus, social changes led to strong relational ties, which formed the basis of social organization of the country. Woodfork argues that money, gender, age, family, and profession are other elements that categorize families.[18] Family ties influence society because the family line defines and identifies everyone; and people's achievements help them achieve social status in society. In this non-static formation of societal relations, politicians use

---

12. Alice Harrison, *Blood Timber*, 4.
13. Woodfork, *Culture and Customs*, 3.
14. Woodfork, 3.
15. Woodfork, 130.
16. Woodfork, 130.
17. Woodfork, 9.
18. Woodfork, 129.

ethnic affiliations as an instrument to achieve their ambitions. In CAR, the main ethnic groups are Gbaya (33 percent), Banda (27 percent), Mandja (13 percent), Sara (10 percent), Mboum (7 percent), Yakoma (4 percent), and Biaka (4 percent). Further divisions are made in all groups.[19]

During the colonial period, indigenous people fought against Europeans to preserve the structures of initiation such as *Labi*, *Soumalé* and *Ngakola*, which imparted socio-religious knowledge to the youths. Dieudonné Kpamo argues that colonial looting, portage, tax, forced labours, and similar treatments put an end to these traditional structures of education.[20] Jacqueline Woodfork also claims that, because they did not understand African social organization, "Colonizers used anthropology as a way to construct differences between people to justify imperialism and its workings. They also used anthropology to create hierarchies among Africans people, finding some groups to be superior to others because of lifestyle, social organization, or other factors."[21] This view reflects the way, for example, Europeans have categorized people according to social structures in Sierra Leone, as I pointed out earlier.

4. Economic Situation

A colonial official, whose name is not recorded, reported in 1934 that, among the French Equatorial Africa (in French, AEF) territories, Oubangui Chari had enough potential in terms of agricultural and thus economic development.[22] However, despite its considerable natural resources and unexplored wealth, decades of political instability that occurred after independence affected the development of the country. The country's geographical position makes it dependent on neighbouring counties in terms of imports and exports. In general, CAR's economy is based on agriculture and mining, but also on forestry activities. Before 1990, while men were occupied producing cotton, coffee, and tobacco for export, women were producing cassava, maize, groundnuts, bananas, and yams for the family.[23] However, frequent instability

---

19. Woodfork, *Culture and Customs*, 8.
20. Kpamo, *La Christianisation*, 9.
21. Woodfork, *Culture and Customs*, 8.
22. ANOM, "Affaires Politiques No. 831."
23. Woodfork, *Culture and Customs*, 148.

and the lack of good policy to preserve and develop agricultural activities have plunged the sector into crisis. Mining and forestry are another sector of economy. Centrafricans who are engaged in mining are called *nagbata* (artisanal miners). Foreign companies have been involved in considerable exploitation of mineral and timber resources and people have not benefitted.[24] During the last two decades of conflict, illegal mining and logging activities have increased with the complicity of foreign industries.

Robert Klosowicz notes that the weakness of economic development in CAR is due to political instability, the problem of skilled labour, poor transport infrastructure and corruption.[25] This is evidenced by the fact that political leaders who ruled the country have been responsible for economic crimes through corruption and mismanagement of public interests. Roland Marshall argues that many Centrafricans consider these as "insecurities [that] manifest themselves frequently in the form of tensions over wealth, accumulation and social status."[26] They also complain when someone uses an official position to enrich himself or herself, or suspect that someone who runs a business and becomes wealthy has used occult means to do so. He goes on to explain that, "This mistrust is part of the reason why nearly the entire commercial class is composed of foreigners."[27] Even though they do not say it openly, many non-Muslims resent Muslims who own businesses in the country, alleging that the foreigners have corrupted the authorities who are more favourable to promoting the commercial activities of the latter than their own.

Another major problem of the CAR economy is its dependence on the French CFA currency. Since the creation of this colonial currency, two community zones use the CFA, the West African zone, and the Central African zone. The currency has been pegged to the French franc since 1948 and now to the euro.[28] In January 2019, Italy's Deputy Prime Minister, Luigi Di Maio, accused France of causing migration into Europe by using the CFA currency to exploit and impoverish its former colonies.[29] The late Chadian president, Idriss Déby Itno, felt the CFA franc could continue to exist but not under

---

24. Woodfork, *Culture and Customs*, 148.
25. Klosowicz, "Central African Republic," 35.
26. Marshall, "Being Rich, Being Poor," 53.
27. Marshall, 53.
28. Kappel, "Future Prospects for the CFA," 269.
29. Locke, "The CFA Franc," 1.

the French system because its arrangement does not promote African economic growth.[30] Many French-speaking Africans have protested against the use of CFA, which prevents the economic growth and development of their countries. In May 2020, France yielded to pressure from West Africa, which decided to create a sub-regional currency called "*eco,*" although the monetary alternative raised questions and has caused debates up to the period under current research.[31]

5. Religious Worldview

Scholars argue that the definition of "religion" varies because it is not "clear to everyone"[32] or has no "single universally accepted definition."[33] While Mbiti points out that "religion can be discerned in terms of beliefs, ceremonies, rituals and religious officiants,"[34] Terry C. Muck describes it as a "human experience as it relates to a transcendence."[35] Kwesi Dickson helpfully explains the crucial role that religion plays in the establishment and functioning of social relations, and how culture and religion are interrelated:

> . . . in African society culture and religion are not easily separated. Religion is a regular accompaniment in a person's life; the chief's role, the relations between members of a society, morality, the stages in person's life (birth, puberty and marriage, and death), the practice of medicine, architecture, warfare, traditional education, etc.: all these areas are not dissociated from religion in traditional African society.[36]

Reflecting on the case of CAR, Woodfork notes the respect Centrafricans have for religion as it unites them and enables them to enjoy moral principles and codes. Through religion, they worship and perform rituals together to

---

30. Locke, "The CFA Franc, 2.
31. Pigeaud, "Reforme du franc CFA."
32. Magesa, *African Religion: The Moral*, 13.
33. Bonsu, "African Traditional Religion," 108.
34. Mbiti, *African Religions*, 1.
35. Muck, "Religion," 818.
36. Kwesi, *Theology in Africa*, 47.

strengthen the bonds of community that exist between them.³⁷ The above arguments suggest that, before the arrival of Western Christianity, Centrafricans developed their primal faith, which helped to bind them together and to seek for solutions to various problems they faced.

Research shows different figures that determine the religious groups in the CAR. For example, Woodfork explains that indigenous religious groups represent 35 percent of the population, while Christians, including Catholics and Protestants, represent 50 percent and Muslims 15 percent.³⁸ Other studies, such as that by the Pew Research Center in 2020, shows that the country's main religious groups are Christians (90.7 percent) and Muslims (6.2 percent),³⁹ while the Joshua Project maintains 71 percent, including Catholics and Evangelicals.⁴⁰

Before Islam and Christianity reached CAR, people were involved in the primal religious faith. They believed in a "supreme being" as the one who created the earth, human beings, plants, animals, and everything that exists. The supreme being according to them "lives in the skies and is all-powerful."⁴¹ Some ethnic groups believed that, after creating all things, the creator distanced himself and charged deities and ancestors to play different roles for

---

37. Woodfork, *Culture and Customs*, 21.

38. Woodfork, 22.

39. Pew Research Center, "Religious Composition by Country, 2010–2020." https://www.pewresearch.org/religion/feature/religious-composition-by-country-2010–2020/. Accessed 21 August 2025.

40. Joshua Project, 2022. "Country: Central African Republic," Accessed 20 June 2022, https://joshuaproject.net/countries/CT. Considering the above figures, someone who identifies as "Christian" is counted as Christan, even if they rarely attend church and primarily practice indigenous rituals. In many post-colonial African countries, "Christian" is a default cultural and ethnic identifier as much as a theological one. Therefore, Pew's high percentage reflects nominal or cultural affiliation. However, Woodfork's categorisation attempts to measure the actual religious landscape rather than just labels. The 35 percent indigenous figure likely represents people for whom traditional beliefs are the primary framework, plus the vast number of Christians who seamlessly blend Christian worship with indigenous practices like ancestor veneration and/or consultation with healers. The 50 percent Christian figure here probably represents those whose practice is more exclusively aligned with formal Christian doctrine. The violent civil conflict since 2013 has drastically altered the demographic map. Indeed, the conflict, often framed along religious lines, has led to the mass displacement and killing of Muslims by Anti-Balaka. Hundreds of thousands of Muslims have fled to neighbouring countries like Chad and Cameroon. This explains the Pew's figure of 6.2 percent Muslim since a significant portion of the Muslim community had been forced out. However, Pre-2013, the Muslim population was estimated at around 10–15 percent. Woodfork's 15 percent figure likely reflects the pre-war reality.

41. Woodfork, *Culture and Customs*, 25.

human beings.⁴² Centrafricans have various names for the supreme being. The Biaka named him *Komba*, the Zandé named him *Mboli*, the Banda *Yilingu*, the Mandja *Galé*, and the Karré *Won*, to mention but a few.⁴³ To reach the creator, they prayed through the deities and ancestors. In this spirituality, ancestors occupied a central place in a family. Woodfork says that "people make offerings of food, drink, prayer, and other things that the deceased enjoyed in life (such as tobacco) to placate and please their forebears and try to curry their good favour."⁴⁴ In doing so, Centrafricans believe in spirits. Some spirits are benevolent and others, malevolent. To protect themselves from malevolent spirits, people wear charms. For example, *Téré* is a "spirit [that] plays a great role in legends and stories." Elders told tales and riddles and sang songs to the youngsters about *Téré*.⁴⁵

Woodfork claims that both primal religious people and Western missionaries fought against colonialism in CAR. While this was obvious for primal religious people, it was not quite the case for Western missionaries who favoured colonial activities and only partly contributed to the fight against the system.⁴⁶ In the spirituality of the Azandé people, while prophets and diviners used oracles to deal with issues such as adultery and death, they were also concerned with "security, good health, fecundity, stability, peace of mind and harmony."⁴⁷ With the introduction of Western Christianity during colonialism as an "imperial religion," Western missionaries attempted to eradicate the indigenous religious practices, as they considered many features of the African culture as inappropriate for Christianity. For example, they considered the Biaka dances to be satanic.⁴⁸

Indeed, archival documents show that even indigenous religious movements were a threat to Western colonial policy and Christianity, because it enlightened people. For example, on 19 May 1932, the lieutenant governor of Moyen Congo sent a report to Raphaël Antonetti, the General Governor of the AEF, concerning the rise and influence of the *Eglise Kimbangu* (Kimbangu

---

42. Woodfork, *Culture and Customs*, 24–25.
43. Woodfork, 25.
44. Woodfork, 26–27.
45. Woodfork, 29.
46. Woodfork, 32.
47. Woodfork, 32–33.
48. Woodfork, 36.

Church) originated from the DR Congo in the colony. On 19 May 1932, the General Commissioner of the Belgian Congo provided, in a letter to Antonetti, detailed information on the whereabouts of people who had followed the Kimbanguist "black prophets" since 1931.[49] The aim was to control people who had fled the colonies and taken refuge in the localities where the Kimbanguist movement was established. In his reply of 21 July 1932, the General Governor instructed the lieutenant governor to monitor the movement and keep him updated.[50]

Woodfork argues that, in Oubangui Chari, missionaries used the schools they built for education and hospitals for health to Christianize indigenous people. Only converts worked in or attended mission schools and health centres.[51] Such a practice was in contradiction with the policy of the Catholic mission school that Barthélemy Boganda attended in Congo. An archival document shows that missionaries begged parents to enrol their children in school so that they could receive a formal education.[52] Moreover, in Oubangui Chari, colonial policy favoured French missionaries more than foreign (protestant) missionaries, as shown in a letter from the General Governor dated 3 July 1952:

> Vous avez demandé à l'Inspecteur Général des Services de Sécurité de vous entretenir de la question de l'entrée en A.E.F. des missionnaires protestants étrangers. La position actuelle de la Fédération est la suivante : Nous souhaitons que les missionnaires protestants soient par priorité français ; cette manière de voir étant malaisée à maintenir de façon impérative puisque le protestantisme français peut difficilement assurer son recrutement nous voudrions au moins que les missionnaires aient fait un stage en France (langue – culture etc . . .).
>
> You have asked the General Inspector of Security Services to speak to you about the entry of foreign Protestant missionaries into the A.E.F The position of the Federation is as follows:

---

49. ANOM, GGAEF 5D 95–96, Confidentielle, No. 3861/430 (19 Mai 1932).
50. ANOM, Direction des Affaires Politiques, Kimbanguisme No. 575/c (21 Juillet 1932).
51. Woodfork, *Culture and Customs*, 36.
52. ANOM, GGAEF 5 D 87d (1928–1959), Les Missions Catholiques en Afrique Equatoriale Française.

> We wish Protestant missionaries to be French missionaries as a priority; this approach being difficult to maintain in an imperative way since French Protestantism can hardly ensure its recruitment, we would at least like the missionaries to have done a training course in France (language - culture etc . . .).[53]

In this context, some indigenous people disapproved of the way Western missionaries brought and presented Christianity to them. They set up an indigenous Church, which combined the practices of Christianity and traditional religion, and became the alternative that made Christianity more relevant to them, as was the case with *Mission ti Africa* among the Azandé people.[54] In the Zandé society, for example, a Zandé prophetess, Awa Marie Sibonguirete, founded the Mission ti Africa (MTA) in 1934. Woodfork highlights that, according to the story, Sibonguirete was saved from an accident and was said to have received God's vision to spread his word and heal Zandé people. Woodfork writes,

> African Christian denominations rose when there was a call from a charismatic individual to follow him or her. In Zandéland, the Mission ti Africa (MTA) churches fall into this category. According to oral tradition, the MTA began in 1934 when a young girl named Awa Marie Sibonguirete survived a severe accident. While unconscious, she met God who asked her to spread His word on earth. God decided that his white male prophets, Moses, Jesus, and Mohammad had not been able to bring Christianity to the Zandé, so He selected an African woman to accomplish the goal. He wanted her to be a healer and gave her a bottle of medicine to cure people. God proposed to make her white and send her down to earth on a wire, but His advisors convinced him to let her remain black. According to colonial documents, Awa Marie Sibonguirete's house was burned down by a Catholic priest and the colonial government

---

53. ANOM, GGAEF 5 D 87d, Dossier en Communication, No. 1645/APA (3 Juillet 1952). (Translation mine).

54. Woodfork, *Culture and Customs*, 32.

jailed her. Colonial officials saw the MTA as antimissionary and antiwhite.[55]

In fact, like many other indigenous prophets such as Simon Kimbangu in DR Congo, or Karnu, the indigenous "prophet" of the Gbaya people who led the non-violent resistance against the colonial officials, Sibonguirete suffered oppression from colonizers and missionaries to the point that the latter jailed her until death. However, even though her religious movement, *Nzapa Zandé* (literally, "God Zandé"), continues to draw people, there is no evidence that it is the indigenous church of the Eglise Evangélique en Centrafrique (ECC), one of the official church denominations in CAR. Despite the atrocities caused by colonizers, traditional religious practices have not disappeared. To this day, Centrafricans consider religion to be the expression of their belief in the existence of the supreme being, the way in which they approach him, find answers to their problems, and bind themselves into communities.

6. Conclusion

The analysis of social, political, economic, and religious contexts of CAR helped understand the societal organization and values that bound people in the past. The chapter explained that shortcomings in the societal organization of CAR caused the sideling of traditional methods of reconciliation and that of traditional leaders in the process of national healing. It also revealed that, despite challenges in its economy, the country has potential to build a nation of peace, harmony, and development. However, as is pointed out in the chapter that follows, the colonial and modern systems perverted the socio-religious values and harmonious bonds that existed in traditional societies. Therefore, colonial dehumanization and over-exploitation of resources laid the foundation for atrocity that the country experiences till today.

---

55. Woodfork, *Culture and Customs*, 37.

CHAPTER 4

Overview of Institutionalized Violence in CAR

1. Introduction

The current chapter gives an overview of the violent conflicts, especially, that erupted in 2013, and it discusses peace and reconciliation initiatives in this context. This overview reflects on uprisings during the colonial period as a backdrop to the Séléka conflict. It comprises the history of institutionalized colonial violence and indigenous uprisings as the background to the Séléka outbreak, the potential factors underpinning it, and the process and actors involved in the search for reconciliation as well as the prospect of transitional justice.

The interest of this overview is to show that the different methods used so far to achieve peace and reconciliation have marginalized traditional initiatives and leadership. Rather, these methods emphasized foreign approaches that proved ineffective to the local/national context and insufficient to resolve the conflict.

2. Insurgencies in the Colonial Period

Barka Ngainoumbey, known as Karnu, a Gbaya indigenous leader, led the revolt known as the *kongo-wara* war. Alain Degras dates the beginning of *kongo-wara* war to June 1928 and its end to December of the same year.¹ To describe the fiercy of the revolt, Peter Baxter states that, "This was the most significant peasant uprising within French colonial territory and was suppressed only with great difficulty."² In archival documents, Batallion Chief Fonferrier explains that Amada Gaza area, where the indigenous resistance took place, was a "region douteuse" (dangerous area).³ Europeans mistakenly equated another uprising, the Pana revolt of the 1930, known as the "cave war", with *kongo-wara* insurrection.⁴

Christensen notes that the presence of Fulbe "whose further immigration into Gbaya territory had been discouraged after a similar conflict in 1896"⁵ fuelled the conflict. During the pre-colonial period, the Gbaya populations lived among the Fulbe of Cameroon. The Fulbe drove the Gbaya out of Cameroon following tribal wars. As a result, the Gbaya migrated to the lands where they live in CAR. They, therefore, expressed resentment of past oppression and opposed the Fulbe presence on their lands during Karnu's insurrection. However, Karnu's method during the revolt was simple: he opposed the use of Europeans' cloth and other items. According to Christensen, he wanted the white people to leave the Gbaya territory. He declared that "their departure could be hastened and encouraged by the application of a medicine he provided. The Gbaya would be freed from white domination . . . if they bore the sign of kongo-wara 'handle of the hoe' on their skin."⁶ In other words, Karnu believed in a power that was greater than the white's weapons to the point that he told his fellow people: "Never shed the blood of the white men and their soldiers with your spears and knives. Just let the bees chase them away."⁷

Karnu's movement influenced many people groups in the colonial period. Even though he stood for non-violence, between 1928 and 1931, the insurgency spread over the AEF and reached the south of Chad, Cameroon, and

---

1. Degras, *Tengbi ti Abakoro Zo*, 22.
2. Baxter, *France in Centrafrique*, 6.
3. ANOM, GGAEF 5 D 47, Oubangui-Chari: Situation Politique.
4. Degras, *Tengbi ti Abakoro Zo*, 21–22.
5. Christensen, *An African Tree of Life*, 119.
6. Christensen, "Karnu: Witchdoctor or Prophet?," 233–246.
7. Christensen, *An African Tree of Life*, 123.

the west of Oubangui, the Moyen Congo, and Gabon.[8] His attitude shows a respect for human dignity and search for justice, equality, and human rights. His peaceful and nonviolent attitude is a possible model for addressing conflict today. Christensen writes that, according to him, the "shedding of blood in warfare is not the way to attain justice."[9] Rather, there were other ways of resolving conflicts than through shedding blood. Few archival records exist of *kongo-wara* resistance, as it appears records were suppressed to avoid publicity.[10]

The second story worth analysing is that of colonial oppression, which led to the outbreak of another revolt, the *guerre aux cailloux (bilo gbalata* in Gbaya) or "stone war."[11] Dieudonné Kpamo writes that in April 1954 in Berberati province, a colonial master, Guy Bontemps, killed his cook, Antoine N'Zembé and his wife, Pauline Zouangama. The following day, in the morning, a crowd surrounded the colonial office of the Berberati province and demanded revenge for the death of N'Zembé and Zouangama. As the colonial senior official refused to comply with their request, "the local populations revolted and started throwing stones at the white people."[12] The colonial rulers tried unsuccessfully to dialogue with the Gbaya notables and headmen, but the population considered them as accomplices of Bontemps.

Analysing the event, Kpamo comments that the aim for the Gbaya population was not only to kill Bontemps but also to take revenge as required in Gbaya tradition.[13] In contrast, the insurgency by Karnu in 1928 was pacifist, although he too was from the Gbaya ethnic group. One can ask why the *guerre aux cailloux* embarked on a bloody revolt. Kpamo argues that the insurgents had expressed their anger and resentment vis-à-vis the colonial officials for the atrocities they went through.[14] This argument corroborates what Didier Fassin describes when he says that in a context of violence and oppression, oppressed people express "rancor, bitterness, acrimony, anger, ire,

---

8. Kalck, *Histoire Centrafricaine*, 235–236.
9. Christensen, *An African Tree of Life*, 118.
10. Woodfork, *Culture and Customs*, 11–12.
11. Kpamo, *La Christianisation et les Débuts*, 136.
12. Kpamo, 115–116.
13. Kpamo, 131.
14. Kpamo, 131.

and indignation"[15] for the suffering and injustice, they experience. However, the day before the event, N'Zembé asked his master to increase his salary as compensation for the extra task he had been doing daily. His demand displeased Bontemps and the two exchanged virulent words to the point that Bontemps murdered N'Zembé.[16] This implies that the root cause of the murders was the argument between N'Zembé and his master.

To settle the problem, the governor of Oubangui Chari sent emissaries to Berberati. Kpamo points out that "Barthélémy Boganda and San Marco then had to personally intervene to bring back peace. The rioters were then sent off to the Faya-Largeau [Chad] penitentiary, where they served a ten-year sentence."[17] Kpamo further notes that Boganda used a strategy when he attended the funerals of N'Zembé and his wife. During the burial, Boganda spoke in the Sango language to the population, which Kpamo translates into English in the book's summary, as follows: "Very soon justice will be the same to be applied to the whites and the blacks."[18] These words encouraged the population and put an end to the tensions. However, the colonial officials arrested about one hundred individuals, accusing them of being responsible for the insurgency and for having injured Arthur Poirier, Unghero, Bongard, and Remusat.[19] Woodfork notes that, "the more than 100 Gbaya . . . allegedly shouted ant-French anti-French slogans and sang anti-French songs."[20] The insurgencies in the colonial era laid the foundation for other violent conflicts, the bloodiest of which was launched by the Séléka rebellion. On the other hand, the the partiality of Europeans in privileging some ethnic groups to the detriment of others was a root cause of resentment that cause conflicts.[21]

---

15. Fassin, "On Resentment and *Ressentiment*," 249.
16. Kpamo, *La Christianisation et les Débuts*, 124–125.
17. Kpamo, 115–116.
18. Kpamo, 134.
19. Kpamo, 134.
20. Woodfork, *Culture and Customs*, 12.
21. Woodfork, 12.

3. Background to the Conflict

Andreas Mehler suggests that in CAR, as in many African states, violence has become a normalized way to compete against others.[22] While Yannick Weyns et al. argue that many of CAR's political leaders use violence as "the most effective strategy . . . to occupy the country's highest office;"[23] others use the national army to get to power or to maintain it. Consequently, the country experienced successive coups, marked by one democratic election in 1993 that brought Patassé to power. However, from David Dacko to the Séléka, each regime was characterized by corruption, authoritarianism, and tyranny.[24]

Commentators claimed that the untimely and mysterious death of Boganda in a so-called air crash in 1959 was a conspiracy of France.[25] Some said it was "a conspiracy of local businessmen and the French secret service."[26] Before his death, Boganda advocated for a Federation of Latin African States, which comprised Rwanda, Burundi, Angola, the DR Congo and Congo Brazzaville, Chad, Gabon, and the geographical position of CAR in the sub-region made it the capital. His dream never came to fruition as he was killed earlier. After his death, Abel Goumba served as a "president-apparent" for few weeks and Dacko, Boganda's nephew, took the command of the newly born republic.[27] Writing about the first coup d'état which occurred in the country, Woodfork says: "Dacko's repressive and dictatorial rule came to an abrupt end on January 1, 1966, when Colonel Jean-Bédel Bokassa, Dacko's cousin and Boganda's nephew, led an almost bloodless coup and took control of the government."[28] Baxter adds that France was aware of Bokassa's coup and did not support Dacko because he "had slipped out of alignment and was not quite the friend that he had at first promised to be."[29]

---

22. Mehler, "Rebels and Parties," 116.
23. Weys, Hoex, Hilgert and Spittaels, *Mapping Conflict Motives*, 8.
24. Vlavonou, "Understanding the 'Failure,'" 318–326.
25. Baxter, *France in Centrafrique*, 13.
26. Baxter, 13.
27. Quai d'Orsay and the local French administrators supported Dacko to the detriment of Goumba, whom they considered a Socialist and too nationalistic. Later on, Dacko put in prison Goumba and his supporters, and in July 1962 instituted a one-party-state. See Baxter, *France in Centrafrique*, 13.
28. Woodfork, *Culture and Customs*, 15.
29. Baxter, *France in Centrafrique*, 14.

Indeed, France incited Bokassa to overthrow Dacko because "Dacko began establishing close ties with China."[30] After taking over, Bokassa ruled CAR with authoritarian and despotic power after he abolished the Constitution of 1959 and dissolved the National Assembly. He crowned himself Emperor on 4 December 1977 with the support of French President Valéry Giscard d'Estaing whose companies received in return diamonds, uranium, and ivory from Bokassa's hands.[31] Thus, soon after independence, CAR experienced dictatorship. Subsequently, France considered Bokassa's relations with the former USSR and with Muammar Gaddafi as a threat because of its interests in CAR. The French government overthrew him in 1979 through Operation Barracuda.

Operation Barracuda aimed at bringing back Dacko to power. The French troops landed in Bangui on 20 September 1979 and reinstalled him while Bokassa was out of the country, visiting Gaddafi. Two years later, people accused his regime of corruption and mismanagement. Therefore, the national army took over in 1981 and the senior military officer André Kolingba led the country until the presidential election of 1993 that Ange-Félix Patassé won.[32]

The history of the current crisis goes back to 2003 when the late Idriss Déby sponsored Bozizé, the chief's staff of the army, to seize power.[33] Douglas-Bowers also assumes that this was an opportunity for Déby to send "his forces to operate in the north of the CAR to eliminate Chadian rebel groups using the territory as a staging ground for attacks" against Chad.[34] During the rebellion, Bozizé made a deal with Chadian mercenaries concerning the power. Mahamed Bahar, one of the mercenaries, asserted that,

> Bozizé made sweeping promises to secure support. 'He said he would be the last Christian President, and that the next President would be Muslim' . . . He promised his Muslim supporters elevated positions in the Army. Instead, once he was

---

30. Douglas-Bowers, "Colonialism, Coup and Conflict."
31. Woodfork, *Culture and Customs*, 15.
32. Al Jazeera News, "CAR government Sings Deal with Rebel Groups."
33. Baker, *Central African Republic*, Kindle 10.
34. Douglas-Bowers, "Colonialism, Coup and Conflict."

in power, he jailed some Muslim soldiers and disenfranchised the rest.[35]

The above show that, among other aspects, the current conflict is the result of a political identity crisis. Such a selfish deal was contrary to the CAR's Constitution and the principles of democracy. The former president of the interim government, Catherine Samba-Panza, observes that the real problem of CAR is not the hatred against the Muslims, but the ambitions for power and interests by the politicians.[36]

Two years after he took over, Bozizé ran and won the 2005 presidential election. In 2011, he ran another election and was re-elected. The opposition parties and observers claimed that the elections were fraudulent.[37] During his regime, the opposition parties, civil societies, and Human Rights organizations denounced corruption, mismanagement, social injustices, imprisonment, and political assassinations. In addition, Francis Kpatindé writes that the international media accused Bozizé of being responsible for the murder of Charles Massi, a former minister, and founder of one of the rebel groups.[38] Moreover, his regime was nepotistic and ethnocentric as he placed his family members, friends of the *Kwa Na Kwa* (KNK) party and his mistresses in different positions in the administration, parliament, national army, and in the lucrative mineral companies.[39] His governing policy contributed to social inequalities and grievances that affected the country until the outbreak of the 2013 coup.[40] The search for a resolution to the conflict involved parties such as individuals, states, and institutions.

4. Conclusion

This short chapter attempted to describe how violence and conflicts have become institutionalized in CAR. It showed that colonial violence has led the foundation for the political and military crises that have erupted in the last

---

35. Baker, *Central African Republic*, 49.
36. Baker, 29.
37. Lombard, "Central African Republic," 1.
38. Kpatindé, "Pourquoi Bozizé a-t-il été lâché par ses frères?" Radio France Internationale.
39. Lombard, "Central African Republic," 1.
40. Lombard, 1.

decades. Colonial abuse and policy of discrimination have caused mistrust and resentment between various ethnic groups. This led to political manipulation and social clashes since the 1990s. The chapter also helped to understand that the lack of traditional initiatives has contributed to delaying the process of healing and restoration of the country. The chapter that follows explores various parties involved in the conflict.

CHAPTER 5

Parties Involved in the 2013 Armed Conflict

1. Introduction

This chapter explains that the parties involved in the armed conflict included the Séléka and Anti-Balaka as non-state armed groups[1], and some soldiers of the Armed Forces of CAR (FACA). Injustice, corruption, human rights

---

1. The Uppsala Conflict Data Program defines a non-state armed conflict as "the use of armed force between two organized armed groups, neither of which is the government of a state, which results in at least 25 battle-related deaths in a year." See Pettersson, "UCDP Non-State Conflict Codebook Version 19.1," 3. Non-state armed groups perpetrate and direct attacks on the state that does not address poverty, political dissatisfaction, autocratic regimes and social exclusion. This happens in many African countries as it has happened in CAR. To add to the discussion, Wendy Isaacs-Martin points out that non-state armed actors influence the socio-political landscape of many countries in Africa, Eastern Europe, and Latin America, as well as Central Asia. See Isaacs-Martin, "The Motivations of Warlords." For Mary Kaldor, non-state armed groups refer to "the new types of war ... taking place in Africa and perhaps also other places." See Kaldor, *New and Old Wars*, 1. In this context, the ideology according to which "the government alone possesses the legitimate use of violence" is no longer the norm. See Isaacs-Martin, "The Motivations of Warlords." Isaacs-Martin points out that the motivations of the armed groups are diverse. For some, it is ideological as they seek "to bring about changes in their social and political recognition." While economic gains attracted some rebels, "territorial interests that do not include the well-being of populations or contribute to political stability" motivated others. See Isaacs-Martin, "The Motivation of Warlords." However, in analysing the civil war in Sierra Leone, Macartan Humphreys and Jeremy M. Weinstein argue that whatever their motivations, armed groups challenge the sovereignty of a country and the legitimacy of the government. See Humphreys and Weinstein, "Who Fight? The Determinants," 439. This is also the case in CAR. The question arises as to which of the categories above best describes the motivation of the CAR rebel groups that have proliferated in the country over the past two decades.

abuses, and similar practices have weakened the country's institutions and allowed non-state armed groups to emerge and take advantage of them to challenge the government. It is also understood that the parties involved in the conflict contributed to sabotaging pre-Christian heritage like *Mbuki* which linked many ethnic groups in peaceful coexistence in traditional context. They also challenged the authority of local/traditional leaders. The first to launch the conflict were the Séléka.

2. The Séléka

The wave of conflicts that disrupted peace and fragile democracy in CAR began with the army mutinies in 1996. During this period, the national army launched three mutinies against the government regarding the payment of salaries, the transfer of the armoury, and the formation of a new government.[2] Patassé sparked the tension when he fired Bozizé, his army chief of staff, on 26 October 2001, accusing him of supporting the attempted coup of May 2001 led by Kolingba.[3] The conflict between the two men caused Bozizé to join Sahr, in southern Chad, where he recruited some Chadian combatants, and his one hundred deserted soldiers from the national army, to launch the coup d'état on 25 October 2002 from the north. On 13 March 2003, when Patassé was out of the country, Bozizé's troops seized power aided by the Chadian *liberators*[4] who came back ten years later as Séléka to overthrow him.

When the relationships between Bozizé and Déby "began to falter, the former turned to South Africa."[5] As Déby realized that Bozizé had not kept his vow, he supported the fighters' march to Bangui.[6] The battle occurred from 22 to 24 March 2013, and a large number of the Séléka rebels marched toward Bangui putting an end to the presence of two hundred and fifty South African Special Forces (SASF) of whom thirteen were killed and twenty-seven wounded.[7] With regard to the armed conflict and the loss of their soldiers in

---

2. Woodfork, *Culture and Customs*, 16.
3. Woodfork, 17.
4. Thomas, *Centrafrique: un destin volé*, 79.
5. Käihkö and Utas, "The Crisis in the CAR," 72.
6. Baker, *Central African Republic*, 10.
7. Vreÿ and Esterhuyse, "South Africa and the Search," 1–27. See also McGregor, "South African Military Disaster," 1–10.

CAR, South Africans demanded explanations from former President Jacob Zuma, as a report showed that the SASFs were sent in 2011 to protect Bozizé.[8]

After taking power, the Séléka rebels and some individual theft engaged in large-scale looting of Bangui. Indeed, economic interest was one of the main motivations for the Séléka coup. Jeremy M. Weinstein calls these "opportunistic rebellions."[9] However, before the coup, a mostly Muslim population from the northeast and northwest of CAR threatened Bozizé's regime.[10] They included the Union of Democratic Forces for Unity (UFDR), led by Dramane Zakaria and Michel Djotodia, the Convention of Patriots for Justice and Peace (CPJP) led by Noureddine Adam and the Convention of Patriots for *Salut ti Kodro* (CPSK) by Mohamed-Moussa Dhaffane.[11] On 18 December 2012, they named their group "Séléka" (in Sango, "alliance" or "coalition"). Other faction groups joined these such as the Patriotic Group for the Liberation of the Central African Republic (GAPLC), the Movement of Central African Liberators for Justice (MLJC) and the Central African Democratic Front (FDPC) led by Abdoulaye Miskine.[12] Djotodia proclaimed himself president and was recognized by the sub-regional presidents and France in April 2013.[13]

The Séléka rebellion included mercenaries originating from Niger, Chad, Sudan, and Cameroon who coveted CAR's resources. After seizing power, the number of Séléka rebels increased exponentially, as numbers of rebels joined the ranks of the troops.[14] In their rivalry for interests and power, they divided into fourteen groups that proliferated throughout the country, controlling more than half the territory while this book is put on paper. In Baker's opinion, the "unruly factions" fought over money, control of territory, and power. This prompted Djotodia to disband the movement, but his decision had little impact, as "The Séléka kept up their atrocities: burning people alive, killing hospital patients, throwing bound prisoners off bridges to drown."[15]

---

8. Thomas, *Centrafrique: un destin volé*, 91.
9. Weinstein, *Inside Rebellion: The Politics*, 10.
10. Isaacs-Martin, "The Motivations of Warlords."
11. Thomas, *Centrafrique: un destin volé*, 87–88.
12. FIDH, "Central African Republic."
13. Thomas, *Centrafrique: un destin volé*, 87–88.
14. Thomas, 95. Le Roux and Sandoua argue that among the rebels, "only 10 percent of the Séléka are CAR nationals – the rest are from Chad and Sudan." See Le Roux and Sandoua, "Leadership Responses during Armed Conflict," 88.
15. Baker, *Central African Republic*, 52.

Although the country had experienced violence and coups d'état in the past, the Séléka rebellion was more brutal. In January 2014, sub-regional leaders deposed Djotodia for being unable to stop the atrocities committed by his men.[16] Even though he disbanded the Séléka movement, his decision did not have any effect "as they felt Djotodia was still indebted to them."[17]

In an interview, the late Franco Mbaye-Bondoi gave a variety of reasons for the increasing violent tensions between armed groups. Of the Muslim groups he stated,

> They wanted to take back power because they thought it was a mistake to let Djotodia go. They had not yet filled their granaries and had left in a hurry. The fact that they left in a hurry without filling their granaries, they wanted to come back. France gives them hope by saying that they are in a minority group, they had taken power and left in a hurry; but they could come back to power. I think this has remained in their minds, especially the foreign Muslims who have invaded the country. There are many of them at Km 5 as I have heard from Centrafrican Muslims who complain about this situation. When we go to meetings, they tell us the truth that in the minds of foreign Muslims, the day they take power; they will make the Centrafricans suffer. France makes false promises to these Muslim bandits. Therefore, between themselves and the Muslims in Km 5 there is no agreement.[18]

In 2014, an interim government was then put in place, led by Catherine Samba-Panza and Faustin-Archange Touadéra was elected in March 2016. However, violent attacks continued, and the measures put in place to stop fighting were still far from bearing fruit, partially because of the rise of the Anti-Balaka militia.

Indeed, economic interest was one of the main motivations for the Séléka coup. Jeremy M. Weinstein calls these "opportunistic rebellions."[19] According to Mary Kaldor, non-state armed groups refer to "the new types of war . . .

---

16. Weys, Hoex, Hilgert and Spittaels, *Mapping Conflict Motives*, 8.
17. Käihkö and Utas, "The Crisis in CAR," 70.
18. Mbaye-Bondoi, Interview, 24 July 2021, Bangui (Translation is mine).
19. Weinstein, *Inside Rebellion: The Politics*, 10.

taking place in Africa and perhaps also other places."[20] The ideology according to which "the government alone possesses the legitimate use of violence"[21] is no longer the norm. Isaacs-Martin points out that the motivations of the armed groups are diverse. For some, it is ideological as they seek "to bring about changes in their social and political recognition." While economic gains attracted some rebels, "territorial interests that do not include the well-being of populations or contribute to political stability," motivated others.[22] The question arises as to which of the categories above best describes the ideology of the rebel groups that have proliferated in the country over the past two decades.

I explain in this chapter that the atrocities committed by the Séléka rebels against the Christian population prompted some politicians and scholars to allege the formation of an Islamic identity through the use of Islamic jihadist ideology in CAR (see chapter 6, section 5). Others, like Baker, however, refuted these allegations and argued that the Séléka against whom the Anti Balaka opposed were not "fundamentalists" but were instead motivated by "prosperity and power."[23]

3. The Anti-Balaka

The Séléka rebellion led to the rise and consolidation of the Anti-Balaka militias, which the international community did not expect. They were galvanized into action by the Séléka's tortures, killings, rapes, burning of houses, looting of churches and villages, public and private goods, and abduction of young boys and girls. According to Weyns *et al.*, the Anti-Balaka militias represent "long-standing village self-defence groups restructured to fight the Seleka."[24] Thomas rightly points out that the Anti-Balaka were made up of three groups: the self-defence militias, Bozizé's supporters and the brigands.[25] One can add

---

20. Kaldor, *New and Old Wars*, 1.
21. Isaacs-Martin, "The Motivations of Warlords."
22. Isaacs-Martin, "The Motivation of Warlords." In analysing the civil war in Sierra Leone, Macartan Humphreys and Jeremy M. Weinstein argue that whatever their motivations, armed groups challenge the sovereignty of a country and the legitimacy of the government. See Humphreys and Weinstein, "Who Fight? The Determinants," 439.
23. Baker, *Central African Republic*, 41.
24. Weyns, Hoex, Hilgert and Spittaels, *Mapping Conflict Motives*, 8.
25. Thomas, *Centrafrique: un destin volé*, 95.

to these groups the "false Anti-Balaka," which comprise those who pretend to be Anti-Balaka militiamen but in reality are not. They were involved in crimes, robbing, looting and extorting people. Originally, the movement, which aimed to counterattack Séléka groups, began in September 2013 around Bossangoa, the hometown of Bozizé.[26] Dieudonné, one of the Anti-Balaka leaders admitted that after the Séléka took power, they committed several crimes.[27] He went to Bossangoa with his colleagues in the security forces loyal to Bozizé, where they "set up a secret base in the jungle and began assembling recruits . . . Soon, the militia had two thousand trained men."[28]

The militiamen saw themselves as a self-defence movement. One of the fighters declared: "No one helps us when the Séléka came to power. If someone comes and puts a boot on your head and knife to your neck, what do you do? You defend yourself."[29] They developed a distinctive identity because, according to Baker, "inspired by animist traditions . . . they were protected by magic. They festooned themselves with wings, costumes, and amulets to ward off attacks, and assembled an arsenal of bows with poison tipped arrows, and a few hunting rifles."[30] Etienne Ngaka, the mayor of Miskine, asserted that his area was secured thanks to "the efforts of our sons [Anti-Balaka]."[31]

The Anti-Balaka used charms or amulets to protect themselves against their "enemies" in battles.[32] They said they may be in danger or may die if they lose the charms. The movement became widespread as former soldiers and presidential guards of Bozizé got involved.[33] People saw them as holding mystical super-powers. As they aimed to expel the Muslim population from the country, some said: *Tonga na sessé so a ayéké ti a Arabo, ala ga a mou ni i ba. Sessé so a ayéké to a kotara ti i la*, meaning, "If this land is the Muslim ancestors' land, let them come and take it over. This is our fathers'

---

26. FIDH/LCDH, "Central African Republic," 18.
27. Deiros, "Central African Republic: The Invetion."
28. Baker, *Central African Republic*, 53.
29. Baker, 54.
30. Baker, 54.
31. Baker, 24.
32. Voice of America, "'Détérioration' de la Sécurité."
33. Reports declare that Bozizé was the political leader of the AB movement. See FIDH/LCDH, "Central African Republic," 59.

land."³⁴ Dejé, one of the Anti Balaka's commanders, said that he had received a "holy" call to set his people free. He asserted, "The earth [land] belongs to us through our ancestors, and foreigners – Muslims – came to try and take it, but they cannot . . . When we invoke the spirits of the ancestors in our dreams, they help us in the fight."³⁵

Such a statement on the one hand explains resentment and revenge against the Séléka but also an unjustified feeling of hatred towards some non-Séléka Muslims. On the other hand, some CAR Muslims became accomplices of the rebels and betrayed non-Muslim individuals. This led some non-Muslims to reject some Muslims, which in turn led to a socio-religious divide between the two groups. The communal divide became the basis for identifying conflicting groups.³⁶ Attempts to resolve the conflict need to take into account the socio-religious identity crisis resulting from the division between the communities. However, both the Anti-Balaka militias and Séléka were responsible for crimes and human rights violations. Since their failure to take Bangui in December 2013, the originally self-defending Anti-Balaka have ceased operating in the country. Only the politicized groups and brigands continued to operate in several parts of the country until the attempt to take power again in 2020. In an interview, Mbaye-Bondoi explained that,

> As Bozizé wanted to return to power, he is using the Anti-Balaka he had used yesterday. In this sense, he made promises to the young people in this movement to become soldiers, to occupy positions of responsibility. As a result, many are killed. Among the Anti-Balaka, there are many churchgoers. I went to Ngaragba prison and Camp de Roux; the Anti-Balaka prisoners I met were mostly Christians. Some said they were Flambeaux or church singers. All those I spoke to were members of prayer cells and evangelical church movements. They told me that they had been promised positions of responsibility. Thus, the politicians made them false promises. Now the consequence is that they end up in prisons or are killed by soldiers from the other side.³⁷

---

34. Baker, *Central African Republic*, 52.
35. Baker, 53.
36. Thomas, *Centrafrique: un destin volé*, 102.
37. Mbaye-Bondoi, Interview, 24 July 2021 (Translation is mine).

Mbaye-Bondoi's explanation shows that young people have been involved in violence. As a result, many Christians among them have been in prison. Andreas Mehler explains that in CAR, as in many African states, violence has become something normal to compete against others.[38] While Yannick Weyns et al. argue that many CAR political leaders use violence as "the most effective strategy . . . to occupy the country's highest office,"[39] others use the national army to get to power or to maintain it. If the Séléka rebels were motivated by political, economic, and religious ideologies when they launched the 2013-coup, the Anti- Balaka were motivated by political and economic ones as political leaders sought to regain power and militiamen to plunder coutry's mineral resources. It is important to observe that politicians used naïve and unemployed people to cause and spark violence for their own political benefits. This is what Mbaye-Bondoi explains above when he states that politicians have enlisted young believers from church youth associations to fight as Anti-Balaka militiamen.

It is, therefore, important if not imperative for policymakers and peace-building organizations to work at creating spaces for continual dialogues between conflicting parties "to avoid the escalation of violence."[40] Currently, in CAR, the national and international courts have arrested and put in prison some leaders of Anti-Balaka and Séléka. Nevertheless, in the ranks of the Anti-Balaka, were some soldiers of the national army loyal to Bozizé.

4. The Armed Forces

Since the fighting began in Bangui, some CAR soldiers and gendarmes loyal to Bozizé have joined the Anti-Balaka.[41] After independence, several political regimes used the national army as an instrument to destabilize other

---

38. Mehler, "Rebels and Parties," 116. In describing a story of inter-communal clash between the Kokombas and Dagombas in northern Ghana in the 1990s, John Paul Lederach explains that customary leaders used young Kokombas and Dagombas to cause violence between the two ethnic groups. He states that during the clash that opposed the two communities over a land issue, "young men . . . were hidden and fighting in the bush." He also goes on to assert that, fortunately, a peacebuilding NGO working in the region "began to push for a peacebuilding effort." See Lederach, *The Moral Imagination*, 8, 12.

39. Weys, Hoex, Hilgert and Spittaels, *Mapping Conflict Motives*, 8.

40. Lederach, *The Moral Imagination*, 8.

41. Thomas, *Centrafrique: un destin volé*, 64.

governments, as they made it political and ethnic in order to achieve their ambitions.[42] I pointed out earlier that similar problems occurred in Sierra Leone causing the resentment and social grievance that led to civil war. According to Siân Herbert, Nathalia Dukhan, and Marielle Debos, the FACA are part of the internal actors of the CAR's crisis because "The majority of the soldiers – 1200 – are stationed in the CAR capital Bangui. The FACA army is under-resourced, under-armed, poorly trained, and has a weak control structure."[43] Since the formation of the national army in 1966, many officers and soldiers received their military training in France or from French officers. After independence, representatives of the CAR state signed "bilateral agreements with France" including a defence agreement with French political elites.[44] When Bozizé appealed to the French president for help in repelling the rebels, the latter refused.[45] Today, instability among the soldiers is partly due to the inappropriate quality of the training they have received.

After the coup started, the UN Security Council (UNSC) decreed an arms embargo on the national army. This made "The country . . . dependent on the UN peacekeeping troops to maintain a certain level of stability."[46] According to Thierry Irénée Yarafa, the reform of the defence and security services is a prerequisite for security and peace in the country:

> Le défi majeur de la RCA, en définitive, reste donc de pouvoir suppléer efficacement les fréquentes interventions extérieures et, plus encore, d'élaborer et de décliner une stratégie de prise en charge effective de la sécurité dans son espace territorial, en se dotant d'une capacité – surtout militaire – de dissuasion, d'anticipation et de gestion de ses conflits et crises internes, ou pour juguler les actes de brigandage et les menaces terroristes venant du Sahel.
>
> The major challenge for CAR remains, ultimately, to be able to effectively ensure frequent external interventions and, above all, to develop and implement effective security management in

---

42. Thomas, *Centrafrique: un destin volé*, 64.
43. Herbert, Dukhan, and Debos, *State Fragility*, 5.
44. Woodfork, *Culture and Customs*, 15.
45. Thomas, *Centrafrique: un destin volé*, 90.
46. Fiedler, *The Contribution of the Interfaith*, 3.

its territory, by equipping itself with a capacity – particularly a military capacity – to dissuade, anticipate and manage internal conflicts, or to curb terrorist flights and threats from the Sahel.[47]

The government and CAR partners have been working on Security Sector Reform (SSR) scheme in order to reform the national army into a professional one. To achieve this, the International Community and the CAR government were involved in recruiting and training soldiers to cope with security issues and guarantee peace in the country. However, one can observe shortcomings in this process as many Centrafricans criticize the methods used to recruit new soldiers.[48]

5. Conclusion

I have tried to show in this chapter that, whether Séléka, Anti-Balaka, or soldiers of the national army who joined the fighting, political ambitions underpinned the actions of the different parties involved in the conflict. This was justified by their actions which consisted of sabotaging the authority of the traditional leaders to contribute to national healing but also of putting aside the contribution of initiatives and traditional leadersip to reconciliation. It is possible to stress that the conflict was motivated much by political and economic reasons. It is also possible that other reasons have motivated the militia groups to join the rebellion. However, all groups have committed crimes and human rights violations.

---

47. Yarafa, "La Refonte des Forces," xvii. (Translation is mine).
48. This argument derives from my personal observation.

CHAPTER 6

Possible Factors Underpinning the Conflict

1. Introduction

In this chapter, I aim to explain that various factors allow to identify the outbreak of the 2013 conflict. While the French media claimed the conflict to be inter-religious, Trinidad Deiros considers this label to be an invention.[1] Other authors suggest that such a label "oversimplifies and distorts the matter."[2] Scholars highlight that, "The most recent outbreak of violence, in 2012, is thus not a religious conflict as often pinned by the international media."[3] Rather, coupled with poverty and social grievances, each party fights for power and economic interests.[4] The International Federation of Human Rights (FIDH) also argues that the major problems of the CAR were elections cut short, lack of dialogue with politics, public mismanagement, corruption, and failure in organizing the army and proceeding to effective disarmament and demobilization of combatants.[5] Socio-ethnic splits contribute to the plight of the country.

---

1. Deiros, "Central African Republic."
2. Le Roux and Sandoua, "Leadership Responses," 87.
3. Akasaki, Ballestraz and Sow, "What Went Wrong."
4. Deiros, "Central African Republic," 4.
5. FIDH, "Central African Republic," 7.

2. Socio-Ethnic Cleavages

One cannot understand the 2013 conflict without exploring the socio-ethnic divisions. I explained earlier that in the past, different ethnic groups shared a common language, heritage, and culture that bound them. Since colonization, the way the Europeans imagined, defined and ruled, and the policy they applied in Oubangui Chari has shaped its history and culture and affected its societal organization. It is what Klosowicz explains when he says that the colonizers "delineated boundaries of their zones of influence, but failed to take into account ethnic and cultural differences."[6] As a result, various ethnic groups competed against each other to get to power. Woodfork notes that, "A recent trend in Bangui sees more ethnic conflict between groups based upon political affiliations . . . Presently, new peripheral areas of the city are often inhabited by a single ethnic group."[7]

The policy of social exclusion and that of divide-and-rule has created socio-ethnic divisions that resulted in violence/conflict.[8] George Baker laments that "The violence is causing deep social fractures relatively new to the country and left many communities traumatized."[9] Today, social unity is more fragile than ever before, although, in recent past, people from different ethnic groups celebrated peaceful coexistence with others through intermarriage and other social activities. Apart from the socio-ethnic roots of the conflict, economic interests are also another aspect of the crisis.

3. Economic Interests

Non-state armed groups not only commit political crimes but also loot. In February 2020, a report by Fiona Mangan, Igor Acko, and Manal Taha showed that in CAR, "Lucrative markets of cattle, timber, diamonds, gold, and other minerals have been linked to pervasive conflict."[10] Edouard Epiphane Yogo also points out that, in the context of conflicts, illegal trade operations usually take place in the "grey zones,"[11] because the use of resources as part

---

6. Klosowicz, "Central African Republic," 36.
7. Woodfork, *Culture and Customs*, 9.
8. Vlavonou, "Understanding the 'Failure,'" 319.
9. Baker, *Central African Republic*, 9.
10. Mangan, Acko, and Taha, "The 'Green Diamond': Coffee and Conflicts," 1.
11. Yogo, *L'Etat et les Groupes*, 52.

of the conflict economy creates disincentives for profiting armed groups to participate seriously in the peace process.[12] He goes on to say that over the past decade, the DR Congo, Rwanda, Uganda, and Burundi were considered the grey zones of the Central Africa sub-region.

A grey zone is an area/country where political-military groups control conquered areas and impose political and economic rules on the populations. The weakness of the state/government to control its territory highlights this situation. Currently, the grey zone of the sub-region of the Central Africa includes the DR Congo, CAR, Chad, Angola, and the borders between Rwanda and DR Congo. It also includes Chad basin, where Boko Haram operates. Table 3 below shows how economic interests play a key role in a conflict context.[13]

Table 3: Armed groups' use and trade of resources in the Central African sub-region[14]

Rebel's Sources of Funding	Countries of Origin	Delivery Routes	Countries of Delivery
Gold	DR Congo and CAR	Airplane, road, and sea	Dubai, India, Lebanon, Burundi, Uganda, Tanzania.
Diamonds	Angola, DR Congo, and CAR	Airplane, road, and sea	Belgium, China, India, Israel, South Africa, Emirate Arabia, Armenia, Sri Lanka, Mali, Cameroon, Chad, Congo Brazzaville, Namibia, Zambia, and Burkina Faso.
Timber	CAR and DR Congo	Road	Burundi, Kenya, Rwanda, Sudan, South Sudan, and Uganda.

Table 3 above depicts a system of illegal transactions of conflict-related mineral resources to finance armed conflicts. It also gives an idea of influence in the relation between the countries in the sub-region. For example,

---

12. Mangan, Acko, and Taha, "The 'Green Diamond': Coffee and Conflicts," 1.
13. Yogo, *L'Etat et les Groupes*, 51–52.
14. Adaptation from *L'Etat et les Groupes*, 51–52.

in July 2015, a Global Witness (GW) fact-finding report showed that, during the Séléka government, the EU and China participated in the illegal trade of CAR's timbers. It concluded that timber industries have played a role in funding CAR's conflict through the "bois de sang" (blood wood).[15] The same can be said for oil, uranium, diamonds, gold, ivory, and coffee.[16]

After the Séléka overthrew Bozizé, they took control of strategic zones of mineral resources, which they exploited illegally. They also collected taxes and acted as agents of the police or the army, as agents of local administration, or justice. For example, in 2016, at Ndassima where gold is mined in the locality of Bambari, Séléka men extorted about fifteen kilograms of gold per month from villagers, selling it for about US$350,000 on the local market or more abroad.[17] Giulio Coppi also claimed that the Lord's Resistance Army (LRA) has been involved in the exploitation of "natural resources such as gold and ivory and illegal trade" since it started operating in CAR.[18] Whether Séléka or Anti-Balaka, armed groups were looking for economic gains: they extorted money from civilians or forced those who did not have money to work in the mine or coffee plantations.[19]

In August 2018, a report showed that "Armed groups often fight each other for control over strategic points . . . to block or facilitate the movement of livestock."[20] Furthermore, in March 2019, after the announcement of a new government that included members of rebel groups, as required by the APPR-RCA recommendations, the FDPC militia group barricaded the Bangui-Garoua-Boulai corridor, preventing the supply of goods from Cameroon to the population. Supported by some Anti-Balaka, the leader of FDPC demanded "more ministries since they controlled the most territory."[21] It was, therefore, obvious that political and economic interests were a central focus of the armed groups.

---

15. Harrison, *Blood timber*, 22–40.
16. Thomas, *Centrafrique: un destin volé*, 167–188.
17. Isaacs-Martin, "The Motivations of Warlords."
18. Coppi, "Focus on Central African Republic," 5.
19. FIDH/LCDH, "Central African Republic," 14–17.
20. International Peace Information Service, *Central African Republic*, 42.
21. Beevor, "How Rebels Became Kingmakers." See also, International Peace Information Service, *Central African Republic*, 42.

Amelia Broodryk and Hussein Solomon have argued that the West has fuelled wars in Africa, as a "source of profit."[22] Since the 1990s, several conflicts in developing countries have been over resources.[23] Floris Endjito also pointed out that CAR's oil has been a source of conflict. He argued that, in 1973, under Bokassa, the US Company Conoco had explored 14,700 square kilometres of land for oil in the Doleo and Salamat basin on the border of Chad and CAR. The important oil deposit in CAR was estimated at ten billion barrels. France requested Bokassa to stop exploring the site. As he disagreed, they overthrew him in 1979. Chad also had an interest in that oil site because preventing CAR from extracting it would allow N'Djamena to drill its own oil site easily.[24]

In 1999, Patassé authorized the exploration of the oil by Greenberg Texas Company covering fifty-five thousand square kilometres but Bozizé suspended it in 2012. Before he was ousted, Bozizé granted exploitation of the oil site to two Chinese companies, PTI-IAS and PTI-AL.[25] In a public speech on the issue in December 2012, he declared that before giving oil to the Chinese, he met with Total officials in Paris and granted the company to exploit the oil, but they did nothing. He finally decided to grant the oil to the Chinese companies and the French made an issue of it. To solve this, he sent his advisor, Maidou, to Paris to discuss the Uranium contract, but the French refused again. Therefore, he gave it to the South Africans.[26] According to the evidence here, French leaders were not comfortable with the fact that CAR has been collaborating with other countries such as China and Russia. To my opinion, this disagreement has probably contributed to the country's slide into chaos. Decades of conflicts in CAR's neighbouring countries have also exposed CAR to violent crises.

---

22. Broodryk and Solomon, "From War Economies," 1.
23. Chauvin, Lallau, and Magrin, "Le contrôle des ressources," 7.
24. Endjito, "La Guerre du Pétrole."
25. Endjito.
26. Douglas-Bowers, "Colonialism, Coups, and Conflict."

4. Subregional Armed Conflicts

Emmanuel Chauvin links CAR's crisis to the conflicts in Darfur and Chad.[27] According to Peter Berg, the situation is "crisis-complex, not complex crises."[28] These crises, occurring in the tri-border area of Sudan, Chad, and CAR constitute a serious concern for the sub-region and beyond. The movements of insurgents such as Boko Haram, the LRA[29], and a range of criminal organizations in DR Congo are a threat to security beyond the borders of the country. Human Rights Watch reports several crimes and human rights violations such as killings, abductions, burning of villages, rapes, and displacement of people, as being the spill-over from the Darfur crisis.[30] It contends that in 2007, France, Chad, Sudan, and DR Congo meddled in the domestic affairs of CAR and even contributed to instability.

> France, the former colonial power, continues to play a dominant and influential role in deciding who governs. The CAR has also been affected by conflicts in neighboring Sudan, Chad, and the Democratic Republic of Congo, with rebel groups and government forces from neighboring countries freely using remote rural areas as rear bases or for military operations. This has created a significant flow of small arms, further fueling (sic) instability, particularly in northern CAR. Conflict in its neighbors has also generated refugee flows into the CAR, which is housing some 11,000 recognized refugees from Sudan, Chad, and the DRC [DR Congo].[31]

One can notice that today, the world is in a dynamic relationship of who rules and who is ruled. Scholars argue that the geographical position of CAR in the sub-region makes it vulnerable to the invasion of external forces. In this sense, France imposes its influence over this country in a dominant-dominated relationship.[32] Thus, one can argue that, in general, several conflicts

---

27. Chauvin, *La Guerre en Centrafrique*, 46; Berg, "The Dynamics of Conflict," 33–40.
28. Berg, "A Crisis-Complex," 72–86.
29. Katongole, *The Sacrifice of Africa*, 6.
30. Human Rights Watch, *State of Anarchy*, 4.
31. Human Rights Watch, "Background: The Varied Causes."
32. Chauvin, Lallau, and Magrin, "Le Contrôle des Ressources," 37.

in contemporary times have geopolitical and geo-strategic scope. It is also important to determine whether the 2013 conflict acts on a religious basis.

5. Theories of Interreligious Conflict

While the international community claimed that, "the Central African Republic (CAR) is facing widespread religious violence that could take on genocidal proportions,"[33] Stephanie Burchard pointed out that "CAR violence has been painted in largely religious terms, obscuring deeper dynamics."[34] Proponents of the interfaith conflict claimed a polarisation between the majority groups (Christians) and minority groups (Muslims), which some scholars have refuted. Even though the Anti-Balaka and Séléka have committed crimes and gross violations in CAR, it is difficult to support the claim that the conflict was inter-religious. Rather, due to weak state institutions and social inequalities, each party fought for power and economic gains.[35] Woodfork observes that in CAR, "Tensions between people of different religious faiths are few and far between; usually, they are ethnic or economic problems."[36] In some sense, the root of the conflict is largely political.[37]

Until recent time, many Centrafricans did not see Islam as a religion of violence, but rather that of peace and cohesion that some ethnic groups embraced.[38] For example, the ethnic groups with high numbers of Islamised populations are Gula, Runga, Banda, and Mandja. However, with the radicalization of Islam, some Muslims have become involved in extremism. The rise of jihadism in the mind of these followers has led them to engage in the conflict.[39] Thomas writes that in August 2012, during a visit to Paris, Bozizé warned French authorities of a hypothetical risk of jihadism in CAR, which they did not consider.[40]

---

33. Burchard, "The Central African Conflict."
34. Burchard.
35. Deiros, "Central African Republic," 4.
36. Woodfork, *Culture and Customs*, 23.
37. Welz, "Briefing: Crisis in the Central," 602; Langa, "The Role of Religion," 5–8.
38. Woodfork, *Culture and Customs*, 11.
39. Pastoor, "Vulnerability Assessment," 5.
40. Thomas, *Centrafrique: un destin volé*, 99.

For Dennis Pastoor, the Islamic *jihad*, which aims at subjugating and waging war on unbelievers, has shaped the mind-set of Muslims in sub-Saharan Africa. This gave rise to the Muslim-Christian religious overtones occurring in Nigeria, among Arabs and blacks in the Sudan civil war, and in Darfur and Chad. Pastoor also maintains that the "legacy of the traditional jihadist perspective with strong Muslim-Christian religious overtones so prominent in the region is witnessed in the present crisis in CAR as Séléka members exempt Muslims in their gross human right abuses of the population."[41] The high percentage of the CAR Muslims who have supported the coup, the statements and writings of Séléka leaders, and the complicity between some Muslims and the rebels led Pastoor to assume that the coup was motivated by an Islamic agenda. However, Elizabeth Le Roux and Yolande Sandoua considered the allegations of the religious conflict as a distortion and over-simplification of the truth.[42]

While these arguments underline the rise of *jihad* in the Central African sub-region, one militia member said of the Séléka rebels, "These guys are not Islamic fundamentalists . . . They are here for prosperity and power; they are not here to change anyone's confession."[43] According to respondents, internally, foreign Muslims fuelled tensions. For example, Mbaye-Bondoi claimed that mercenaries from Chad and Sudan encouraged those in CAR to keep fighting so that they would not lose the power to a non-Muslim president.[44] Other elements may help us to refute the idea that the current conflict is an inter-religious crisis. First, Anti-Balaka militias were not "the Christian militia"[45] as many people claimed, but "a group . . . of young men whose families had been killed in the Séléka's brutal campaign, and who are now seeking revenge."[46] Second, as described above, the Anti-Balaka militias are traditionalists and villagers who followed rituals used to protect themselves with mystical power for combat.

Third, when the aggressive attacks against the Muslims reached the peak, many churches in the capital city or in provinces sheltered those who escaped

---

41. Pastoor, "Vulnerability Assessment," 5 (footnote 3).
42. Le Roux and Sandoua, "Leadership Responses during Armed Conflict" 85.
43. Baker, *Central African Republic*, 41.
44. Mbaye-Bondoi, Interview, 24 July 2021.
45. Baker, *Central African Republic*, 6
46. Welz, "Briefing," 603.

the killings by the Anti-Balaka.[47] Many Centrafricans struggle to explain why such a situation occurs in a country "where different communities and religions appear to have coexisted peacefully for many years."[48] Fourth, in her conclusion on the role of religion in the CAR conflict, Felicia Langa states that, "the Christian majority and Christian leaders in CAR have officially and vehemently distanced themselves from the anti-Balaka violence."[49] Thus, this inter-religious claim seems to be a strategy of the CAR and French political leaders to 1) deny their responsibility for the chaos caused by their policy of supporting of the Séléka rebellion, and 2) draw the international community's attention to the crisis.

Based on the above, it is possible to argue that the socio-religious divide was not the cause of conflict, but a result. As the UN failed to see the hidden side of the conflict, they also failed to provide effective responses to it. Furthermore, the new coalition between the Séléka and Anti-Balaka factions launching the attempted coup of January 2021 was further evidence that the allegation of the religious character of the conflict distorted the truth. Deiros rightly states that, "Despite the religious bias acquired by the attacks on civilians in the Central African Republic, the reasons of the current crisis should be referred not to religion, but to political and economic reasons."[50]

6. Conclusion

In this chapter, I explained the possible factors underpinning the CAR conflict that are the structural socio-ethnic divide, the economic greed, and the consequences of regional violence. In general, armed groups are motivated by political ambitions and/or the pursuit of economic interests. However, according to some respondents, the religious claim of the conflict is a misinterpretation of the situation. Evidence showed that this claim distorts the truth. They argued that the religious allegations of the conflict are the consequences of the crisis rather than their causes. Nevertheless, peace actors have been working towards achieving reconciliation and recovering peace.

---

47. Ajiambo, "In Central Africa, a Cathedral."
48. Weyns, Hoex, Hilgert and Spittals, *Mapping Conflict Motives*, 8.
49. Langa, "The Role of Religion," 15.
50. Deiros, "Central African Republic," 13.

CHAPTER 7

Peace and Reconciliation Processes and Actors

1. Introduction

This chapter examines the processes used to achieve peace, and the main actors involved in these processes. These include the interfaith platform and the peacekeeping mission. It is to be understood that according to several respondents, the processes put forward in this context did not provide effective responses to the conflict. Participants's efforts were undermined by leadership rivalries and competitions over the conflict, particularly rivalries that emerged within UN peacekeeping organizations. Additionally, the chapter describes the misconducts and unethical behaviour of some UN troops, resulting in sexual abuse, paedophilia, gold and diamond dealings, and other human rights violations, which jeopardized peace processes. It can also be argued that the influence or control of foreign countries and international community over the processes have led to traditional methods and leadership being ignored or considered unimportant. However, the religious leaders remained in the forefront.

2. The Interfaith Platform

Since the killings started, a group of the religious leaders have come together in an Interfaith Platform (IP), to initiate a peace process, engaging in dialogue with communities to promote social cohesion.¹ At the forefront of the Council were Cardinal Dieudonné Nzapalainga of the Roman Catholic Church, Reverend Nicolas Guerekoyamé-Gbangou, the former representative of the Evangelical Alliance, and the late Imam Omar Kobine Layama, head of the Central African Islamic Council. They focused on working together to plead for reconciliation and to seek humanitarian responses for needy people.[2]

With the conflict falsely labelled inter-religious, the religious leaders have led campaigns at national, regional, and international levels to refute these allegations. Rebekka Fiedler asserts that they encouraged Christians and Muslims, "to demonstrate through their friendship that the root cause of the conflict is not religious."[3] As militia groups have burned down churches and mosques, and looted belongings and properties of Christians and Muslims, they worked to stop the violence. Fiedler pointed out that in 2014, the leaders of the Interfaith Platform helped "to restore the social fabric of the country to persuading (sic) the [UN] Security Council to take action."[4] Thus, thanks to their plea, the UNSC allowed in September 2014 the deployment of twelve thousand peacekeepers in CAR.

Fiedler also asserted that they engaged in dialogue at community level with the militias, but also with the local populations to promote tolerance and forgiveness rather than hatred and division. They organized seminars and workshops on peacebuilding for church leaders and mobilized Christians from various denominations to pray for the peaceful resolution of the conflict.[5] The faith leaders also attended to victims of the conflict and paid visits to the internally displaced peoples. Their exemplary unity transcended all religious cleavages. To facilitate their task, the EU provided material and financial support to help them establish peace committees across the country.[6] However, the large-scale politicized attacks by the militia groups in 2017,

---

1. Chonghaile, "Central African Republic Still." Accessed 5 May 2020, https://www.theguardian.com/global-development/2015/aug/21/central-african-republic-powder-keg-sergio-vieira-de-mello-prize-interfaith-peace-platform.
2. Chonghaile, "Central African Republic Still."
3. Fiedler, *Making Peace a Reality*, 10.
4. Fiedler, *The Contribution of*, 3.
5. Fiedler, *Making Peace a Reality*, 11.
6. Coppi, "Focus on Central African Republic," 10.

which resulted in the APPR-RCA, showed for example, that much remained to be done.[7]

3. Peacekeeping Missions

As in the DR Congo, Sierra Leone, Liberia, Uganda and other sub-Saharan African countries, the international community has increased military interventions in CAR. These include peacekeeping or peacebuilding missions carried out by the Economic Community of Central African States (CEEAC), the African Union (AU), the EU, France, and the UN.[8] Lombard and Carayannis explained that, according to some scholars, over the last two decades CAR has been the world's champion of peace missions, while others argued that prior to the crisis of 2013, the international community did not pay much attention to the critical situations in the country.[9] Some also said CAR was a "low priority for the international community"[10] while others stressed that the international response to the country's condition was scarce.[11]

Bjørn Møller argued that the AU "neither intends to manage, nor would be capable of managing the . . . armed conflicts or other problems" in Africa. The reason, he claimed, was that the AU expected the sub-regional organization to solve the problems in the states, but there was a lack of capacity to do so. Furthermore, the lack of clear political decisions to support fragile states, protect civilians, provide effective responses to humanitarian needs, stop and prosecute rebels could explain Møller's observations.[12] The UNSC voted the resolution 2127 that allowed the Mission Internationale de Soutien à la Centrafrique (Misca) to deploy to CAR in September 2013.[13] While French

---

7. Voice of America, "Détérioration de la Sécurité."

8. Brosig and Sempijja showed that, from 2000 to 2015, the UN carried out ten peacekeeping missions in sub-Saharan Africa. These missions are in Burundi (ONUB), Central African Republic (MINUSCA), DRC (MONUSCO), Ivory Coast (ONUCI), Liberia (UNMIL), Mali (MINUSMA), Somalia (AMISOM), South Sudan (UNMISS), and Sudan (UNAMID). See Brosig and Sempijja, "Does Peacekeeping Reduce," 4.

9. Lombard and Carayannis, "Introduction," 1. See also Welz and Meyer, "Empty Acronyms."

10. Lombard and Carayannis, "Introduction," 1.

11. Welz, "Briefing," 601.

12. Møller, "Africa's Sub-Regional Organisations," 1.

13. Thomas, *Centrafrique: un destin volé*, 108.

authorities harboured ambitions to intervene again in CAR, they activated the political and diplomatic levers and while seeking UN legitimization to intervene in CAR, which took time, they decided in mid-November 2013 to deploy Sangaris's troops.[14]

The Mission of the United Nations for the Stabilisation of the CAR (Minusca) was mandated to stabilize the country under the Resolution 2149 adopted on 10 April 2014, taking over from AU troops. Its tasks consisted of protecting civilians, providing "humanitarian assistance, protecting human rights, supporting the rule of law, and ensuring the disarmament,"[15] demobilization, reintegration and repatriation of former combatants. In January 2020, the total number of UN personnel was 14,708.[16] There are more civillian humanitarian workers than troops tasked with fighting insurgents.

Séverine Autesserre argues that there is no peacebuilding when there are no actions, interests, and strategies of national actors, and that the foreign actors can, at best "support peace initiatives and undermine efforts to resume violence."[17] In his investigations on the relationship between peacekeepers and their responses to the current crisis, Martin Welz writes:

> Several regional and international organizations, including the African Union (AU), the Economic Community of Central African States (ECCAS), the European Union (EU), and the United Nations (UN), became involved in the process of crisis solution, with all of the organizations deploying troops to the CAR. Their efforts have thus far born limited results; fighting and human suffering continue . . . It shows that there is competition between them for visibility, relevance, and control over the process, leading to strained relations between the key organizations, particularly between the ECCAS and the AU and between the AU and the UN. These strained relations in turn have led to delayed responses to the crisis and are only understandable through a consideration of the interests of the organizations'

---

14. Thomas, *Centrafrique: un destin volé*, 104–106.
15. Security Council Report, "Chronology of Events."
16. Council on Foreign Relations, "Global Conflict Tracker."
17. Autesserre, *Peaceland: Conflict Resolution*, Kindle Loc. 38.

member states. Particularly interesting in this context are Chad and France, the two states with most influence over the CAR.[18]

Rather than uniting their efforts to help civilians and provide effective responses to the crisis, peacekeeping organizations compete against each other. Baker opined that, if the peacekeepers "could freeze the conflict into a stare down, which would be precarious but bloodless,"[19] their efforts would have brought positive results. In 2019, the estimated number of internally displaced people was approximately 581,362 and 2.9 million were in need of humanitarian assistance.[20]

The media reports have also revealed the involvement of peacekeepers in practices such as paedophilia and sexual abuse.[21] J. E. Maximiliano Jimenez Villarreal and D. A. Jimenez Montalvo have shown that French soldiers sexually abused children. This occurred at the internally displaced camp (IDP) near M'poko airport from December 2013 to June 2014 in exchange for chocolate, biscuits, or bottles of water.[22] To ascertain the allegations of paedophilia, the former General Secretary of the UN (GSUN), Ban Ki-Moon, assigned Adres Kompass to investigate. Kompass documented, with evidence, the facts detailing acts of rape, sodomy, and oral sex by peacekeepers on children. The reports arrived at the desk of the officials of the UN High Commission for Human Rights (UNHCHR). Although Kompass did his job, there has been no response to the report on rape in CAR, either from the French authorities or from the UN. The former head of the UN-led mission in CAR, Parfait Onanga-Anyanga, acknowledged "the existence of 100 sexual abuse allegations from 2013 to the beginning of 2014" and between 2015 and 2016, 513 girls and boys were raped. Although the UN General Assembly (UNGA) adopted measures to punish the perpetrators of sexual abuse, the sanctions the member states impose should be "representative and symbolic rather than punitive."[23] This situation requires the establishment

---

18. Welz, "Briefing," 601–602.
19. Baker, *Central African Republic*, 24.
20. Council on Foreign Relations, "Global Conflict Tracker."
21. Villarreal and Montalvo, "Sexual Violence in Post-Conflict," 505–523.
22. Villarreal and Montalvo, 512–518. This situation requires the establishment of a Special Court to judge cases of sexual misconduct in accordance with International Humanitarian Law (IHL).
23. Villarreal and Montalvo, "Sexual Violence in Post-Conflict," 505–523.

of a Special Court to judge cases of sexual misconduct in accordance with International Humanitarian Law (IHL). Critics also claimed that groups of UN contingents only acted out of self-interest while others worked with the rebels to continue fuelling the conflict.[24]

These practices have called into question the ethics of the UN peacekeepers and the credibility of the institution,[25] resulting in delays in the peace processes and resentment among the population. For example, in February 2020, over a thousand demonstrators marched in Bangui to demand the expulsion of three Minusca staff members, accused of "sabotaging the CAR's peace agreement between the rebels and the government."[26] Vladimir Montero, the spokesperson for the Minusca said it was a manipulation aimed at escalating the crisis. When the CAR authorities demanded that Minusca officials dismiss the accused officers, they resisted with an iron fist and refused to accept the injunction. In many ways, the organization's impartiality was called into question.

4. The Non-Governmental Organizations (NGOs)

Since the beginning of the conflict, community, religious, and political mediations have been involved in the search for peace and reconciliation. Subsequently, the mediation process has reached a multidimensional level.[27] The spill over of the conflict affecting inter-communal and inter-faith relations from 2014 onwards required community and religious mediations with civil society actors, and political settlements under the auspices of the international community. Prior activities motivated by the BNF recommendations, such as those carried out on the ground to bring Christians and Muslims together for eventual social cohesion, included community reconstruction work. This led NGOs to support the repair of public markets or places of worship. It also allowed them to encourage the local populations to engage in sports and artistic games (songs and plays related to conflict and peace),

---

24. Villarreal and Montalvo, "Sexual Violence in Post-Conflict," 505–523.
25. Villarreal and Montalvo, 509.
26. Bambi, "Protesters in Bangui Call."
27. Virculon, "A la Recherche de la Paix," 10.

as well as meetings and exchanges on peace.[28] For example, the NGOs have established local peace committees in Carnot, Berberati, Bambari, Mbres, Kaga Bandoro and Bouar. The Danish Refugee Council has set up in the towns of Ouham and Ouham-Pendé and thirty-nine social cohesion committees in Bangui. NGOs such as the Danish Refugee Council, Mercy Corps, Search for Common Ground, Catholic Relief Service, Cordaid, and Conciliation Resources were involved in this process. The actions carried out gave rise to local peace committees established in the neighbourhoods of Bangui and in several towns.[29]

The peace structures that NGOs set up in neighbourhoods and in some rural areas aimed to promote and support dialogue at the local level, and thus to prevent inter-community violence. They included neighbourhood chiefs, community leaders, shopkeepers, teachers, students, religious leaders, and government representatives.[30] Although neighbourhood leaders were included among others to promote peace and reconciliation at community level, this was further evidence that they did not hold a key position in the process.

Nevertheless, the work of NGOs has been insufficient. During field research, seventeen respondents (17.34 percent) claimed that they support the work carried out by NGOs in their area/locality, while seventy-five respondents (76.53 percent) said they did not support NGOs' activities and six interviewees (6.12 percent) had no answer. This is evidence that, despite the contributions of state and non-state organizations to the search for reconciliation, most people are dissatisfied because indigenous authorities are not fully involved in the process. It implies that if the latter had been effectively involved, they would have have probably brought significant changes.

5. The Sidelining of Indigenous Leaders

In CAR, indigenous leaders claimed to be sidelined in peace processes. While some interviewees pointed to internal weaknesses of indigenous leaders to

---

28. Virculon, "A la Recherche de la Paix," 10.
29. Virculon, "A la recherche de la paix en Centrafrique," 10 (see footnote 8).
30. Virculon, 10 (Translation is mine).

engage in peace processes, others pointed to external constraints. Table 4 below summarizes the responses of twenty-three participants.

Table 4: A description of internal weaknesses to indigenous peace processes[31]

Internal Weaknesses	# of Responses	%
Indigenous leaders involved in armed groups	2	8.69
Lack of formal education	1	4.34
Indigenous leaders involved in bribe	2	8.69
Lack of fearing of God	1	4.34
Lack of good leadership	5	21.73
Indigenous leadership is outdated	1	4.34
The uprooting of tradition	5	21.73
Indigenous leaders involved in political parties	1	4.34
No tax collection	4	17.39
Some indigenous leaders accused of sorcery	1	4.34
Total	23	

To describe what caused the loss of power of indigenous leaders and the weaknesses in conflict resolution, twenty-three respondents pointed to certain weaknesses as obstacles to these. They provided a variety of evidence to support their arguments. Some claimed that indigenous leaders were involved in the conflict as members of the Séléka or Anti-Balaka. Others claimed that some indigenous leaders took bribes, and still others said that some had no formal education. To explain other facts that corroborate these arguments, Nongo-Aziagbia declared:

> The traditional chiefs have lost their authority over their people. Authority is now in the hands of young men who smoke hemp and take drugs that make them lose their minds. How to put everything back in order is now the challenge of the government. One can claim on the radio to restore the authority of government officials, but such a restoration requires that of parents, traditional chiefs and headmen. To do this, the right people must be appointed to the right position. The traditional

---

31. Plaisance Rivoli M'Bara (sources from field research).

fabric of CAR has been completely erased. The colonial administration did not help us in this area. Today, with the spread of modernism and new technologies, people try to imitate what is outside the country, what comes from the West. Therefore, we have lost our soul in this context. How do we combine modern knowledge with the traditional wisdom of our ancestors? We have to find a balance.[32]

In addition to internal weaknesses, indigenous leaders face external constraints that challenge or minimize their effective contribution to reconciliation and social cohesion. These constraints relate to the internalization and geopolitical stakes of the conflict. In table 5 below, of ninety-eight interviewed, ninety-one respondents (92.85 percent) linked the crisis to external influences, indicating a variety of responses.

Table 5: A description of external constraints to indigenous peace processes[33]

External Constraints	# of responses	%
Colonial policy eradicated the authority of indigenous leaders	2	2.10
Proliferation of armed groups	9	9.89
Control of Western powers on CAR	6	6.59
Complicity of politicians and foreign forces to gain power	7	7.69
France's involvement in the internal affairs of CAR	25	27.47
CAR's neighbouring countries interfering in its internal affairs	10	10.98
Search for resources-conflict	6	6.59
Duplicity of international community	5	5.49
Western modern system caused the loss of traditional system	11	12.08
Lack of political and financial supports	10	10.98
Total	91	

Some respondents pointed out that most interventions by international communities were interest-based, with states and organizations competing for dominance, economic interests and strategic resources. As a result, they

---

32. Nestor Désiré Nongo-Aziagbia, Interview, 10 November 2020, Bossangoa (Translation is mine).

33. Plaisance Rivoli M'Bara (sources from field research).

influence not only peace operations but also peace processes, affecting the search for justice, peace, reconciliation and security, and the contribution of indigenous leaders.

6. Conclusion

This chapter revealed that peace actors external to cultural and traditional contexts dominated peace processes in CAR. In this context, local initiatives and traditional actors have not been used or have not been fully involved in the reconciliation processes. Consequently, several peace deals that peace actors carried out did not take into account the realities of Centrafricans. Another reason is that policymakers concluded peace agreements outside the country, using the French language. As a result, the outcomes of processes did not meet the expectations of the populations. During field research, some respondents pointed out that, apart from being set aside from the peace processes, some traditional leaders have been involved in corruption, bribery, and violence, as they have joined or helped armed groups in one way or another.

CHAPTER 8

The Political Settlements of the Conflict

1. Introduction

This chapter examines the different political settlements of the conflict. These include the several peace agreements, transitional justice, and an assessment of peacebuilding policies. It also highlights that the approaches used so far are far from implementing the local/traditional methods of conflict resolution and reconciliation such as *Mbuki*. Actors involved in the political settlements comprised the militias, the Community of Economic States of Central Africa (CEEAC), African Union (AU), France, the European Union (EU), UN, and Russia.

2. Peace Agreements

Regional and international organizations have been involved in the conflict resolution as a third party. Julius Mutwol argues that a third party can be successful in the peace process because of "its leverage, interests, and impartiality, as well as the strategies of mediations."[1] He adds that conflicting parties accept peace through third party mediation "if the mediator is perceived as *able* and *willing* to help them reach [an] agreement."[2] The question is,

---

1. Mutwol, *Peace Agreements*, 8.
2. Mutwol, 8.

"Why despite various mediations are peace deals are still not bearing fruit?" Furthermore, what strategies are needed to successfully resolve the current conflict? From 2003 to the time of this research, approximately nine peace agreements have been signed between the CAR government and representatives of the armed groups under the auspices of the international community. Serge Simon Bozanga saw the 2003 peace dialogue, the Dialogue National Centrafricain (DNC), as the gathering of all Centrafricans under the palaver tree to solve their problems in the traditional way. He said,

> La sagesse africaine se manifestait jadis par le principe du dialogue et de la concertation sous l'arbre à palabre; (sis). Arbre sous lequel se réunissent les notables, les anciens, les gens du village. En cas de démêlés ou de différends entre certains membres de la société Böro, le peuple, sur convocation du chef coutumier, se réunissait sous l'arbre à palabres afin de trouver un terrain d'entente. Le conseil des sages siégeait donc à l'ombre d'un baobab. Plus exactement du grand arbre du village pour démêler l'écheveau d'un conflit latent et quelquefois en gestation au sein d'une communauté ou l'opposant à une autre.
>
> African wisdom was manifested by the principle of dialogue and concertation under the palaver tree. Tree under which met the notables, the elders, and the people of the village. In the event of disputes between certain members of the Böro society when convened by the customary chief, met under the palaver tree to find common ground. The council of wise men, therefore, sat in the shade of a baobab tree. More precisely of the big tree of the village to untangle the skein of the latent conflict and sometimes in gestation within a community or opposing it to another.[3]

The meeting, chaired by the late Isaac Zokoué, discussed the root causes of the political instability, military coups, economic plight, and social harm that ruined the country.[4] About three hundred and fifty people attended the forum and were charged with debating peace issues. Of the six commissions

---

3. Liliane PREVOST et Barnabé LAYE, *Guide de la sagesse africaine* (Paris : L'Harmattan, 1999), p. 95 cited by Serge Simon Bozanga, "Dialogue National Centrafricain." (Translation is mine).

4. Bradshaw and Fandos-Rius, *Historical Dictionary*, 219.

charged to discuss key problems of the country, four worked on issues related to truth and reconciliation, politics and diplomacy, defense and security, education, and socio-cultural affairs. A truth commission was set up with the view "to investigate human rights abuses committed during the period 1960 to 2003" and to bring the people involved in the crisis "to publicly recognize the negative impact of their actions, and assume official commitments for the future."[5] Despite the fact that the Commission proposed a solidarity fund to compensate the victims of the conflict, nothing came of it.

In general, the lack of the political will to implement the recommendations of the fora on the part of the government and the sabotage of the recommendations on the part of armed groups have hampered the peace processes. Since the conflict broke out in 2013, negotiations held in Gabon, Chad, Congo Brazzaville, the Vatican, or Khartoum have been controversial. For example, the Brazzaville negotiations on 23 July 2014, "involved dozens of members of armed groups, about 170 Central African officials and civil society members."[6] At the "Sant Egidio's' meeting [Vatican], the representatives of the government and those of the political-military groups met in June 2017" and signed an "immediate ceasefire deal" under the mediation of the Roman Catholic Peace Group.[7] Whether in Gabon or Khartoum, the scenario was the same. The general impression of Centrafricans was that, for some participants, taking part in such meetings made them famous before the world and gave them opportunities to claim or maintain a position in the government.[8] Such an attitude clearly shows that their presence in the peace processes was not in the interest of the affected populations.[9]

Furthermore, the Dialogue Politique Inclusif (Inclusive Political Dialogue [DPI]) held in 2008 and the FNB in April 2015 under the interim government, as well as the APPR-RCA in 2019, focused more on political deals. Each peace forum brought together members of the government, political parties, civil society, and rebel groups as well as representatives of the regional and international organizations. Each forum ended with recommendations for a

---

5. Coppi, "Focus on Central African Republic," 5.
6. Neill, "What Hope."; Relief Web, "A Tentative Ceasefire in CAR."
7. Al Jazeera News, "CAR Government Signs Peace Deal."
8. My observation of the processes helps me to reach the same conclusion.
9. Olayiwola, "A Leadership Perspective."

new consensus government, free and fair elections, a truth commission, and the disarmament, demobilization, reintegration, and repatriation (DDRR) of rebels, and participants agreed to work towards implementation.[10] However, they have always failed, and a new spectrum of violence erupted.[11]

The last peace meeting, the "Dialogue Républicain" (Republican Dialogue), held in Bangui from 21 to 27 March 2022, brought together over four hundred and fifty participants. It attempted to address the issues that have caused much weeping, hurt hearts and desolation in communities, and that have undermined CAR development and nation-building. At the summit, participants discussed political, economic, security and diplomatic issues and made around six hundred recommendations for implementation.[12] It is questionable whether power-sharing is the best way out of a conflict like this. Such a question allows us to assert that the current situation explains a politico-cultural identity crisis. In reality, the challenge to address the wrongs of the past through the process of transitional justice is great. It is, therefore, important to adopt appropriate strategies.

3. The Prospect of Transitional Justice

Transitional justice is key in the quest for reconciliation and peace. Colleen Murphy argues that this justice is not about retribution but rather about "societal transformation."[13] It addresses the past to inform the present in terms of truth, justice, reparation, and reconciliation.[14] In CAR, the interim government organized the "Consultations populaires" (popular consultations) in 2014 to gather views of the populations on peace and security, governance and reparation, reconciliation, and economic recovery.[15] The objective of the consultations was to tap into the unexplored and untapped depths of people's collective knowledge and wisdom to find innovative and catalytic alternatives

---

10. Bradshaw and Fandos-Rius, *Historical Dictionary*, 220, 271.
11. Bradshaw and Fandos-Rius, 271.
12. Radio Ndeke Luka, "Dialogue Républicain: Plus de 600."
13. Murphy, *The Conceptual Foundations*, 119.
14. Bloomfield, "Reconciliation: An Introduction," 14.
15. Ministère de la Réconciliation Nationale, du Dialogue Politique et de la Promotion de la Culture Civique, "Rapport des Consultations Populaires," 5.

as ways to address the problems of the nation.[16] The ideal was to address the country's problems from the bottom up, and in a participatory manner.

Gregory Leberger revealed that "A total of 1,977 participants from different components of society . . . were consulted and the results compiled in a report serving as a basis for the bill" included in the FNB's recommendations.[17] The FNB suggested, and the APPR-RCA emphasized the creation of the CVJRR. In January 2020, the Committee for the preparation of the CVJRRC bill presented the document to the President of CAR.[18] The document approved by Parliament proposed that the Commission should investigate the crimes, establish the truth, and situate responsibility for the events between Boganda's death on 29 March 1959 and 31 December 2019. The Commission comprised eleven members selected from all the regions of the country including at least four women. A committee selected the candidates, which the President appointed in December 2020.[19] The mandate of the Commission was for five years. Its role was to investigate public confessions of perpetrators of crimes and human rights violations, heal relationships and reconcile communities. They have "autonomy" and "independence of action."[20]

To facilitate the Commission's investigations, the bill recommends that, "any group of persons suffering from an individual, collective or massive violation of human rights can seize the CVJRR by filing a complaint."[21] According to Dominique Saïd Paguindji, president of the Conseil d'Etat, "The Truth Commission will deal with minor offences, such as putting up illegal roadblocks, racketeering [and] petty thief with no aggravating circumstances."[22] However, whether they are minor offences or not, the CVJRR is the alternative solution to address the problems of conflicts in CAR.

While the national jurisdictions and ICC continue investigating or prosecuting criminals, a hybrid jurisdiction, the SCC, was set up. During the interviews, respondents shared their opinions on the effectiveness and reliability

---

16. Ministère de la Réconciliation Nationale, du Dialogue Politique et de la Promotion de la Culture Civique (MRN), "Rapport des Consultations Populaires," 5.
17. Picco, "Can the Central African."
18. Leberger, "Central African Republic."
19. El Gantri, "Pourquoi, en Centrafrique."
20. Leberger, "Central African Republic."
21. Leberger.
22. Bouessel, "Central Africans Still Waiting."

of national courts, the SCC, and the ICC. Out of ninety-eight individual interviews, sixty informants (61.22 percent) stated that they had confidence in the national jurisdictions, twenty-one people (21.42 percent) stated that they did not have confidence, while seventeen people (17.34 percent) knew nothing about the judicial system. Those who do not trust justice pointed out shortcomings such as political interference, corruption, slow procedures, unfairness to victims, and impunity.

The ICC lost credibility for releasing DR Congolese Jean-Pierre Bemba in 2018, whose men committed war crimes in CAR between 2002 and 2003.[23] Thus, in order to bring a new impetus to the people, expectations for the SCC are high.[24] To date, some cases related to the current conflict are before the ICC. It arrested Patrick Edward Ngaïssona in 2017, Alfred Yekatom in 2018, Mahamat Said Abdel Kani in 2021[25] and Maxime Jeoffroy Eli Mokom[26] on 14 March 2022, for being responsible for war crimes and crimes against humanity.[27] In the light of the above, an assessment of the justice and peace processes helps determine the major obstacles to the implementation of peace in CAR.

4. Assessing Peacebuilding Policies

Kendrick Foster points out that in CAR, "previous peace agreements failed because they focused too much on elite support."[28] Policymakers may encourage indigenous methods of conflict resolution and appoint indigenous leaders to settle minor disputes related to conflicts among the local population. As external actors have imposed their agenda on reconciliation processes,[29] the peace initiatives they have led were ineffective and irrelevant, as they do not "create peace at the local level."[30] Most of the peace talks were held out of the

---

23. Bouwknegt, "Between Truth, Justice and Tradition," 63.
24. Cruvellier, "CAR Special Court."
25. Amnesty International, "République Centrafricaine."
26. ICC, "Situation in Central African Republic II."
27. International Criminal Court, "Questions and Answers: Situation in the Central African Republic II – The Procurator v. Alfred Yekatom and Patrice-Edouard Ngaïssona." Last updated 11 December 2019. Accessed 30 April 2020, https://www.icc-cpi.int/itemsDocuments/201912110-coc-hearing-carII-eng.pdf.
28. Foster, "From War to Peace."
29. Idris, "Supporting Reconciliation," 2.
30. Foster, "From War to Peace."

country. During the mediations, some participants used French rather than Sango, which made it difficult for most of indigenous people to understand the discussions.[31]

In contrast to top-down approaches to peace, in 2015 the national consultations attempted to address CAR's problems from bottom up. This approach was unique and genuine, as it required the participation of members of the population over the country to give their opinions on the reconstruction of the country. However, parties into peace processes have not implemented the recommendations.[32] The reconciliation process obviously needs the insights of culture and tradition to inform people. Mbiti asserts that, "traditional concepts could shed light on understanding and implementing peace in our times."[33] Therefore, it is important to explore the insights into tales, songs, proverbs, and stories in order to effectively address the conflict in CAR. In doing so, Centrafricans could learn from indigenous values and leadership. It would be instructive to understand how, in the pre-colonial period, sultans and lamido resolved conflicts.[34] Honoré Douba lamented about the lack of an indigenous process of reconciliation in the APPR-RCA.[35] Indigenous leaders and initiatives may be significant to provide useful insights into addressing the current conflict.

Indeed, the lack of accountability and justice for armed groups, in addition to weakening the judicial system, does not deter future unilateral attacks.[36] Thus, given that indigenous leaders are concerned about the application of customary laws in rural areas and that their authority on this matter has been diminished, how can policymakers empower indigenous leaders to deal with minor offences and promote peace and reconciliation in their areas?

5. Conclusion

The above discussions showed that, in the political settlements of the conflict, regional states, the international community and its organizations have

---

31. Franco Mbaye-Bondoi, Interview, 27 July 2021, Bangui.
32. MRN, "Rapport des Consultations Populaires," 5.
33. Mbiti, "Relating Peace in African Religion," 110.
34. Bagayoko, *Comparative Study of Transitional Justice*, 6.
35. Douba, "L'importance du Jugement Coutumier."
36. Foster, "From War to Peace."

influenced the processes, putting forward those that are alien to the realities of CAR. Since the outcomes of the processes did not meet or have been slow to meet people's expectations, it is necessary to develop an alternative approach that builds, in the context of this study, on *Mbuki* tradition. This consists in investigating *Mbuki* as a vital line of defence against conflict and to foster sustainable reconciliation. The following chapter explores the conceptual understanding of *Mbuki* and its characteristics.

CHAPTER 9

The *Mbuki* Blood Pact for Reconciliation

1. Introduction

The chapter on *Mbuki* (or *Mbèlé*), a Sango word meaning "blood pact," "blood covenant," or "blood brotherhood"[1] aims at examining the characteristics of the ritual pact, its conceptual understanding, its significance, and contrqution to reconciliation in traditional context. As examined in chapter 2 in the case of Sierra Leone on *Fambul Tok*, one traditional practice that could help Centrafricans to deal with national healing and reconciliation in CAR is *Mbuki*. This chapter highlights that *Mbuki* is about sharing blood. Blood refers to, and means life. Therefore, sharing blood is sharing life. Such an understanding, deriving from the practice of *Mbuki* in traiditional societies, could help promote reconciliation in armed and divided CAR's societies and even beyond.

Central to *Mbuki* culture was the notion of identity belonging, the relational blood pacts that bound generations together for various purposes. E. E. Evans-Pritchard argued that blood covenants were "exceedingly common" in Africa and widespread in many parts of the world.[2] In CAR, the Azandé people had institutionalized it in their culture, but several ethnic groups also performed it. According to T. O. Beidelman, the institution of blood

---

1. In this book, I use the terms interchangeably.
2. Evans-Pritchard, "Zande Blood-Brotherhood," 369.

brotherhood in the Kaguru culture in East Africa is now obsolete.³ This is the same in CAR. Nevertheless, from these ancient practices, Centrafricans may learn how to build peaceful relationships in contemporary times.

To guide the analysis in this chapter, I raise the following questions: "What was the practice of *Mbuki* in CAR context?" How was it originally understood? What was the context in which it was used and how has it changed? In the field research, I asked respondents additional questions to further elicit their understanding of the practice of *Mbuki*. I also draw on literature on this topic from other parts of CAR and Africa to help in the analysis of blood pact.

2. Conceptual Understanding of *Mbuki*

Evans-Pritchard who studied the Azandé "blood brotherhood" defines it as "a pact or alliance formed between two persons by a ritual act in which each swallows the blood of the other . . . It may also involve the social groups of which they are members."⁴ In Azandé culture, the ritual bound men as blood brothers and by extension their clans into a kinship. Swallowing each other's blood was a means of bonding and mutual assistance.

In pre-colonial societies, processes of building peace and preserving unity through blood pacts were pervasive. David W. Shenk identified several covenants in traditional Africa. These included the "friendship pact," "blood brotherhood," "kinship pact," "adoption pact," "marriage pact," "land pact," and "peace pact."⁵ Béatrice Epaye pointed out that in the CAR context, blood pacts, marriages, the council of the elders, and initiation were the "mechanisms" of conflict resolution in traditional societies.⁶ Luise White asserts that the blood pact "raises questions about what is kinship and what it is not."⁷ In traditional societies, blood pacts helped to establish new social, political, and economic orders between people.⁸

---

3. Beidelman, "The Blood Covenant," 322.
4. Evans-Pritchard, "Zande Blood-Brotherhood," 369.
5. Shenk, *Justice, Reconciliation and Peace*, 44–72.
6. Epaye, "Les Conflits Centrafricains," 114–155.
7. White, "Blood Brotherhood Revisited," 359.
8. In Azandé culture, the priests and priestesses were responsible for maintaining harmony in a community. They used the oracles (*benge*) to determine the causes of evil and to punish those who disrupted the social order and harmony between people. Molefi Kete Asante states that, "The Azande believe that Mbori, the almighty God, is responsible for the creation of the

One purpose of people who used *Mbuki* in CAR was to prevent conflict between two communities. Father Godart and Cyprien Zondé argued that the two exchanged blood after carefully defining the terms of the relationship between them.[9] Writing about the Bantu peoples, namely the Bashi (in DR Congo's West Kivu), the Banyarwanda and Barundi, originating from Rwanda and Burundi, and located in the East Kivu and Lake Tanganyika, Vincent Mulago pointed out that the three groups of people were linked by communion.[10] He goes on to argue that in the Mashi language, "blood pact" is translated *Okunywana*, in Kinyarwanda and Kirundi, it means, *Ubunyawanyi* or *Ukunywana*. The verb *Kunywa* means, "drink" and *Kunywana* translates as "drink each other, being a drink for each other."[11] Thus, to exchange blood means to drink the blood of another or to make the blood of another flow into one's own blood. In other words, it means becoming one with the other in an indissoluble unity.

Irrespective as to the purpose of people exchanging blood, whether to build new social relationships, promote commercial activities, resolve conflicts, and maintain peace, Luise White, writing about East Africa, claimed that the ritual processes are almost the same. She states,

> Local realities varied considerably, and sometimes varied within a society, but the ritual followed this schematic form: two men met at an appointed time, and each made a small cut on a specific part of his body. Each man offered the other some of his blood, either on a coffee berry or a nut or from his hand. Each then drunk or ate the other's blood, they were solemnly declared blood brothers, and the ceremony ended.[12]

Evans-Pritchard also stated that, in *Mbuki* rituals, there were "variations in the order and composition of the rites as they occur in one area, there also appear to be regional differences."[13] For example, while the Azandé blood pact

---

world, but they do not have shrines, temples, rituals, or ceremonies to worship Mbori." See Asante, "Azande," 84. Although *Mbuki* rituals were well developed in the Zandé tradition, the Azandé consulted the oracles to find the cause(s) of their misfortunes that befell them.

9. Godart et Zondé, *De l'esclavage*, 28.
10. Mulago, "Le Pacte de Sang," 172.
11. Mulago, 172–173 (Translation is mine).
12. White, "Blood Brotherhood Revisited," 359.
13. Evans-Pritchard, "Zande Blood-Brotherhood," 381.

was exclusively patrilineal,[14] the Kaguru blood pact in east-central Tanganyika was matrilineal.[15] As I pointed out earlier, Mulago argued that between the Banyarwanda and the Bashi, or between the Banyarwanda and Barundi, there were no barriers related to race or social rank. However, only those who were members of different clans could perform it.[16] In asking why Azandé blood brotherhood was limited to men, excluding women, Evans-Pritchard argued that a blood covenant with another's wife was considered "an adulterous union" and that with a female relative as absurd since the two were related.[17]

To understand the context in which people performed the *Mbuki*'s practices, Bernard Simiti stated that,

> In the past, our ancestors had no court of justice, but internally they had their ways of settling disputes. This explains why they concluded many alliances. Most often, alliances sealed the reconciliation that settled conflict. Therefore, when someone went somewhere, he would hear people say, 'This person is our slave', and the other one would say, 'No! You are our slave because we defeated you [your clan].' There were many pacts in the past, especially blood pacts. People drew a drop of each other's blood and drank or sucked it. This definitely ended conflict. One of the most popular pacts still in force is that between the people of eastern CAR, such as the Nzakara and Zandé, those of Bangassou and Ndélé. Between them, war and mixed marriages are forbidden.[18]

Bienvenu Mbomba confirmed what Simiti said about the blood pact between "slaves" and "masters." He noted that, during a war, when two clans fought and one of the clans won the battle, both clans entered into a blood pact to establish peace. However, the defeated clan agreed to serve their masters as slaves by transporting the leader of the winning clan on *tipoye* (portage) and performing other tasks.[19] The notion of master and slave in

---

14. Evans-Pritchard, "Zande Blood-Brotherhood," 371.
15. Beidelman, "The Blood Covenant," 322.
16. Mulago, "Le Pacte de Sang," 173 [Translation is mine].
17. Evans-Pritchard, "Zande Blood-Brotherhood," 373.
18. Bernard Simiti, Interview, 16 March 2021, Bangui (Translation is mine).
19. Bienvenu Mbomba, Interview, 10 May 2021, Bangui.

this context was not the same as that practised by colonial rulers in Oubangui Chari. It was not about the subjugation of one group to another, but rather about a social relation that brought cohesion, peace, and harmony between the former rival groups.

Slave raiding flourished before the Europeans set foot in the ancient region of CAR. Slave raiders entered the northern part of the country from Chad and Sudan and attacked non-Muslim populations, taking captives, forcing migration and reducing the population.[20] This phenomenon led various ethnic groups that lived together to conclude blood pacts, either to stand together against a common enemy (in this case the advance of the slave raiders) or to oppose the arrival of new migrants who fled the raids from their home villages. This explains the pervasiveness of *Mbuki* practices in CAR and is an aspect of the context in which the practice was developed.

Epaye claims that between 1908 and 1909, the Sultan of Bangassou and the Sultan of Rafaï entered into a blood alliance with the slave-owning Sultan Mohamed es Senoussi.[21] In an interview, Samuel Doguela declared, "The blood pacts existed in the past, when we think of the kingdoms of Senoussi and Rabah, in the south-east and north-east respectively. This was what they found as a way to cease hostilities, to sympathize, and to start afresh."[22] Rabah and Senoussi were Arab sultans, probably originated from the Sudanese kingdom. Rabah, a slave trader seized Dar-el-Kouti (now Ndélé) and installed his nephew Senoussi, providing him with weapons to rule under his leadership. Senoussi murdered the French explorer Paul Crampel in April 1891 and later Gabriel Biscarrat, seizing their weapons. Colonial officials played along as if to support his raids but killed him in 1911.[23] However, before his assassination, and in order to end violent hostilities that broke out due to the slave trade, the sultans of Bangassou, Rafaï and Ndélé concluded pacts with Rabah and Senoussi in order to stop violence and promote peace.[24] This event among others illustrates how people from Muslim background and

---

20. Woodfork, *Culture and Customs*, 33.
21. Epaye, "Les Conflits Centrafricains," 144.
22. Doguela, Interview, 12 March 2021 (Translation is mine).
23. Mayneri, *Sorcellerie et Prophétisme*, 30–31.
24. Epaye, "Les Conflits Centrafricains," 145.

some ethnic groups in CAR have a long story of relations, associated with mixed marriages.

In the light of the above arguments, it can be argued that a high sense of humanity underpinned the blood pacts that lessened or prevented conflict in traditional times. Instead of shedding blood and seeking forgiveness after committing evil, people made pacts to avoid shedding even a drop of blood and strengthened their relations.[25] Furthermore, the above analysis suggests that there was expansion in the practice of blood pacts from pacts between individuals to traditional leaders and then to pacts between communities. These blood pacts also included trade, new kinship relationships and other social orders.

Another form of pact that indigenous people made with those who invaded their territory was the trusteeship pact during the colonial period. Documents in the archives show that the colonizers have initiated protectorate agreements that sultans signed, thus conceding their authority to their new masters. For example, on 23 March 1909 Governor Merwart concluded a protectorate agreement with the sultan Labassou of Nzakara ethnic group and later with N'Doura the sultan of Zandé ethnic group.[26] The agreements stipulated that the sultans and their people had placed themselves under the sovereignty of France and the prescriptions of the French authority. Such agreements were contrary to the *Mbuki* pacts, as they led to the subjugation and total control of indigenous people. However, another document also reveals that, before the colonial policy of subjugation in Oubangui Chari, among the Azandé people, war captives did not experience slavery, but were integrated with the conquerors who treated them as equals.[27] This makes clear that the equal relationships that existed between masters and slaves prior to colonialism were based on respect and value of the latter as a human being.

When I asked the participants what they understood about the practice of *Mbuki* in CAR, out of the ninety-eight interviewees, fifty-one respondents

---

25. Epaye notes that this blood brotherhood is still maintained to this day. See Epaye, "Les Conflits Centrafricains," 145. Some of those interviewed about this culture shared the same view, as the chapter shows.

26. ANOM, GGAEF 4(3) D 16, Politique à l'égard des Sultans du M'Bomou (1909–1917). See also ANOM, GGAEF 4(3) D 16, Le Petit Temps, No. 2710 (16 mai 1909).

27. ANOM, GGAEF 5 D 95–96, Esclavage: Rapport de la Commission Consultative d'experts – Société des Nations, n° official C. 189 M 145, Vol. VI (1936), 29.

(52.04 percent) gave an explanation, but fourty-seven respondents (47.95 percent) did not know (see Table 6 below).

Table 6: Participants' understanding of *Mbuki*[28]

Participants' Understanding of *Mbuki*	# of respondents	%
Performed in case of rape or thief	1	1.02
Performed in case of violent conflict between clans	18	18.36
Performed through exchange of children	4	4.08
Performed through sharing of food/animal	2	2.04
Performed when a strong clan defeated a weak clan	2	2.04
Performed to seek a change in a *Mbuki*	1	1.02
Violation of a *Mbuki* without reparation causes curse	2	2.04
A peace talk is a form of *Mbuki*	2	2.04
Mbuki was more that the political agreements	2	2.04
Mbuki sealed unity, cohesion, kinship	10	10.20
Intermarriages are a form of *Mbuki*	1	1.02
Gula, Runga, Yakoma, and Zandé respect their *Mbuki*	2	2.04
No need to call on *Mbuki* today	4	4.08
Do not know	47	47.95

Respondents defined *Mbuki* more in relation to conflict and peace than to social ties or economic activities. Of the fifty-one respondents who know about *Mbuki*, eighteen interviewees (18.36 percent) specifically associated it with reconciliation after a violent war. Very few associated it with reconciliation after a rape, theft, or a farm issue. Barthélemy Dimanche said, "Blood pacts bound two clans and ended conflict. During the ceremony, the conflicting parties exchanged food or drink to confirm that they were permanently bound by blood."[29] To confirm that the ritual appeases tensions and conflicts, Doguela argued that people performed blood pacts "to stop hostilities, to sympathise and to start afresh."[30] However, the respondents' answers about *Mbuki* were superficial because they had never participated in the rituals. The reason for this could also be that the younger generation did not learn

---

28. Plaisance Rivoli M'Bara (Sources from field research).
29. Barthélemy Dimanche, Interview, 14 April 2021, Bouar (Translation is mine).
30. Samuel Doguela, Interview, 12 March 2021, Bangui (Translation is mine).

about *Mbuki*, making it difficult to understand the insights and depth of the rituals. However, during fieldwork, many interviewees expressed their desire to reconnect with the insights into culture and tradition such as *Mbuki*.

In addition, when I asked them how people performed *Mbuki* in their culture, it emerged from the responses that some ethnic groups used human blood and others used animal blood to make pacts. Joseph Kondia stated that in the Yakoma tradition, "the elders would take an animal that they killed and poured the blood on the ground. The conflicting parties would jump over the spilled blood. From that moment on, the members of the two opposing clans or villages became allies."[31] Franco Mbaye-Bondoi also explained that, "Sometimes, in order to conclude a covenant, the two parties would eat chicken together. They would kill a chicken, perform rituals and then eat it together. The chicken was a symbol of blood."[32] Beyond CAR, other people also performed blood rituals by exchanging animal blood to seal their pact. This was the case for the Kaguru as Beidelman depicts.[33] These examples show that, some ethnic groups performed *Mbuki* rituals by killing an animal and eating it together to seal their covenant. The exchange of little boys or girls was another way of practising *Mbuki*. Magloire Dobigue explained:

> In the Dagba culture, people practised traditional pacts in a different way. They exchanged young girls, aged between 8 and 12, between two communities in order to establish peaceful ties after a war. In addition, to avoid conflict with a community that had powerful warriors, a traditional leader would establish a relationship by offering his daughter to the village chief who was militarily powerful. This prevented the two communities from waging a war.[34]

Jean Allia also described a similar example,

> We are from the Banda ethnic group. There was a bloody war between the Banda Linda and the Dakpa. The Dakpa attacked the Banda Linda, the Banda Linda fought back and blood was

---

31. Joseph Kondia, Interview, 6 May 2021, Bangui (Translation is mine).
32. Franco Mbaye-Bondoi, Interview, 24 July 2021, Bangui (Translation is mine).
33. Beidelman, "The Blood Covenant," 325.
34. Magloire Dobigue, Interview, 26 October 2020, Bossangoa (Translation is mine).

shed. The Banda Linda chased the Dakpa into caves. The Banda Linda gathered dry grass and placed it on fire at the entrance of the caves, adding the chilli pepper. They blew on the grass. The Dakpa smelled the smoke in the caves and ran out to escape. They went to ask for forgiveness. As a covenant, the Dakpa took a girl from their clan and gave her to the Banda Linda and the Banda Linda gave a girl from their clan to the Dakpa. Their act both sealed a covenant. Therefore, between the Banda Linda and the Dakpa, no war. They swore that if either clan violated the pact and attacked a member of either clan in a future war, the people of that group would all perish.[35]

Evans-Pritchard researched and participated in the ritual with an Azandé chief. In his description of the obligations between blood-brothers, he states, "I was surprised that my blood-brother did not take advantage of my being European to make extravagant request for gifts and exercise of political influence."[36] His description also provided some insights. First, he explains that his partner did not use the blood pact opportunity to request for some advantages or to envy any political position. This explanation shows that honesty was a quality that guided blood brothers, as any dishonesty in the conclusion of the pact would result in danger and misfortune. Second, for the ceremony to take place among the Azandé, two potential blood brothers agreed on the blood exchange, the day, and the place of the ceremony. They ensured that only close relatives and friends knew about it and gathered where preparations were made. A relative checked if everything was ready for the ceremony to start. If not, the owner of the place gathered pieces of benge wood, salt, and some groundnuts. These were the ingredients to be chewed and swallowed dring the ritual pact. Then, the blood partners or their relatives made a slight incision with a knife on the arm or chest of the other to draw blood.[37] He then stated,

> One partner takes a small rectangular piece of *banga* (sic) wood, or several ground-nuts, and soaks in the blood which oozes

---

35. Jean Allia, Interview, 23 July 2021, Bangui (Translation is mine).
36. Evans-Pritchard, "Zande Blood-Brotherhood," 390.
37. Evans-Pritchard, 375.

from the body of the other. Often the two men consume each other's blood at the same time, each taking some ground-nuts, rubbing them in blood, and dipping in salt. They eat the nuts with exaggerated relish. When the ground-nuts are used they consume nut and blood together, but when *benge* wood is used they chew the wood into pulp which they spit out after swallowing blood, salt, and wood juices.[38]

Table 5 above shows that eighteen respondents (18.36 percent) indicated that *Mbuki* promoted human blood exchange for conflict resolution, peace and reconciliation. While, in the Azandé culture, people made an incision on each other's arm or chest,[39] in the Gbaya tradition, they made it on the abdomen.[40] Then, the Azandé partner chewed on a "piece of benge wood" soaked in his blood brother.[41] Mulago also claimed that the Bashi, Kinyarwanda and Hamite performed the ritual in the same way, except that the Bashi mixed blood with traditional beer and drank it, while the Hamite dropped blood in a bottle of milk and drank it.[42] After Azandé partners exchanged blood, they addressed each other by saying that the one who assisted or helped his blood brother or his partner's clansmen would live by blood, and the one who would not do so would die by blood.[43] Likewise, the 52.04 percent of respondents who declared that they had some idea of *Mbuki* stressed that breaking its rules would lead to misfortune. Therefore, these practices shaped the sociological organization of Azandé and other ethnic groups in CAR. There is evidence that ethnic groups, and largely the entire population of CAR, were bound by the blood pacts, yet they are still ignorant about the existence of these social bonds to the extent that some continue to shed the blood of their blood brothers and sisters.

---

38. Evans-Pritchard, "Zande Blood-Brotherhood," 375–376.
39. Evans-Pritchard, 375.
40. Thomas Christensen, *An African Tree of Life*, 88.
41. Evans-Pritchard, "Zande Blood-Brotherhood," 380.
42. Mulago, "Le Pacte du Sang," 173.
43. Evans-Pritchard, "Zande Blood-Brotherhood," 375.

3. Significance of *Mbuki*

Pierre Ambroise Tako-Ali stressed that exchange of blood was the method people used in the past to resolve conflicts and to prevent them from harming each other. He went on to say that the population of Obo no longer exchange blood to resolve conflicts.[44] Ricardo Dimanche also explained that such a practice is outdated and that, using it would lead to the spread of diseases. Nevertheless, according to him, to ease violence, other forms of conflict resolution are today possible in Obo.[45]

In order to understand why people used blood to make pacts, Father Nazaire Diatta noted that blood, not only expresses life, communion, reconciliation, and peace; it is also the basis of the culture and spirituality of reconciliation.[46] Evans-Pritchard sees it as "a concrete magical substance."[47] Drawing from these comments, *Mbuki* not only evokes the spirituality of reconciliation, but also expresses the vital substance that gives life and engenders communion. In other words, sharing blood means sharing communion and life.

Mbiti argues that life is vital for human beings, whether individuals or groups, because "Life is a unity, and human-life depends on other life."[48] Thus, to secure a community requires securing the lives of the people in it. This idea reminds us of Karnu who advocated respect for human life.[49] His concern was to avoid violence and to preserve people's lives as precious gifts from God. In an interview, an anonymous man emphasized that everyone's life is sacred, "When the blood of the conflicting parties mixed, it means that they are united."[50] In this sense, several ethnic groups used *Mbuki* to institute a new social order, uniting blood brothers and, subsequently, large families. Thus, an exchanged blood pact was for life, and ended with the death of its members. Any violation brought misfortune on the part of the person who broke the rules.[51]

---

44. Tako-Ali, "Les Méthodes Traditionnelles."
45. Dimanche, "Les Méthodes Traditionnelles."
46. Diatta, "Le Concept de Réconciliation," 71.
47. Evans-Pritchard, "Zande Blood-Brotherhood," 400.
48. Mbiti, "Relating Peace in African Religion," 112.
49. Christensen, "Karnu: Witchdoctor or Prophet?," 244.
50. Anonymous 25, Interview, 3 November 2020, Bossangoa (Translation is mine).
51. Diatta, "Le Concept de Réconciliation," 63.

For this reason, to avoid such situations, the Azandé took precautions to consult the *benge* oracle to find out what would happen in the course of the concluded pact. Evans-Pritchard points out that the Azandé were experts in using *benge* to administer poison to fowls in order to ascertain the causes of a misfortune. He also noted that people used *benge* to reveal the future. This comprises the success in a marriage, in a journey, or in carrying out an essential project. This ritual method was a way of finding the truth that the Azandé considered more satisfactory than the ritual performed by traditional doctors. Evans-Pritchard goes on to explain the ingredients of the benge. He states,

> The poison used is a red powder manufactured from a forest creeper and mixed with water to a paste. The liquid is squeezed out of the paste into the beaks of small domestic fowls which are compelled to swallow it. Generally, violent spasms follow. The doses sometimes prove fatal, but as often the fowls recover. Sometimes they are even unaffected by the poison. From the behaviour of fowls under this ordeal, especially by their death or survival, Azande receive answers to the questions they place before the oracle.[52]

Addressed as if it were a person, the *benge* oracle or *benge* poison answered according to the fowl. If the fact is true, *benge* killed the fowl but if it is not true, *benge* spared the fowl.[53] In addition, before entering into a blood pact, the candidate sought the consent of his family members, as they would share the responsibility and the obligations of the pact. However, some did not seek the consent of their relatives before concluding a blood pact.[54]

3.1 *Mbuki*: An Alternative to Social Ties

From table 5 above, ten respondents (10.20 percent) associated blood exchange with the search for social bonds. According to them, *Mbuki* built an alternative to social ties. Diatta states that when members of two clans or villages exchanged blood, they shared the same blood, which circulated in

---

52. Evans-Pritchard, *Witchcraft, Oracles, and Magic*, 120.

53. Evans-Pritchard, 120.

54. de Dampierre, *Un Ancien Royaume Bandia*, 267. See also Evans-Pritchard, "Zande Blood-Brotherhood," 371.

each of them, including members of their groups, linking them to each other.[55] A Gbaya Kara proverb states, *Yi neè ne kay yi go*, which means, "The river that flows alone eventually deviates."[56] In other words, *Mbuki* stops people from deviating. This saying warns against individualism, and encourages community spirit, which is of a great help. In relation to the analysis, the proverb highlights the issue of sociability in solving problems that arise in society, in the sense that the community shares the burdens of others.

Mulago also stated that, "L'échange de sang symbolise la fraternité, le dévouement mutuel, mais il est une donation réciproque, une façon d'entrer dans la famille de l'autre" ("The exchange of blood symbolises brotherhood, mutual devotion, but it is a reciprocal gift, a way of entering the family of the other").[57] He went on to say that, in the political or public context, indigenous Bashi, Banyarwanda and Barundi leaders concluded "traités d'alliance" (friendship treaties) with each other to maintain good neighbourly relations.[58] Thus, in general, *Mbuki* promoted life in community, sharing, interdependence, being supportive and convivial. Jack Donovan argues in this direction when he states that, in a blood pact, "Allied tribes or states, while retaining their separate identities and their independence, are expected to support one another in conflict, to favour one another according to the terms of their agreement, and to assist one another wherever possible."[59]

As I noted earlier, respondents who were aware of *Mbuki* rituals did not fully understand their extent and pervasiveness in society. As a result, coexistence between some communities in CAR was superficial or fragile. When I researched the state of relationship between Christians and Muslims before the 2013 conflict, 99 percent of interviewees opined that it was good. For example, Danboy said that some Christians and Muslims lived under the same roof.[60] Mandje-Ndjapou maintained that young Christians and Muslims went to school or played together.[61] Ghislain Ngoma contended that Christians and

---

55. Diatta, "Le Concept de Reconciliation," 76.
56. Dimanche Barthélemy, Interview, 14 April 2021, Bouar (Translation is mine).
57. Mulago, "Le Pacte de Sang," 174 (Translation is mine).
58. Mulago, 172.
59. Donovan, "A Timeless Way," 5.
60. Fidèle Danboy, Interview, 9 November 2020, Bossangoa.
61. Fernand Mandje Ndjapou, Interview, 26 August 2021, Bangui.

Muslims were involved in commercial activities[62] and Blaise Malitongo noted that some Christians and Muslims had mixed marriages.[63] Mbaye-Bondoi revealed that Christians and Muslims supported and helped each other. During the Islamic festivals of Ramadan or of Tabaski, Muslims invited pastors to mosques and Christian relatives to their premises to celebrate. Christians also invited Muslims to participate in their Christmas celebration and other religious activities such as baptism or weddings.[64]

Even if the 2013 conflict was not religious, the violence between Christians and Muslims has affected relations between them, as eighty-eight respondents (89.79 percent) acknowledged. Imam Balla Traoré highlighted the depth of the problem when he said:

> Christians said that Muslims were foreigners and they should go back to their countries of origin. Take my case. My family name is Traoré. My distant origin is West Africa. Our ancestors were snipers brought by the French colonisers to fight during the war. At the end of the war, they decided to stay in CAR. My grandfather married a woman and gave birth to my father, who in turn married a Gbaya woman and gave birth to me. My first child is from an Ngbaka-Mandja woman and my second child is from a Kabba mother. If I am told to go home, what can I claim as my roots?[65]

It was unfortunately true that people discriminated against some Muslims today, as Balla pointed out. Such an attitude was evidence of hidden xenophobia on the part of those who promoted it. Considering Balla's statement, his family members were married to Christian women from several ethnic groups. Marital relationships established social links between the Traoré lineage and the Christian lineages. However, because of the conflict, the promoters of xenophobia attempted to drive them out. Epaye pointed out that in the CAR culture, marriage prohibited violence between in-laws. In case of conflict, the elders of each family acted as mediators.[66] Due to the ineffec-

---

62. Ghislain Ngoma, Interview, 11 March 2021, Bangui.
63. Blaise Malitongo, Interview, 16 March 2021, Bangui.
64. Mbaye-Bondoi, Interview, 24 July 2021 (Bangui).
65. Balla Traoré, Interview 27 January 2021, Bangui (Translation is mine).
66. Epaye, "Les Conflits Centrafricains," 145.

tiveness of conflict resolution methods implemented so far by peace actors, ongoing violence has disrupted social relations between many Christian and Muslim communities in general, and marital homes in particular, affecting the future of children.

In the same vein, speaking about the violence in Bossangoa after the conflict broke out, Ouanekpone said, "If we look carefully, those who understood the kind of relationship they had with Muslims, those who had a strong coexistence with Muslims before the 2013 conflict, were not much more brutal than the youth. The youth were in the forefront."[67] Here, Ouanekpone pointed out that people who had good relations with Muslims before conflict did not act like the youth, committing gross violations on the Muslim community when the conflict broke out. He went on to point out that, in Bossangoa, "There were mixed marriages between Christians and Muslims. Muslims who were in the locality were brothers and sisters-in-law of the local people. There was no reason to reject them."[68]

Despite existing ties, violence has broken social bonds, if not in the whole country, at least in most communities. Imam Traoré said, "Neither Christians nor Muslims have won. The conflict has affected both communities and broken relations between them. Until today, they have not found a solution to end it."[69] Therefore, to help CAR emerge from this situation, Tatiana Carayannis and Louisa Lombard argue that it is important to address the root causes of the conflict rather than the "symptoms."[70] This means, addressing the issues that have broken down relationships between communities, making them fragile and easier to tear apart through manipulation and resurgence of violence.

As I explain below, there were rules that guaranteed the relational ties that existed in the past through blood alliances that each party had to respect, including the future generation. Respecting these principles was more advantageous and more humane to avoid conflicts and to maintain a good harmony between communities. If the rules of harmony and cohesion are violated today, is it possible that reviving some aspects of the *Mbuki* ritual may open

---

67. René-Patrice Ouanekpone Interview, 31 October 2020, Bossangoa (Translation is mine).
68. Ouanekpone, Interview, 31 October 2020 (Translation is mine).
69. Traoré, Interview 27 January 2021 (Translation is mine).
70. Carayannis and Lombard, "Making Sense of CAR," 2.

the way to a better alternative for reweaving the bonds of reconciliation and national unity than the modern processes of reconciliation that have not proven successful? Indeed, the bond of kinship formed through *Mbuki* ritual creates ties beyond biological kin.

3.2 *Mbuki* for Mutual Assistance

In traditional societies, initiation rites served to build the community life among initiates. During initiation, elders shared their life experiences with the young people in order to shape their character and personality to forge their socialization and integration into the community. In addition, elders imparted on young people secrets of life, wisdom of ancestors and work skills.[71] During initiation, elders taught young people how to promote mutual support. Maurice Dimanche Arsy emphasized the richness of the initiation when he said:

> At the initiation the candidates were taught the alphabets a, b, c and d in the *LaBi* language. I remember my father reciting these alphabets in that language: a = watarake; b = wataralai; c = kumbasse; and d = kumbalai. The initiates memorised also the names of trees, insects and many other things in the *LaBi* language. It was a reservoir of oral tradition. The problem was that they did not preserve their knowledge in writing.[72]

Arsy did not elaborate on what the initiates had learned. He rather regretted the lack of written documentation on this indigenous knowledge. Kevin Kossi pointed to the loss of the educational function of ancestral values, including initiation. He emphasized that modern education has contributed to the loss of these fundamental values.[73] However, in the past when young people attended initiation rites such as the *LaBi*, *Soumale* or *Ngakola*,[74] they learned to build solidarity, community spirit, and to deal with various issues, including conflict issues. According to Ninga Songo, during the *LaBi* initiation, the novice learned and recited the eleven principles that consecrated *LaBi*

---

71. Woodfork, *Culture and Customs*, 131–133.
72. Maurice Dimanche Arsy, Interview 2nd April 2021, Bouar (Translation is mine).
73. Kossi, "La Passation des Valeurs Ancestrales."
74. *LaBi* was a secret society among the Gbaya and Karré ethnic groups, while *Soumale* and *Ngakola* were among the Banda. See Kpamo, *La Christianisation et le Début*, 9.

education, the second of which stated, "Il faut s'entraider pour vaincre les difficultés" (It is necessary to help each other in order to overcome difficulties).[75] This view does not contradict Woodfork's statement that "Initiation is also a bonding experience; those who go through initiation together are a family of a sort and individuals identify themselves as a member of their initiation group throughout their lives."[76] According to Christensen, the performance of *LaBi* has been extinct since the 1960s.[77] One can also say so of the *Ngakola* and *Soumale* initiation rituals.

Nevertheless, an important aspect of the initiation rite was the blood pact when the *LaBi* master (*Narninga*) performed the rite of blood pact by making an incision of a few centimetres on the abdomen or back of the novices.

> Then he dips a raw manioc tuber into the bloody incision and gives it to the boy to eat. 'This is your blood', he says. 'Now that you eat this blood, if you ever reveal the secrets of *labi* to anyone who is not an initiate, may your own blood kill you! May you die by the knife! May the buffalo kill you with his horns! May the spear run you through! If you reveal the secrets of *labi*, may all that God has made kill you!' . . . The boy eats the manioc that has been dipped in his blood. If he simply licks the blood, he does not make a covenant. Manioc and blood are genuine food; they must be consumed to seal one genuine covenant.[78]

Once the initiates became immersed in the LaBi covenant, their lives were linked to its spirit, and their blood mixed with cassava, the "genuine food" of the covenant.[79] They learned what a covenant was and committed themselves to living with its secret. In an interview, Nathalie disagreed with the argument that the LaBi initiation bound people in Gbaya traditional societies. She recalled that in Bossangoa, the Gbaya were attached to tradition, but for nothing serious, they could resort to violence: "The more they were attached

---

75. Ninga Songo, "Le LaBi, 'rite d'initiation' des Gbaya." In *Peuples et culture de l'Adamawa (Cameroun)*, 181–186. Edited by Adala H. and Boutrais Jean. Paris: ORSTOM, 1993.
76. Woodfork, *Culture and Customs*, 131.
77. Christensen, *An African Tree of Life*, 84.
78. Christensen, 88.
79. Christensen, 89.

to their tradition, the more quickly their path became divided."⁸⁰ When I asked her if traditional leaders could contribute to peace in Bossangoa, she said, "A pastor leads the local peace mediation committee. I believe that God does not take into account our traditions; he wants us to be detached from tradition. The CLPR [local committee for peace and reconciliation] has an assistant leader who is a woman; she is from the Catholic Church."⁸¹ Such an argument is understandable, given Nathalie's experience in this situation. However, it is possible that she has misunderstood the meaning of the Gbaya tradition, as she is not from that ethnic group. Conversely, if the Gbaya people behaved as she has described, then it is also possible that they have lost the memory of cultural traditions and their treasuries.

Mulago describes the advantages of the "solidarity agreements" between the Bashi, the Banyarwanda and the Barundi, as groups of people linked by blood pact. He writes,

> Dans la vie journalière, ils se montrent beaucoup de simplicité; ils s'intéressent à la vie les uns des autres, se rendent visite, s'invitent réciproquement à manger, à boire, à passer ensemble de joyeuses soirées dansantes. Quelqu'un construit-il une hutte, tout le voisinage accourt l'aider, et comme récompense de sa peine, il se contentera d'une gorgée de bière de bananes. On se fait aussi aider pour les cultures . . . La vie de Bashi, Banyarwanda et Barundi est une communion avec l'autre.
>
> In everyday life, they are very simple; they take an interest in each other's lives, visit each other, invite each other to eat and drink, and spend happy evenings dancing together. If someone builds a hut, the whole neighbourhood comes out to help and, as a reward for their effort, they will settle for a sip of banana beer. They also help each other to cultivate their farms . . . The life of the Bashi, Banyarwanda and Barundi is a communion with each other.⁸²

---

80. Nathalie, Interview 24 November 2020, Bossangoa (Translation is mine).
81. Nathalie, Interview 24 November 2020 (Translation is mine).
82. Mulago, "Le Pacte de Sang," 171–172 (Translation is mine).

Just as the Bashi, Banyarwanda and Barundi found great benefits in building a community of solidarity through blood pacts, so the Azandé also exchanged blood to seek benefits or to compensate for "the deficiencies of ordinary brotherhood." Indeed, when a Zandé man was disappointed with the attitudes of his family members, he entered into a blood pact, partly "to show disdain for and distrust of his biological brothers."[83] This explains how beneficial blood pacts were in societies, as the following clarifies.

Addressing the 2013 conflict means addressing the root causes of the problem. People make the *Mbuki* pact for mutual assistance and one outcome is the sense of "love each other." A community that promotes *Mbuki* as mutual assistance does not need to resort to violence and then seek forgiveness and reconciliation. Promoting love through mutual assistance could enable greater cohesion and unity. There are, therefore, theological implications of this understanding. I develop, in this book, a scriptural interpretation of the *Mbuki* ritual to understand its significant contribution to reconciliation.

3.3 *Mbuki* for Socio-Economic Purposes

During the interviews, none of the interviewees referred to the socio-economic purpose of *Mbuki*. It is possible that they were not aware of it, probably because, as I noted earlier, people no longer perform the ritual. It may be also because elders did not pass on stories about the rituals to new generations. However, other sources provided insights into the particularity of this practice. Evans-Pritchard observes that Azandé exchanged blood not only for security reasons, but also for "favourable economic conditions."[84]

> It is also common for men to make a blood-pact for purposes of trade in which there is no high degree of personal danger. A man living in the heart of Zande country finds difficulty in acquiring various luxuries which are plentiful in districts. Thus Azande people sometimes make blood-brotherhood with the semi-Zandeized Mbegumda and Mberidi of the extreme north with the purpose of obtaining dried meats and vegetable oils. At the time of the year when these articles of food are abundant the Zande pays his blood-brother a visit and asks him for presents

---

83. White, "Blood Brotherhood Revisited," 362.
84. Evans-Pritchard, "Zande Blood-Brotherhood," 373.

of oil and dried meats. He may bring some articles with him as return gifts or he may just demand them *gine kure*, 'in the path of blood'. In any case his blood-brother will have anticipated the visit and will have reserved part of his surplus oil and flesh to meet the occasion. When he feels inclined the northerner will pay a visit to the centre of Zande country where he will enjoy the hospitality of his blood-brother from whose home he will return laden with one or two spears, or some bark-cloth, or other such articles which are difficult to obtain in his far-off district.[85]

The Azandé developed commercial activities for economic purposes. In doing so, they laid the foundation for successful economic investments. For example, a person from the centre of Zandé land could travel to the northern part in search of partners to develop economic exchanges. Evans-Pritchard gave further evidence of the growth of these activities through people who were given the preferential treatments they needed in economic exchanges and were assured of the security of the transactions they made. Thus, in this tradition, blood brothers helped each other according to what they had and/or wanted.[86] In this context, the privilege of blood brotherhood was to share interests.[87]

Beyond CAR, some ethnic groups in Kenya also practiced blood pact exchanges. Thomas J. Herlehy has argued that in the pre-colonial era on the Kenyan coast, economic activities linked the Swahili, Arabs, Waata, Orma, Akamba and Taita through "the demand for palm wine and other commodities, and the social cohesion sustained by blood-brotherhood and intermarriage."[88] According to him, "This increased economic unity was complemented by the forging of social bonds, especially through the pledging of blood-brotherhood and intermarriage."[89] What he stressed corresponds to the interests that the Azandé people sought in the exchange of blood with partners. Today, the rediscovery of these practices would allow Centrafricans to understand how, in pre-colonial era, people strengthened

---

85. Evans-Pritchard, "Zande Blood-Brotherhood," 373.
86. Evans-Pritchard, 373.
87. Donovan, "A Timeless Way," 5.
88. Herlehy, "Ties that Bind," 285.
89. Herlehy, 286.

their relationships through economic exchange. For example, young boys and girls were trained not only to be fully involved as active members of society, but also to be creative and skilled workers to develop their families and communities, socio-economically.[90]

4. Widespread Practice of *Mbuki* in Traditional Society

Writing on the customs and culture of CAR, Woodfork observes that social customs bound people together. The rituals they practiced linked them to each other.[91] This explains the prevalence of *Mbuki* practices in ancient societies. Victor Bissengue asserts that, among the Azandé, the king was not only of the Zandé or of Nzakara ethnic group. Ethnic mixing led a person from one ethnic group being chosen as chief of another group.[92] Of the ninety-eight individual interviews, none of the fifty-one respondents who knew about *Mbuki* indicated the widespread practice of the ritual in the past. They simply said that their clans had made a blood pact with another clan as a sign of reconciliation after a war. Consequently, the allied clans could not wage war against each other. Thus, they were not aware of the pervasiveness of the blood pacts. However, Diatta argues that the practice of blood pacts was widespread in traditional societies.

> Il y a pacte de sang, entre Ndi et Sabanga ; entre Kaba et Gbaya-Kara ; entre Gbaka et Itei ; entre Kare et Tali ; entre Benam et Betokomia ; entre Bengormbo et Bessa ; entre Gbaya et Dakpa ; entre Mondjombo et Mbasse ; entre Sango et Ngbuku ; entre Ngbaka-Mandja et Ali ; entre Banda-Ndele et Nzakara ; entre Banda et Zandé ; entre Yakoma et Nzakara ; entre Yakoma et Ngbougou ; Entre Banda et Mandja ; entre Banda-Sango et Langba-Kabou-Goula ; entre Mbati et Gbaka ; entre Yakoma et Zandé ; entre Zacara de Bangassou et Banda ndele ; entre Ngbougou de Mobaye et Yakpa d'Alindao ; entre

---

90. Woodfork, *Culture and Customs*, 14.
91. Woodfork, 129.
92. Bissengue, *Les Maux de la République*, 85.

Ngbougou et Boroto ; entre Tongo et Careins ; entre Langbachi-Gbeyere et Banda.

The assertion translates as follows:

> There is a blood pact between Ndi and Sabanga; between Kaba and Gbaya-Kara; between Gbaka and Itei; between Kare and Tali; between Benam and Betokomia; between Bengormbo and Bessa; between Gbaya and Dakpa; between Mondjombo and Mbasse; between Sango and Ngbuku; between Ngbaka-Mandja and Ali; between Banda-Ndélé and Nzakara; between Banda and Zandé; between Yakoma and Nzakara; between Yakoma and Ngbougou; between Banda and Mandja; between Banda-Sango and Langba-Kabou-Goula; between Mbati and Gbaka; between Yakoma and Zandé; between Zacara de Bangassou and Banda ndele; between Ngbougou de Mobaye and Yakpa d'Alindao; between Ngbougou and Boroto; between Tongo and Careins; between Langbachi-Gbeyere and Banda.[93]

Diatta's research shows evidence that the majority of ethnic groups in the pre-colonial period exchanged blood with each other. Evans-Pritchard also says that when two Azandé men, for example, exchanged blood, they became bukare ("blood brothers").[94] In light of the above, and given the extent to which *Mbuki* was prevalent in the past, it is possible to say that Centrafricans are each other's bakurëmi ("my blood brother") and nakurëmi ("my blood sister").[95] It is also possible that those who give in to ongoing violence continue to mistakenly harm or kill their own "blood brothers" or "blood sisters" in light of this logic.

5. *Mbuki* and the Culture of Peace

In table 5 above, 18.36 percent of respondents associated *Mbuki* with conflict resolution, peace and reconciliation. Ambroise Tako-Ali explained the benefits of blood pact in Obo town, stressing the consolidation of peace

---

93. Diatta, "Le Concept de Réconciliation," foot note No. 76, 78–79 (Translation is mine).
94. Evans-Pritchard, "Zande Blood-Brotherhood," 370.
95. Evans-Pritchard, 370.

between individuals and communities.⁹⁶ He said that blood pact, promoted community cohesion. When people concluded a blood pact, the community was respected. Everyone lived peacefully, because everyone promoted respect of one other.⁹⁷

In his book, *Le Dernier Survivant de la Caravane*, Etienne Goyémidé described the story narrated by the storyteller, Ngalandji, of violent clashes between the Oubanguians and the slave traders, who carried out raids from Chad and Sudan before the Europeans arrived.⁹⁸ The story involved a blood pact between the Dakpa and Linda clans at the Diwa village. The two tribes were fierce enemies, clashing at every opportunity. The warriors of both clans agreed to a new battle. Before they arrived at the battlefield, the women of both clans gathered there, followed by their children.

When warriors arrived at the battlefield, they summoned the women and children to leave. The eldest woman came forward in the middle, accompanied by two small children from both clans. She solemnly told the warriors that women were the bearers of life, which they took care of until it reached maturity. This life, she said, was sacred and precious, but men took it away through violence. Thus, women decided to put an end to it. She called the warrior leaders of the two clans to approach in the middle and stripped them each of their weapons. She made an incision in the hand of the two children of the clans and dropped blood into the palm of her hand, which she mixed with her knife and put it to the tongue of each warrior leader, and of the children.⁹⁹ Then, she stated,

> Chefs des tribus Linda et Dakpa, vous venez d'absorber le sang mélangé de vos propres enfants déposé sur vos langues. En acceptant de la faire, vous vous êtes juré de mettre un terme définitif à toutes vos querelles. Vous venez de conclure un pacte de non-agression et de sceller par le sang une alliance éternelle. Quiconque brisera cette alliance attirera sur sa tribu les pires calamités ayant existé sous le soleil. Par cette même opération, vous avez affirmé devant tous que vos enfants ici présents sont

---

96. Tako-Ali, "Les Méthodes Traditionnelles."
97. Tako-Ali.
98. Goyémidé, *Le Dernier Survivante*.
99. Goyémidé, 84–88.

sacrés et appartiennent à vos deux tribus. La guerre et sa cohorte de misères doivent disparaitre à jamais pour laisser la place à l'amour, aux mariages, à la procréation et à la continuité de la vie.

Chief of the Linda and Dakpa tribes, you have just absorbed the mixed blood of your own children. By accepting it, you have sworn to put an end to all your quarrels for good. You have entered into a non-aggression pact and sealed an eternal covenant with blood. Whoever breaks this covenant will bring upon his tribe the worst calamities that ever existed under the sun. By this very operation, you have affirmed before all that your children here are sacred and belong to your two tribes. War and its attendant misery must disappear forever to make way for love, marriage, procreation and the continuity of life.[100]

Thus, she mixed the remaining blood in the hands of the two children, sealing the unity of the clans, and blew on what was left in her own hand towards the warriors, sprinkling them with the mixed blood so that they became one people. This account of reconciliation takes us to the heart of the peace process in the pre-colonial period through a pact that led to reconciliation, peace, and communion.[101]

In this story, the old woman played a key role of mediator. Diatta said that they chose life and its perpetuation to save the clans and secure the progenitor.[102] They envisaged a peaceful future rather than a community bereaved by violent war. Thus, blood was the reconciling element, vital for keeping the two clans together. The women were opposed to the loss of any member of the clans because they knew the value of blood. They were united by blood, for they shed it to give life to all, while the two children shed blood, to seal unity, peace, and reconciliation, which they consumed to unite future generations. The clan leaders were included in the blood they consumed. The rest of the warriors too became part of the blood the old woman blew onto them, to make them one clan, one army, and one people, reconciled by blood.[103]

---

100. Goyémidé, *Le Dernier Survivant*, 88 (Translation is mine).
101. Diatta, "Le Concept de Réconciliation," 71.
102. Diatta, 72.
103. Diatta, 75–78.

It is important to emphasize the instructive nature of this story and the reconciliatory values it highlighted. The story describes the love and unity between the women of the two clans, their sense of forgiveness (the women of the Linda clan forgave the husbands/warriors of the Dakpa clan and *vice-versa*) and the reconciliation that took place through the consumption of the mixed blood of the children belonging to the two clans. The ritual put an end to the violence between the two groups of warriors and led the two clans to reconcile.

I have shown ealier that parties to the conflict in CAR have concluded several peace agreements inside or outside the country, with recommendations for implementation, which they violated. Out of ninety-eight individual interviews, forty-nine participants (50 percent) indicated that the violation of the recommendations was the primary cause of the recrudescence of violence. In doing so, the armed groups have broken the life-sustaining pact to make a deadly pact. Doguela thought that today, peace agreements represent blood pacts in the traditional period, except that in the past people scrupulously respected their covenants, and "there were no mistakes, there were no half measures for those who violated them."[104] While many Centrafricans blamed Muslims for the conflict, Jean-Pierre Dounia Nambate highlighted the existing blood pacts between the non-Muslim Centrafricans who have converted to Islam and Muslims. For him, the religion that united them could be enough to initiate peace and reconciliation.

> Among the Muslims, there were some people from the Mandja ethnic group who were Islamised, there were some from the Banda group who were Islamised, there were some from the Yakoma group who were Islamised, because Muslims came from the eastern regions. Therefore, how and on what basis did these people become Islamised, let alone Goula and Runga? Based on this argument, can they not build peace, social cohesion and unity? They have been Islamised, but how have they lived with their co-religionists? Could we not go back to this starting point to consider the future? Today, because of selfish interests, people

---

104. Doguela, Interview 12 March 2021 (Translation is mine).

no longer take into account the alliances that their ancestors made in the past, and this is a problem.[105]

Indeed, this issue requires reflection on the part of Muslims and non-Muslims converts to Islam, and Centrafricans in general, seeing the sympathy that the two communities have felt in the past and reflecting on their rupture today. Mulago and Epaye pointed out that, in addition to tribal pacts, political treaties of friendship strengthened friendly relations and maintained peace between states. Once two parties were united by a political pact, any future conflict could be resolved peacefully.[106] No one could resort to violence without suffering the consequences.[107]

A Sango proverb says, *Vouko bongo a soukoula na ya ti séwa* ("Dirty cloth is washed in the family"). This saying expresses the necessity of dealing with issues that divided people in peaceful ways within the community. I mentioned earlier that respondents criticized the government and international organizations' methods relating to holding peace talks outside of the territory. Such approaches have not provided effective outcomes. They suggested that peace meetings, rather, be held within the territory. When this happens within the territory, participants would assess what bound them and work for peace. As an example, Tako-Ali revealed the existence of *Mbuki* between the Banda-Ndélé and Azandé. He explained that when a member of the Banda-Ndélé ethnic group met a member of the Zandé group, he would put down his weapon and welcome the latter as a brother, more than a brother. Both groups continue to observe this agreement until today.[108]

A further example shows that, in July 2020, gunmen of Goula and Runga ethnic groups reconciled and burned their guns to re-establish their relationship.[109] The main reason remains in the fact that the two groups were, in the past, bound by blood pact. Epaye claims that this relationship dates back to 1908 or 1909 with a blood pact between Sultan Mohamed Senoussi,

---

105. Jean-Pierre Dounia Nambate, Interview 15 March 2021, Bangui (Translation is mine).
106. Mulago, "Le Pacte de Sang," 171–172 ; Epaye, "Les Conflits Centrafricains," 145.
107. Goyémidé, *Le Dernier Survivant*, 88.
108. Tako-Ali, "Les Méthodes Traditionnelles."
109. Radio Ndeke Luka, "Centrafrique: les Communautés." Accessed 28 December 2020, https://www.radiondekeluka.org/actualites/securite/35887-centrafrique-les-communautes-goula-et-rounga-se-reconcilient-a-ndele.html?fbclid=IwAR3yhr1kpPU0LE0Q6R255LF73Bl UGGfifBMwxM-zgiEGrVoav4JceWDlX7M.

Sultan Bangassou and Sultan Rafaï, which is still in force today.[110] Describing a process of blood pact between the Banda-Ndélé and the Zandé, Tako-Ali explained that, through a diplomatic initiative, a clan would come together and sit around a paramount chief to reflect on the issue of their clash with another clan. They sent emissaries to the chief of the other clan to seek reconciliation. When the chiefs of two clans met, they discussed what affected their relationships and agreed to make a pact. He went on to say that the Azandé had exchanged a blood pact with the chief of Birao after several years of war. The pact between the Banda-Ndélé and Azandé is still alive.[111]

In CAR, a Sango proverb says, *Pembé na langue a te tere me ala ke tere ape* ("The tongue and the teeth always hurt each other, but never cease to coexist").[112] This saying means that, when the teeth bite the tongue and blood comes out of it, it affects both parts. However, when the tongue stops bleeding, the two are reconciled and live together. This proverb explains how Centrafricans should strive to stay together despite the problems they may encounter, and to resolve their conflicts peacefully in the interest of cohesion and peace. Nongo-Aziagbia's statement below aligns to the above proverb when he notes that the sultan of Bangassou reminded the blood brothers of Vakaga of the blood pact existing between them.

> The sultan of Bangassou sent a letter, not only it but also the natives of the Mbomou region sent a message on this issue to their brothers in Vakaga or Birao because they saw that their brothers in Birao betrayed the links that united them by the attack that the latter launched against them. Therefore, some mechanisms that existed and continue to exist in our cultures and among our people. In addition, I think we can explore the traditional mechanisms that allow us to revive the process of conflict resolution in our country.[113]

He concluded that such an example proves that Centrafricans can initiate peace and reconciliation based on existing blood pacts that have bound several ethnic groups together. Unlike him and other respondents who thought

---

110. Epaye, "Les Conflits Centrafricains et Leurs Règlements," 145.
111. Ricardo, "Les Méthodes Traditionnelles."
112. Doguela, Interview 12 March 2021 (Translation is mine).
113. Nongo-Aziagbia, Interview 10 November 2020.

that the insights into indigenous practices, including *Mbuki*, could help initiate reconciliation, Ricardo was pessimistic, saying that many young people were unaware of the existence of *Mbuki* between the Banda-Ndélé, Goula and Zandé. The clauses of the pacts stipulated that a member of these ethnic groups should not shed the blood of another. He admitted that young people who belong to these groups and were involved in the conflict ignored the prohibitions and shed others' blood, thus violating the pacts their elders made.[114] As a result, the achievements of the blood pacts have been set aside in today's CAR society, as Balla Traoré noted.

> There were indeed blood alliances according to which certain ethnic groups should not trigger a war against others. However, nowadays, these alliances have been set aside. That is why there is no solution to our crises today. The choice to resolve the crisis by arms brought nothing as a solution, we all lost [because] we have broken the covenants.[115]

Here, Traoré linked the failure of the peace processes to the violation of blood pacts. Although this cannot be the sole cause as he argued, nevertheless reconciliation processes have failed because people have broken the pacts that bound them to each other. Unable to maintain them, some political leaders have made alliances with foreign mercenaries and terrorists to fight for them to rise to power. The picture below shows Niger's Ali Darassa, leader of the armed group UPC, signing a ceasefire to end the clashes that have left many people dead in Bria.[116]

6. The Obligations of *Mbuki*

Out of fifty-one respondents who were aware of *Mbuki*, more than forty-five respondents emphasized the prohibition of breaking its clauses. Father Godart and Zondé reveal that sometimes, during the process, the blood brothers sang a song saying that the one who did not respect the rules of the pact would die, while the one who complied with the requirements would stay alive.[117]

---

114. Ricardo, "Les Méthodes Traditionnelles."
115. Traoré, Interview 27 January 2021 (Translation is mine).
116. Radio Ndeke Luka, "Ali Darassa Paraphant."
117. Godart et Zondé, *De l'esclavage à la Liberté*, 28.

However, it is difficult to know whether the blood brothers always complied with the requirements. With regard to Azandé culture, Evans-Pritchard pointed out that, there were sometimes "flagrant breaches."[118]

In discussing the obligations of blood pact, Donovan asserted that it was characterized by mutual respect, personal sovereignty, and an obligation to support the interests and honour of the other. Otherwise, the "bond would be an exploitative sham."[119] These, therefore, motivated the Azandé people to make a blood pact. Indeed, for the Azandé, society privileged family class or ranking status among brothers, while blood brothers favoured egalitarian interests and absolute equality. Thus, in contrasting blood brotherhood and kinship, they argued that "a blood-brother is a much better friend than a real brother." While the former helped his blood brother "in time of need," the latter bribed his brother's wife or refused to help him when he needed it.[120]

Indeed, the success of blood pacts in the past was due to the fulfilment of mutual obligations by the partners and respect of the engagements, followed by legal sanctions in case of violation.[121] Ngoupandé also argued that no one could violate *Mbuki* and escape disastrous consequences.[122] I raised a question in the introduction about the consequences of breaking the obligations of a pact. In an attempt to answer the question, an anonymous respondent stated, "The alliance of blood is profound. When the blood of the belligerents mingles, it means that they have become united. If they did not respect the covenant, a great calamity befell them. This practice went beyond the agreements that are not respected today."[123] Similarly, Dimanche stated that,

> Blood alliances bound clans and ended conflict. The warring parties exchanged food or drink to signify that they were permanently bound by blood. Nowadays, the dialogues that the warring parties have had to make peace are a form of alliance. Normally, no one is supposed to violate a blood covenant, neither blood brothers nor their descendants who become blood

---

118. Evans-Pritchard, "Zande Blood-Brotherhood," 394.
119. Donovan, "A Timeless Way," 8.
120. Evans-Pritchard, 399.
121. Evans-Pritchard, 400.
122. Ngoupandé, *Chronique de la Crise Centrafricaine*, 135–136.
123. Anonymous 25, Interview, 22 October 2020, Bossangoa (Translation is mine).

relatives. However, today, all those who have signed covenants through peace talks and negotiations do not know their importance and do not respect them.[124]

Some interviewees also agreed that the current political agreements are like blood pacts made in order to achieve peace. However, whereas in the pre-colonial era, people were honest about blood pacts, today they break them, resorting to violence against each other. For this reason, Dimanche thought that blood pacts were superior to the peace agreements that parties involved easily break today.

Referring to the rampant hostilities between rebel groups and the atrocities towards the population, another anonymous respondent declared, "It is forbidden to violate the recommendations of the blood pacts. By resorting to violence against one's ally, they [the armed groups] have already violated the pacts [peace agreements, cease-fire] by killing each other."[125] While Kondia's opinion supported this idea,[126] Simiti pointed out that, because of the existing covenant that still unites them, violence and mixed marriages between the Nzakara-Zandé of Bangassou and the people of Ndélé were forbidden.[127] In all this, Nicaise said,

> When two people were united by the blood covenant, the covenanters and their future generations were bound by the covenant. Neither the parties nor their descendants were to break the terms of the covenant. Today, it is possible to recall the history of *Mbuki* between the ethnic groups who engage in violence that their ancestors were bound by a blood alliance. The fact that they have been killing each other is a violation of the pacts that were made, it would have dramatic consequences.[128]

In view of this social phenomenon and given the inter-group clashes, social unrest, and political violence, Centrafricans bound by blood pacts have broken the existing *Mbuki* bonds while "Traditionally, blood alliances

---

124. Dimanche, Interview, 14 April 2021 (Translation is mine).
125. Anonymous 78, Interview, 30 August 2021, Bangui (Translation is mine).
126. Kondia, Interview, 6 May 2021.
127. Simiti, Interview, 16 March 2021.
128. Nicaise, Interview, 12 June 2021, Bangui (Translation is mine).

advocated unity, non-violence, tolerance, peaceful conflict resolution, peace and cohesion."[129] These views help to understand the gravity of the current situation.

7. Conclusion

The study of *Mbuki* brings a major contribution to the issue being addressed. It shows that this traditional practice, like *Fambul Tok*, could help address conflict issues in modern Africa. Indeed, the *Mbuki* principles emphasize a sacred vital element of life, namely the exchange of human or animal blood, or the exchange of young boy or girl to seal a covenant, symbolizing the sharing of life. Blood pacts already existed between several ethnic groups, consolidating their links and favouring harmony, conflict prevention, and peaceful resolution. The following insights arise from *Mbuki*'s analysis: (1) it is a covenant of a new life, (2) in *Mbuki*, the shedding and exchange of the blood is the death of a blood brother to share a new life with a partner, (3) the blood of each party builds a new kinship, and (4) *Mbuki* brings new benefits in the life of each individual and in that of the extended families/relatives because through it each party cares about well-being and preservation of life. It is important to examine how the Scriptures interpret these insights with the view to achieving lasting peace and reconciliation.

Those who ignored the insights into *Mbuki* broke the rules of the pact and killed a blood-brother or sister. From the discussion so far, one can observe that the existing blood pacts are essential to address "intra-personal, interpersonal and inter-community conflicts" and to forge a lasting peace.[130] This could be a way to reconnect divided ethnic groups based on the established pacts. As a fundamental institution that expresses non-violence, *Mbuki* strongly advocates the preservation of life and the promotion of future generations. To preserve life and future generation, it promotes forgiveness, reconciliation, and coexistence. Thus, the concepts that emerge from the scriptural interpretation of the *Mbuki* ritual help develop the theology of reconciliation. This last point is explored in the chapter that follows.

---

129. Anonymous 78, Interview, 30 August 2021 (Translation is mine).

130. Simiti said that, once popularized, the blood pact could help prevent "intra-personal, interpersonal and inter-community conflicts." See Simiti, Interview, 16 March 2021 (Translation is mine).

CHAPTER 10

Scripture Interpretation and Theology of Reconciliation in Light of *Mbuki*

1. Introduction

The framework that guides the theology of reconciliation concerning this study includes representativeness, pervasiveness, and the scriptural interpretation of the *Mbuki* rituals. Many Centrafricans do not know about *Mbuki*; however, its practice in traditional societies was widespread, linking many ethnic groups. It is important to highlight that when the Azandé made *Mbuki*, they built and maintained new social bonds, cohesive unity, mutual assistance, security, peace, and well-being.

The engagement of the gospel with *Mbuki* culture for reconciliation, and the contribution of the reflection to a theology of reconciliation, as I explore in this chapter, is essential to derive values of love, unity, forgiveness, truth, justice, and others, to put them into practice whether at the community, religious or political level. The values derived from the *Mbuki* practice can take deep theological meaning when interpreted scripturally to ecourage evangelism, discipleship, and theological scholarship. The acquired values could, therefore, lead Centrafricans to "adopt the lifestyle of reconciliation"[1] that is effective to achieve conflict transformation and national healing.

---

1. The Third Lausanne Congress, "Building the Peace of Christ" 68.

2. Scripture Interpretation

The concept *Mbuki* is so amply paralleled in the Hebrew Bible, and the NT ably spiritualizes such occurrences to the extent that some scholars may alert that, in this book, it is a selective ritual practice to Christianize elements of African Traditional Religions (ATR). However, my aim in this book is not to Christianize the cultural practice, rather to allow Scripture to interpret the *Mbuki* culture.

When two Azandé exchanged blood through the *Mbuki* ritual, they established a covenant and called each other *bakurëmi*. Underlying all of Scripture is the theme of covenant and in particular God's covenant with humanity and ultimately all creation. Therefore, the scriptural interpretation of *Mbuki* ultimately brings to the fore God's covenant through the blood of Christ that brings the peoples of the world to fellowship with God, with selves, with others (Ephesians 2:11–19), and with all creation (Colossians 1:19). The ideas that *Mbuki* practice encompasses are key to the biblical writings, especially to Paul's epistles when he refers to the Greek notion of *koinonia*.[2] The notion of *koinonia* that the Sango Bible translates as *bé oko* (fellowship) points to the communion between people. Jesus taught the disciples to love each other and be united (John 13:34–35; 15:12, 17), and he prayed for unity of believers (John 17:1–12). Thus, believers are one, for in Christ there is no division but unity of the "body of Christ" (1 Corinthians 12:13–27). Therefore, the notions of blood, covenant, fellowhip, and unity as seen in the *Mbuki* tradition are also clearly stated in Scripture.

To seal a pact between two people or two clans, blood brothers killed an animal (by shedding its blood), which they prepared and ate together. Other ethnic groups exchanged small boys and/or girls to fulfil the pact. What matters in these pacts were the new relations and new life that emerged from them. In Leviticus (1–7), the sacrifice of animals was intended to keep Israel in the covenant with God, while in the NT, Christ bearing the sins of humanity upon himself was the *Ngassambanga ti Nzapa* (Lamb of God) who atoned for the sins of the world (John 1:29, 36; Hebrews 9:23–28; Isaiah 53). The scriptural interpretation of these rituals shows that Christ is the new *Mbuki* ("new covenant"), the ultimate sacrifice through whose redemptive

---

2. *Koinonia* refers to "The relationship of believers to one another in the common experience of salvation." See O'Brien, "Fellowship, Communion, Sharing," 293–294.

death humanity enjoys God's gifts and life in abundance (Romans 5:1–6:23). What emerges from this analysis, in the light of Scripture and in the practice of *Mbuki*, is that life is abandoned through the shedding of blood to build a bond between people. However, the blood of Jesus is more superior than any other blood to cleanse, atone, forgive, and restore lost humanity to life. So, while the *Mbuki* model of reconciliation is temporary, the reconciling death of Christ is ultimate and permanent to save and to reconcile (Hebrews 9:12).

Furthermore, in the Christian faith, the Lord's Supper establishes communion between believers who participate by sharing bread and wine, and includes believers from around the world as one united people of God (1 Corinthians 10:14–21). Similarly, during the *Mbuki* ceremony, blood brothers solemnly declare their communion with the commitment to live together as they share each other's blood mixed with palm wine in a pot or soaked in a piece of cassava that both drink, chew and/or swallow. It is important to note that the ritual binds also the extended families/relatives of the blood allies to fulfil the rules and obligations of the pact. Here again, the ceremony of *Mbuki* and that of the Lord's Supper concern the sharing of blood. If in traditional societies people shared their own blood or that of animals to bind and unite, in Scripture, Christ shed his own blood on the cross to save sinners. Moreover, in both ritual ceremonies, is the notion of justice. In *Mbuki*, this justice resides in the obligations of the pact: each blood brother is supposed to follow the rules and obligations of the pact; otherwise, they expose themelves to danger and death. In the sacrifice of Christ, however, the death of the cross satisfied the atonement of sins and redemption of sinners. Whether in the Lord's Supper or *Mbuki*, participants to the ritual ceremony are united by the bonds of love, interdependence, compassion, sharing and caring, forgiveness, and reconciliation.

Therefore, from the alaysis done so far, the insights arising from the scriptural interpretation of *Mbuki* are as follows: (1) while *Mbuki* institutes a covenant for life, Jesus Christ is the "new *Mbuki*" (new covenant) who reconciles humanity with God, (2) while in *Mbuki*, the shedding and sharing of blood is the death of a blood brother to offer and receive a new life, in Scripture, the death of Christ is sufficient to forgive, save, heal, and unite divided societies, (3) while in *Mbuki*, extended families are united in the blood brotherhood, the blood of Jesus has broken all barriers and made ethnic divides the new humanity in Christ, and (4) the covenant of Christ is permanent and eternal, and cares more than *Mbuki* does for the oppressed, orphans and the widows.

Emmanuel Katongole stressed that people's stories are fertile ground for an effective theology of politics in Africa that deals with reconciliation issues.[3] This was the case, he said, with Angelina Atyam when the LRA abducted her daughter. Atyam had experienced pain, loss, and anger over her daughter's abduction, but she learned to forgive and "began a ministry of advocacy on behalf of all suffering children."[4] In addition to what Katongole pointed out about Atyam, another story was that of Nelson Mandela, who was kept in prison for life, like Joseph in Scripture (Genesis 45:1–45). However, after his release, he forgave his perpetrators, and his attitude opened a path for new cohesion in the country.

Thus, to formulate a theology of reconciliation, it is important to raise the following questions: Are there any stories related to the CAR ongoing conflict that highlight the values of forgiveness, truth, justice, and reconciliation? How can the stories of women raped or families massacred during the conflict in Sierra Leone teach Centrafricans to develop a theology of reconciliation specific to their context on the basis of indigenous beliefs and practices of reconciliation? These questions help to answer the main question, "To what extent can the insights into the traditional *Mbuki* ritual bring about an emerging theology of reconciliation in CAR?" The best way to explore the theology of reconciliation in light of *Mbuki* is to allow Scripture to interpret the insights that emerge from the traditional practice in the CAR context.

For this theological analysis, I highlight how the Sango Bible interprets the *Mbuki* ritual. Kwame Bediako suggests that any relevant theology allows Scripture to interpret culture. He states that,

> gospel and culture engagement is about the conversion of cultures, the turning to Christ and turning over to Christ of all that is there in us, about us and round about us that has defined and shaped us when Jesus meets us, so that the elements of our cultural identity are brought within the orbit of discipleship.[5]

---

3. Katongole, *The Sacrifice of Africa*, 3.
4. Katongole, 24.
5. Bediako, "Scripture as the Hermeneutic," 2.

Interpreting traditional practices through the lens of Scripture allows Christians to highlight what is key to reconciliation. In the same way, Muslims' understanding of the Qur'an should enable them to do the same.[6] Although people claim that CAR conflict is "inter-religious," it is critical to note that this study is not a comparative study between Christians using Scripture to interpret indigenous practices, beliefs, meanings, and Muslims doing the same with the Qur'an. Andrew Walls makes it clear that,

> Much misunderstanding in Christian-Muslim relations has occurred from the assumption that the Bible and Qur'an have analogous status in the respective faiths. But the true Christian analogy with the Qur'an is not the Bible, but Christ. Christ for Christians, the Qur'an for Muslims, is the Eternal Word of God; but Christ is the Word Translated. That fact is the sign that the contingent Scriptures (also described as Word of God), unlike the Qur'an, may and should constantly be translated.[7]

In addition to seeing how Scripture enables Christians to interpret traditional practices, beliefs, and meanings, I point to relevant passages in the Qur'an that may enable Muslims to do the same related to reconciliation. To begin this chapter, I refer to the story of an incident that occurred in a local church in Bangui, revealing key messages that help to formulate a theology of reconciliation.

3. Theology of Reconciliation in Light of *Mbuki*

Kwesi Dickson states that, "Every Christian theologises."[8] This statement highlights that it is not only people who have formal theological education, who can theologize. Every theological formulation "entails reflection; the reflection has situational reality; and, there is the communication of this reflection."[9] However, the mode of communication in theology could be "through

---

6. For example, theologically, Christians and Muslims confess to share a common faith in the seed of Abraham, or Jesus, who is the promoter of reconciliation. See Bridger, *Christian Exegesis of the Qur'an*, 2.

7. Walls, *The Missionary Movement*, 27.

8. Dickson, *Theology in Africa*, 13.

9. Dickson, *Theology in Africa*, 14.

coherent language" or through "communication by living."[10] Commenting on the prayers of a Ghanaian Christian woman, Christina Afua Gyan (known as Afua Kuma), Bediako acknowledges the "evidence of a theological articulation within Ghanaian Christianity," which may exist "elsewhere in Africa also."[11] This theological articulation depicts the life experience of indigenous people and their faith. Bediako concludes, "It is the evidence of what I call a 'grassroots' theology."[12] His reflection here helps to reflect on the formulation of a theology of reconciliation in light of the *Mbuki* ritual.

In response to the question, "What specific problems did you encounter during this conflict and how did you deal with them?" the late Pastor Franco Mbaye-Bondoi, victim of the Séléka attack in April 2013 with his congregation during a Sunday service, narrated the story of an incident.[13] The incident took place at Fédération des Eglises Évangéliques des Frères (FEEF). He stated,

> On 14 April 2013, in the middle of a service in our local church, the Séléka militiamen launched three shells; two fell inside the church and one outside. This caused a lot of damage. The toll was 37 victims with four deaths. Two people died on the spot and two later in hospital. Four children had their feet amputated, one child had both feet cut off and the other three had their left leg amputated. So, there was a lot of material and human damage in the church. I was in the church that day but God had preserved me. However, I had a shock to my chest for which I spent a few hours in hospital before returning to the campus of the faculty of theology where I spent two years because of the threats. The case of this fatal incident is now before the special court. I was interrogated a few days ago and I am waiting for the results. The Séléka shot in cold blood other collaborators, killed not only in our local church, but also in one of our pastors in Bossangoa. In my village, the Séléka shot two of my younger brothers.

---

10. Dickson, 14.
11. Bediako, *Jesus in Africa*, 8. See also Kirby, *Jesus of the Deep Fores*.
12. Bediako, *Jesus in Africa*, 8.
13. Franco Mbaye-Bondoi narrated the story of the incident in French. I translated it from French into English. However, the small boy's appeal might be in Sango.

I cannot do anything. In spite of all this, God says we must forgive them. We should not hold hatred against them. The child with the two amputated feet was the very first to say, 'Pastor, we have to forgive the Séléka.' I brought this message when I went to Europe to advocate for [the NGO] Africa Service. I showed the picture of this child with his feet cut off and his message that the churches should forgive the Séléka because they were ignorant of what they had done; the devil had used them.[14]

This heart-breaking story provides evidence that some people, in CAR's darkest hours, still have hope for recovery and have sincerely forgiven their perpetrators with a view to lasting reconciliation. It is very difficult to know how many silent victims of rape, abduction, torture, and all form of inhuman treatments have forgiven their perpetrators in this ongoing conflict. This reminds us that reconciliation begins with a story of forgiveness.

From the incident Mbaye-Bondoi recounted, the young Christian Centrafrican boy's appeal reveals key elements of a Christian approach to reconciliation. First, there is a call for forgiveness; second, there is a mandate to churches and all Christians; third, there is a need for forgiveness and justice for the Séléka militiamen; and fourth, the devil used the Séléka to kill people. These elements provide a working framework for a theology of reconciliation. The points constitute the sections under which emerges a theological understanding of reconciliation. The analysis also draws on lessons from Sierra Leone study that shed light on the boy's call. The four elements form the basis of the theological reflection and derive from the understanding of the the insights into the spiritual interpretation of *Mbuki*. It aims to build the understanding of Centrafricans on the need to promote reconciliation.

3.1 Reconciliation Starts with Forgiveness

As noted in the previous chapters, *Mbuki* practice and *Fambul Tok* emphasize forgiveness, even though the latter is not accompanied by the sharing of blood. Indeed, forgiveness prevents reprisals, promotes peaceful coexistence, and preserves life. In the Christian tradition, forgiveness is a central theme

---

14. Mbaye-Bondoi, Interview, 24 July 2021, Bangui (Translation is mine).

of the Bible. If forgiveness exhibits a value of the kingdom, it also exhibits a value that people promoted in *Mbuki* tradition.

In Hebrew, *slh* expresses the idea of forgiving. J. J. Stamm argues that its occurrences relate to "covering or atoning for sin . . . removing it . . . letting it pass . . . wiping it out, washing it away, cleansing it, and forgetting it."[15] In the light of Jeremiah 31:34 and 33:8, the word *slh* has "prophetic promises" for the age come.[16] In proclaiming salvation in Jeremiah 33:1–13, the prophet points to forgiveness as "an eschatological gift" through the rebuilding of Judah and Israel. On the other hand, the book of 2 Chronicles (7:14) emphasizes forgiveness and healing of the land for the people who repent from their sins.[17]

During interviews, church ministers reflected on the themes of the sermons they preached concerning peace and reconciliation. Of the ninety-eight interviewees, thirteen ministers (13.26 percent) stressed that, among other themes, they preached on *tèné ti pardon* ("the word of pardon").[18]

In explaining how he emphasized some themes in his sermons, Innocent Kaibo-Saulet from Elim Church said,

> Because of the conflict, we had changed the way we preached. We taught about the nature of man created by God. The idea was to make Christians understand that human beings are created in the image of God, no matter who they are. Since God is the author of creation, human beings need peace. We have therefore taught Christians about peace, cohesion and love. The theme of love is the last one we have taught in all the local churches of our association. We talked about love and forgiveness by teaching Christians that Muslims are not our enemies but rather our brothers and sisters regardless of their religion.[19]

Jesus's prayer on the cross of Calvary in Luke 23:34 pointed to the foundation of forgiveness for any reconciliation effort. He said, *Baba, pardonné*

---

15. Stamm, "To Forgive," 797.
16. Stamm, 798.
17. Stamm, 802–803.
18. Other themes included *bian ngo légué* (change of one's way or repentance), *mbilimbili ti Nzapa* (righteousness of God), *ndoyé* (love), *yékia mbéni zo* (acceptance of others), *siriri* (peace), *sala ngo songo* (building relationship), and *bé oko* (fellowship), to name but a few.
19. Innocent Kaibo-Saulet, Interview, 25 March 2021, Bangui (Translated from French).

ala, tèti ala hinga yé so ala sala pèpé (Father, forgive them, because they do not know the thing that they do).[20] The word *pardonné* as translated in the Sango Bible is a French word. In Sango, to express forgiveness, people say *gbou guelé*, which literally means, "to hold feet." When someone says to another, *Mbi gbou guelé ti mo* ("I hold your feet"), it means that the former asks for forgiveness or apologizes to the latter. In this spirituality, seeking forgiveness is not only limited to the use of the words such as, "I am sorry" or "Forgive me." It is deeper because, in order to receive forgiveness, the offender goes to the offended and kneels down, holding the feet of the offended as a sign of regret. Such a ritual attitude is significant for forgiveness and reconciliation. Moreover, rather than *pardonné*, the biblical word for forgiveness in Sango is *mbô*.[21] To say, *mèné ti Christ Jesus a mbô siokpari ti dûnîa* means "the blood of Christ Jesus wipes away the sin of humanity." In this sense, forgiveness relates to the act of *mbô* (wiping out) the sin. The act of *gbou guelé* is physical, while *mbô* is abstract and spiritual. However, both aim to achieve the same goal, which is justice and forgiveness.

Jukka A. Kääriäinen argues that although reconciliation has been a *missio Dei*, a *missio Christus* and now *missio ecclesiae*, it remains an incomplete task. He also points out that reconciliation deals with human identity.[22]

> The firmer one's ethnic, political, racial, religious, or personal identity is, the more difficult reconciliation seems to become. To achieve reconciliation, identity seemingly must be compromised, changed, or surrendered. This, in turn, produces resentment, which sabotages genuine reconciliation. Furthermore, the role and use of power in identity formation is challenging. The pre-condition of reconciliation is humility of owning wrong and asking for forgiveness.[23]

The search for reconciliation requires humility and asking for forgiveness, as the author stated. In this sense, the Séléka combatants who killed believers during a Sunday service or the Anti-Balaka who have also been responsible for

---

20. In this chapter and in the entire thesis, all the Sango Bible references are a back translation to allow readers to understand what the Sango speakers say in a more literal sense.
21. Karan, *Kêtê bakari tî Sängö*, 46.
22. Kääriäinen, "The Gospel of Reconciliation," 220.
23. Kääriäinen, 220–221.

crimes and atrocities in the country need to consider their actions as crimes against civilians. In other words, one way to seek reconciliation is for them to acknowledge their crimes and to beg for forgiveness.

In the *Mbuki* tradition, it is easier for a blood brother to ask for forgiveness and/or to forgive his/her fellow brother/sister because the rules of the pact prohibit harming an ally. Assuming that those involved in the 2013 conflict were aware of their blood brotherhood with one another, they might with regret *gbou guelé* of those they had offended, as the *Mbuki* culture taught them. In doing so, the culture of forgiveness could take root not only among believers, it could also spread throughout the country. This lifestyle could help maintain sustainable peace.

In Romans 12:19, Paul tells the Romans, *Aita so mbi ndoyé i mingui, i fouta koula ti i mvèni pèpé, mais i djia lègué na Ngonzo ti Nzapa; tèti Mbéti ti Nzapa atèné, Koula ayèké ti Mbi; fade Mbi fouta koula ni, Seigneur atèné.* This translates as, "My beloved brethren, do not avenge yourselves, but allow the wrath of God; for the Word of God says, vengeance is mine; I will take vengeance, says the Lord." Stephanie Goins argues that in this passage, Paul clearly evokes the "theological justification for forgiving."[24] Indeed, to forgive is a choice for the victim, and it consists in allowing God to do justice, which is different from one's own justice or the popular justice that people commit out of resentment, anger, and hatred. It allows former enemies to come together in a blood pact to forgive wrongs committed and to unite (former) enemies for the well-being of each other. The pact prevents the kinship ties of the two blood brothers from taking revenge. It also enables them to forgive their aggressors and seek to save any broken ties. By promoting forgiveness, the *Mbuki* tradition is in line with the biblical one as it prohibits hatred, harm, and vengeance toward a fellow human being. Rather, it values shared life through mutual communion and commitment to respect the obligations of the pact. However, according to Scriptures, Christ's forgiveness is more precious, ultimate, and eternal; offering a lifestyle of peace and reconciliation to people living in divided societies, as Christ becomes for them the "new *Mbuki*."

In Matthew 18:21–22, perhaps bearing in mind the issue of forgiveness versus retaliation, Simon Peter asked Jesus a question about how many times to forgive one's enemy rather than doing one's own justice. Genesis 4:8 is

---

24. Goins, *Forgiveness and Reintegration*, 44.

about Cain killing his brother, Abel. In Genesis 4:15b, because of his murder, God *amou fa tèti Cain* (made a sign on Cain) so that nobody should kill him. However, the culture or cycle of violence had taken root in Cain's descendants. Therefore, Lamech, the son of Cain, became involved in revenge. The verses 23–24 show that Lamech sang "the Song of the Sword."[25] Regarding the question he asked about forgiveness, Peter expected from Jesus something like "seven times," but Jesus said seventy-seven times. Micah Onserio Moenga points out that "Peter was thinking about the practicality of the whole issue [forgiveness], but Jesus was thinking of how to maintain healthy relationships."[26] Moenga's view is right, however, one can argue that Jesus's response goes beyond maintaining healthy relationships. This statement of Jesus is so profound for breaking the cycle of revenge. By referring to "forgive seventy-seven times," Jesus actually reversed the trend of revenge that Lamech set in place in Genesis 4:23–24.

In an interview, Fidèle Danboy recalled that in one sermon, he preached from Genesis 33:1–16 about the reconciliation between Jacob and Esau.[27] He also quoted Matthew 6:14–15, which urges believers to forgive others of their sins so that God will forgive theirs. In both cases, he stressed that when forgiveness takes place, reconciliation becomes effective. With regard to Genesis 33, Assohoto and Ngewa describe how Jacob was afraid of Esau's approach to meet him. They said that Jacob arranged his wives and children in such a way that, "If Esau was hostile, each mother would be able to plead with Esau for her own children."[28] For reconciliation to occur, the meeting between the perpetrator and the victim is important, while "forgiveness can be offered in the absence of the person involved in the conflict."[29] In this case, Jacob was afraid of Esau's resentment, hatred or revenge while meeting him.

Ramizah Wan Muhammad points out that Islam also emphasizes forgiveness as a virtue to avoid retaliation and violence. It sees forgiveness "as a great virtue that brings forth gratitude, heals broken relationships, and establishes peace at individual and social levels."[30] According to Mohammed Abu-Nimer

---

25. Lasor, Hubbard and Bush, *Old Testament Survey*, 31.
26. Moenga, "A Response," 16.
27. Fidèle Danboy, Interview, 9 November 2020, Bossangoa.
28. Assohoto and Ngewa, "Genesis," 133.
29. Noah, *Reconciliation and Peace*, 54.
30. Wan Muhammad, "Forgiveness and Restorative Justice," 277.

Ilham Nasser, in the Qur'an, the term "forgiveness" includes *Afw*, which means to free from the burden of punishment and restore honour, and *safhu*, which means to turn away from sin or to ignore the wrong, and *ghafara*, to cover up or to erase sin.[31] Thus, it is possible to argue that the Qur'anic understanding of forgiveness does not contradict that of the Christian faith. Both see it as the way of covering up sins and not carrying the guilt of it.

Thus, there would have been no problem in initiating transitional/restorative justice in churches, leading each group to avoid violence, to forgive and to reconcile. This is important, because "forgiveness is the exact opposite of vengeance."[32] If forgiveness is against vengeance, it is not against justice because "forgiveness presupposes that justice . . . has not been done. If justice were done, forgiveness would not be necessary."[33] According to Ephesians 2:14 Christ's mission is to unite divided people. Thus, seeing Jesus as the perfect *Mbuki* opens the way for Centrafricans to surrender to Jesus to heal any sentiment of hatred, revenge, resentment, and deep wounds caused by conflict and to prevent a resurgence of violence.

3.2 Reconciliation: A Mission for CAR Churches

Before examining the boy's second appeal, it is important to note that church reconciliation efforts are not a new phenomenon. Some early church fathers were involved in the process of reconciliation. This was the case with Cyprian, the bishop of Carthage. Rudolf Gaisie points out that, in the context of divisions within the church of Carthage, Cyprian dedicated his life and ministry to unity and reconciliation. Cyprian addressed the division of the Church through the synods held under his leadership. According to Gaisie, his life and work have four characteristics that can inform contemporary Christian reconciliation efforts. First, his sense of service; second, his commitment to pastoral ministry; third, his exemplary leadership in times of conflict, and fourth, his commitment as a mediator.[34] Gaisie's analysis of Cyprian's contribution to the reconciliation of the Church of Carthage is relevant to inform the church's reconciliation efforts in CAR.

---

31. Nasser, "Forgiveness in the Arab," 476.
32. Arendt, *The Human Condition*, 241.
33. Volf, "Forgiveness, Reconciliation, and Justice," 46.
34. Gaisie, "St Cyprian of Carthage."

Linking with this is the boy's second appeal pointed to the churches in CAR. Mbaye-Bondoi said, "I showed the picture of this child with his feet cut off and his message that the churches should forgive the Séléka . . ."[35] This message recalls the mandate of reconciliation that God has given to Christians. Before analysing it further, it is important to remember that the church is a covenantal body, "a community of saints" (*boumbi ti aouamabé*). In his book, *Journeys of the Muslim Nation and the Christian Church: Exploring the Mission of Two Communities*, David W. Shenk takes us into the very understanding of the notion of "community" in the Muslim context: the *Ummah*.[36] Another scholar, Tariq Ramadan, also points out that *Ummah* relates to the "faith community" in Islam. It highlights that Muslims from East and West, North and South are one, united around "the scriptural sources, fundamentals, and practices" that form the basis of their faith.[37] Shenk argues that, although the church and the *Ummah* refer to people as a community, these two communities have been in competition in most parts of the world.[38]

Komi Dzinyefa Adrake, explaining the mission of reconciliation between Christians and Muslims and the role of the Programme for Christian-Muslims Relations in Africa (PROCMURA) in this context, confirms Shenk's view of the conflicting relations between the two religious groups. He explains that, in the Middle Ages, Arabs/Muslims led conquests and expeditions to supplant Christianity. As a result, between 1095 and 1295, eight crusades were "organized by the Western Christian armies to liberate the Holy Land, Jerusalem, which was under Muslim rule."[39] According to him, Christians and Muslims still remember the consequences of the crusades today. However, given that "Both claim the Abrahamic faith and the one God, and each claim they have been vested with a mission responsibility by God," it is important that the two religious groups reconcile.[40]

During the field research, I realized that the labelling "inter-religious conflict" was a political manipulation. Some respondents also shared the same

---

35. Mbaye-Bondoi, Interview, 24 July 2021.
36. Shenk, *Journeys of the Muslim Nation*, 223.
37. Ramadan, "Tariq Ramadan," 206.
38. Shenk, *Journeys of the Muslim Nation*, 223.
39. Adrake, "Mission and Reconciliation," 146.
40. Adrake, "Mission and Reconciliation", 146.

view.⁴¹ Similar events have been taking place in Nigeria. John Azumah explains that violent attacks based on extremism constitute "Islamic militancy."⁴² He argues that this issue has become "the main determining factor for Christian responses to Islam."⁴³ In this context, sometimes, atrocities on civilians are the consequences of Christian-Muslim divisions that follow the bombing of churches and/or the destruction of mosques. Similar incidents occurred in CAR. Balla Traoré pointed out that in Bangui, "Some Muslims destroyed the houses of poor Christians who lived nearby Km 5, and some Christians destroyed the houses of Muslims who lived outside Muslim neighbourhood."⁴⁴

In the face of Islamic militancy/violence, Moussa Bongoyok reflects on how Christians should react in line with their Christian faith. He writes,

> How should the church react when innocent Christians are killed and church buildings are burned, as is the case in Northern Nigeria? There is no easy response. I am personally in favour of non-violence. The use of violence to end violence is not the smartest way to proceed, because it will only generate more violence.⁴⁵

Non-violence is a fertile ground for forgiveness and reconciliation to take root and develop in a post-conflict context. It is not weakness, but rather a strength to overcome hatred and revenge. Jesus taught his disciples to have a non-violent attitude: *I kè pèpé tonga na jo assala sioni na i; Mais jo so apika mo na ngbangba ti mo ti koti, mo tourney mbéni mbagué ni na lo nga.* It roughly translates, "Do not refuse if someone does what is wrong against you; But if a person slaps you on the right, you also turn the other side to him." Here, Jesus warns his disciples not "to ignore basic principles of justice" and do their own justice.⁴⁶ It is important for Christians to live in cohesion to allow justice to function by denouncing injustice and defending what is right. Walter Wink is a promoter of non-violence. He observes that most Christians aspire to non-violence but they do not take non-violent actions

---

41. Balla Traoré, Interview, 27 January 2021, Bangui.
42. Azumah, "Fault Lines in African," 127.
43. Azumah, 127.
44. Traoré, Interview, 27 January 2021 (Translation is mine).
45. Bongoyok, "The African Christian," 212.
46. Kapolyo, "Matthew," 1863.

to end injustice.⁴⁷ In other words, by not taking non-violent actions, they become accomplices of injustice.

In the colonial period, Karnu advocated non-violence. In doing so, he valued human beings more than his oppressors had.⁴⁸ The *Mbuki* ritual, for example, expressed the social bonds, and a way of resolving conflicts and maintaining peace. Covenants in African tradition and in the Christian tradition both symbolize unity and communion. Vincent Mulago explains that in traditional African societies, blood pacts represented a "vital communion-participation" that people exchanged over a common meal or drink to seal a gift of self to the other.⁴⁹

Similarly, the Lord's Supper in the Christian tradition is a symbol of reconciliation of each believer to God and to the other. John 6:56 says, *Lo so até mi-tèlé ti Mbi na lo gno mèné ti Mbi, lo douti na ya Mbi, na Mbi douti na ya lo* ("He who eats my flesh and he who drinks my blood stays in me, and I stay in him"). Mulago says that this verse indicates that a vital communion is established between the Christian and Christ, a sharing of Christ's life to the believer.⁵⁰ In this sense, blood, whether in the traditional context or in the Christian context, refers to sharing, communion, unity, and life. He continues, "Le pain, c'est-à-dire, le Corps du Christ, le Christ lui-même, étant unique, on conçoit que cette unité du pain entrainera l'union de ceux qui y communient." This translates, "The bread, that is to say, the body of Christ, the Christ himself, being unique, one understands that this unity brings unity between those who commune."⁵¹ According to his arguments, believers cannot take part in the Lord's Supper and continue to hate or to be divided. Centrafrican Christians are the first agents of reconciliation; they will contribute to effective reconciliation if they are reconciled with God and with each another. The

---

47. Walter Wink, *Jesus and Nonviolence*, 4.

48. I showed in chapter 4 that Karnu was non-violent because he refused to use his *tikin* (magic stick) to hurt or kill his oppressors, and he objected to his followers who killed whites or the guards who oppressed them (see section 4.4).

49. Mulago, "Le Pacte du Sang," 180.

50. Mulago, 180. The Qur'an also emphasizes that God made a covenant with the people of Israel and they broke it (Qur'an 2:83). Its principle is "To keep God's covenant and fulfil other conditions" (Qur'an 2:35–36, 13:20–23). However, those who violate such a principle "will face God's curse and the fire of hell (Qur'an 13:25)." See Campo, *Encyclopedia of Islam*, 170.

51. Mulago, 181.

sharing of bread and wine, symbolizing blood, cements relations of reconciliation between believers and from them to others.

Therefore, *Mbuki* is a "stepping-stone" for reconciliation. Mulago points out that the Eucharist, the ritual of the Lord's Supper, is one of the mysteries and symbols that bind Christians together. According to him, the celebration of the Lord's Supper reveals this mystery of unity and communion between believers and Christ (1 Corinthians 10:16–17; John 6:22–65). Thus, the Eucharist implies that a believer is united to Christ (John 6:56) and to others.[52] This is perceived in the one bread that believers share, which symbolizes Christ himself, to unite them. They drink the wine, symbolizing blood, to establish a vital exchange, a flow of life from one to another.[53] If through the communion of bread and wine, those who take part in the Lord's Supper are united in Christ (in kinship with Christ), therefore, they are also in unity with all those in whom that blood flows and with all those who feed on the same bread of life.[54] This view establishes that, in the *Mbuki* ritual, the shared food symbolizes bread and the calabash of milk or beer with a drop of blood mixed in it symbolizes the Lord's Supper in Christian tradition. In his article on reconciliation and the blood pacts, Diatta says: "Ici en Centrafrique, l'importance vitale, existentielle, de la réconciliation [est] signifiée et réalisée dans le pacte de sang" (Here in CAR, the vital, existential importance of reconciliation [is] signified and realized in the blood pact).[55]

It is possible to argue that God's original intention for the *Ummah*-community is to get people to build relational bonds. Here is the idea of the unity of the body that Scripture teaches us. In Ephesians 4:3 and 13, Paul exhorts the Ephesians to *béoko* (unity). A Christian community exists to build the *béoko ti Yingo na ya kamba ti siriri so akanga I oko* ("one heart of the Spirit through the bond of peace that binds us together") and *juska ani kouè aga oko na ya mabé* ("until we all become one in the faith"). Therefore, one advantage of unity in a community is to form and maintain the bond of peace.

In Bossangoa town, some interviewees regretted that instead of promoting social bonds, the Anti-Balaka militiamen expelled the Muslim community

---

52. Mulago, 180–182.
53. Mulago, 181–182.
54. Mulago, 182.
55. Diatta, "Le Concept de Réconciliation," 63 [Translation is mine].

from the locality. Respondents claimed that Muslims used to buy products from their fields, while they used to buy items such as sugar, soap, salt, onions, and other items from Muslim shops. For this reason, the commercial activities that existed between the communities before 2013 no longer exist. The above testimonies from both Christians and Muslims provide evidence that, as individuals and as a community, there is the basis for reconciliation in the town. This attitude reminds us of Karnu, who avoided violence against his oppressors because he respected them and valued their identity and dignity.

In his book, *Exclusion and Embrace*, Miroslav Volf analyses how the issue of self-identity and the "other" is at the root of divisions and violence. He points out that, "the problem of ethnic and cultural conflict is part of a larger problem of identity and otherness."[56] Volf estimates that in the face of ethnic-cultural cleansings, it is important for Christians to emphasize the "place of *identity and otherness at the center of theological reflection* on social realities."[57] It is also important to observe that, although the conflict in CAR was allegedly religious, it falls into the category of what Volf points out, since manipulated ethnic divides have also played a role in exacerbating violence. The population of Bossangoa has realized the mistake of the expulsion of the Muslim community. In an interview, Enoch Dokafei said, "I told my people, one person cannot live alone on earth. It takes 51 nations to form the United States."[58] From his statement, he seemed to disapprove of the expulsion of the Muslim community from the town.

On the question about the themes of sermons church ministers preached/taught to instruct believers on the need of reconciliation, Jérémie, a church pastor, said he preached 2 Corinthians 5:18 as one key verse in his sermon: *Lo so assala si ani ga songo na Lo na légué ti Christ, na Lo mou na ani koussala ti sala songo*. The verse literally means, "He made us to be reconciled to him through Christ, and has given us the work of reconciliation."[59] In the Sango language, *songo* means "kinship" or "brotherhood", while *sala songo* means, "entering into a relationship, becoming a family." The expression, *Lo sala si*

---

56. Volf, *Exclusion and Embrace*, 16.

57. Volf, 17 [Italics are from the author].

58. Dokafei, Interview, 19 October 2020 (Translation is mine).

59. Jérémie, Interview, 9 November 2020, Bossangoa. He also cited Colossians 3:5–13 as one of the biblical passages he used to preach on peace and reconciliation.

ani ga songo na Lo translates as "He made us his kin or family."[60] Thus, the idea behind 2 Corinthians 5:18 could be that God values human beings and he allows those who believe in him to become his "family members." He then commissions them to proclaim the message of reconciliation. In light of this passage, *sala songo* is not only between the human being and God, but also between each other. God's intention for believers is to regard their fellow human beings as *songo* because the essence of family and humanity is unity.

Diatta also observes that in CAR, Christians celebrate the Lord's Supper every Sunday as a covenant of reconciliation through the blood of Jesus and as a covenant of reconciliation with one another.[61] However, he deplores that Christians, especially priests, who partake the rite of reconciliation par excellence, in the blood of Jesus, true God and true man, where they become a reconciled people, do not respect the covenant, as they promote divisions among them.[62] I explained earlier that the Dakpa-Linda clan leaders, warriors, women and children swallowed the mixed blood of two little children to seal their reconciliation and unity forever. Diatta asserts that this story describes a culture of peace by the existence of communion and unity among the Dakpa-Linda people, which laid the foundation of communion, unity, peace, and reconciliation between the CAR ethnic groups.[63]

Arguing about the importance of blood pacts in the present-day CAR society, Father Charles-Nasser Koudje stated,

> Whether it is blood alliance or other alliances, these alliances have, in my opinion, one goal, which is for peaceful coexistence. Although today, with the incarnation of Jesus Christ, the advent of God who became Man, from the point of view of the Catholic Church, we can no longer continue to practice these covenants because we are under the only covenant by which blood was shed and which replaced all the other covenants is that of Jesus

---

60. Karan, *Kêtê Bakarî tî Sängö*, 65.

61. In the Sango Bible, the translation of Matthew 26:27 reads, *Lo kamata kopo, Lo mou merci, Lo mou na ala, na Lo tèné, I kouè gno; tèti so ayèké mènè ti Mbi, mèné ti mbèlé so assa na sessé tèti ajo mingui tèti pardon ti siokpari*. This is translated, "He took the cup, he gave thanks, he offered them, and he said: All of you drink; because this is my blood, the blood of covenant that flows on the ground for many people for the forgiveness of sins." Again, in *Lo mou merci* the word "merci" is a French word. The alternative is *Lo mou singuila*.

62. Diatta, "Le Concept de Réconciliation," 64–65.

63. Diatta, 79.

Christ. However, I will say that the ancestral alliances had only one objective, which is how to bring the people to live in peace while respecting each other.[64]

Although Koudje argued that blood pacts in traditional societies were intended to build social bonds, he did not enable the covenant of Christ to interpret the traditional covenant. Rather, he just treated it as an issue of replacement. Walls indicated that conversion of cultural traditions is not a matter of substitution or replacement, as I pointed out earlier. Mbaye-Bondoi interpreted, in the statement below, the blood pacts through the covenant in the Christian faith, and stressed that both covenants are fundamental to transmitting a culture of reconciliation in CAR,

> Today, I believe that we cannot go back to these practices because of pandemics. However, we can refer to the blood of Jesus and preach on God's covenant. We must teach that the blood of Jesus reconciles, forgives men once for all. The Church's message can be taught in this direction to help the new generation to get an idea of the blood covenants that were practiced in traditional society. These traditional covenants were like a foundation that united the ethnic groups in CAR, not only those living on earth but also those in the afterlife. These are very important messages that the Church could transmit to help people at this level.[65]

Mbaye-Bondoi's statement about the unity between the living and the dead through the blood covenant was significant. He perceived it as a crucial message for the church to CAR society. He emphasized that the way people break blood covenants through violence affects their relationship with the departed.[66] He also envisaged the mission of the church in transmitting the message of tolerance, forgiveness, and acceptance of others to rebuild the

---

64. Charles-Nasser Koudje, Interview, 19 March 2021, Bangui (Translation is mine).

65. Mbaye-Bondoi, Interview, 24 July 2021 (Translation is mine). As a Senegalese priest, while serving in CAR, he was amazed at the culture of the blood pacts that have existed and to how pre-Christian African societies, resorted to blood pacts to reconcile and build bonds after a conflict.

66. In short, the scriptural interpretation of blood covenants allows for a deeper understanding of the societal bonds that existed through blood pacts as a prefiguration of the blood of Jesus uniting the divided peoples into a reconciled people.

unity of people with each other and with the departed. Joseph Kondia, for his part, stated:

> In African tradition, two rival clans for example made peace based on a blood covenant. As Christians, we believe that in Christ, we have a covenant with God. Created in the image of God, men rebelled against him and as the epistle to the Ephesians says, we were enemies of God. However, God in his grace has reconciled us through his son. To make the reconciliation effective, Jesus had shed his blood. As in the African tradition, when there is reconciliation, people respected the terms. God also respected it; we also, as Christians, should respect the rules to be in his covenant.[67]

Some significant points emerge from the above reflections on the *Mbuki* ritual. First, there is a sense that the *Mbuki* ritual, stemming from the primal worldview, provide a foundation for the praeparatio evangelica (preparation for the Gospel).[68] Second, the missio ecclesiae (mission of the church) is impacted in terms of evangelism, discipleship, and theological scholarship because *missio Dei* (God's mission), reflected through the gospel and Scripture, enables the *Mbuki* ritual to be interpreted and thus to be modified, purified, and fulfilled. The notion of *missio Dei* encompasses the "five marks of mission" including compassion, justice and injustice, and the whole environment, as well as the proclamation of the gospel and discipleship mentioned above.[69] Interpreting *Mbuki* rituals in light of the above paradigms can enable the church in Africa (or CAR) to "see her mission as bringing wholeness to people as Jesus did."[70] In highlighting the mission of the church in terms of peace, justice and reconciliation in Africa, Philomena Njeri Mwaura's statement below is instructive for believers. She states,

> The Church in Africa should see her mission as bringing wholeness to people as Jesus did. Jesus' ministry was grounded in *Shalom*, an Old Testament concept of peace connoting harmony

---

67. Joseph Kondia, Interview, 6 May 2021, Bangui (Translation is mine).
68. Mbiti, "Christianity and Traditional,"432.
69. The book, *Mission in the Twenty-First Century*, edited by Andrew F. Walls and Cathy Ross focuses on the "five marks of mission."
70. Mwaura, "Reconstructing Mission," 192.

and wellbeing. Shalom bespeaks justice, healed relations between individuals in society, between God and humanity and between humanity and the rest of creation. One of the greatest challenges for the Church is reconstruction in a post war context. This is where confession, forgiveness, reconciliation, and healing are necessary. Reconciliation should not be a hasty process; it should respect and restore human dignity. It should be seen as a process that leads victims to discover the mercy of God welling up their lives. It is discovering God's reconciliation through Christ. It is allowing the Holy Spirit to bring forgiveness and reconciliation among both victims and perpetrators who were hurting.[71]

With regard to the above arguments, the interaction between primal spirituality and the Christian faith makes the AICs vital. This means that the AICs reconcile the pre-Christian and the Christian worldview. Walls also argues that the growth of African independent movements in Africa has been a result of an emphasis on pre-Christian worldviews.[72] Thus, the emergence and growth of the independent movements, appropriating the use of water, prayer, prophecy, healing, and deliverance as elements for worship, conversion, and discipleship, explains the reality of African Christianity in the global context.[73] Bediako also contends that, "the primal religions in Africa and elsewhere in the world have entered upon a new career in Christian scholarship."[74] In other words, this perspective allows Christians to explore, for example, the relevance of the Christological identity and the soteriological work of Christ for Africans in the African context. These also provide a "fertile ground for Christian conversions."[75] The practices that take place in independent movements in CAR point to reconciliation within the churches. In this interaction, the AICs reconcile the pre-Christian to the Christian worldview.

Considering Ephesians 2:11–22, Timothy J. Monger and Marco Methuselah pointed out that Paul emphasized "the reconciliation that God has achieved between himself and the believers." They, thus, applied his arguments to the

---

71. Mwaura, "Reconstructing Mission," 192.
72. Walls, *The Cross-Cultural Process*, 116.
73. Oduro, "Contributions and Challenges," 49.
74. Bediako, *Christianity in Africa*, 83.
75. Bediako, *Christianity in Africa*, 83.

"mutual relationships" that all believers have in Christ, because Christ has broken "the hostility between Jew and Gentile."[76] This reinforces the idea that the initiative of reconciliation between divided groups comes from God. Verses fourteen to sixteen of Ephesians 2 state:

> [14]Teti lo yéké siriri ti ani, Lo so assala si ani ossé aga oko, na Lo fa' deré ti ya da' so akangbi ani, [15]tèti Lo lounguela kèngo tèlé na lègué ti mi-tèlé ti Lo, ndia ti commandement so ayèké na kpingba-tènè; si Lo lingbi créé ala ossé so ti ga jo-ti-fini oko na ya Lo mvèni, tonga so Lo sala si siriri aga; [16]na Lo sala si ala ossé aga songo na Nzapa na ya tèlé oko na lègué ti kèké-ti-croix, tèti na lègué so Lo sala si kèngo tèlé aoué.

> [14]For he himself is our peace, he who made us to become one, and he destroyed the wall that divided us, [15]because he removed our hatred through his body, the law of commandment that has effect; so that he could create the two to become one people in himself, therefore he made peace possible[16]; and he made that the two have become united to God in one body through the cross, by this way he made hatred to end.

Moreover, Scripture presents the blood of the sacrificial animal as a prefiguration of the blood of Christ shed on the cross. Jesus is the "Lamb of God" who takes away the sins of humanity (John 1:36). The Sango Bible translates the lamb of God as Ngassambanga ti Nzapa. The word ngassambanga means the "goat of sin." The ngassambanga is used for covenant rituals in Scripture to take away the wrong that is done. Since the *Mbuki* ritual is a blood covenant, Christ is the ultimate *Mbuki* who laid the foundation for God's covenant because, through his blood, he inaugurated the *fini Mbuki* (new covenant). Therefore, when the CAR Christians allow the gospel to interpret the *Mbuki* ritual, it allows them to see Jesus as the *fini Mbuki*.

From the above analysis, two points are worth highlighting. First, the reconciliation mandate of the churches in CAR is to promote or maintain community links, not only within the Christian community, but also outside. This can be done, for example, by re-emphasizing socio-cultural activities that brought Christians and Muslims together before the 2013-coup, such

---

76. Monger and Methuselah, "God's Masterpiece," 109.

as football games, school cultural activities, intermarriage relationships and others. Second, the mandate of the churches is to encourage Christians (and even non-Christians) to be non-violent in response to conflict and violence, and to advocate for truth, justice, and reconciliation.

Therefore, in the light of Scripture's interpretation of *Mbuki*, a theology of reconciliation enables the articulation of Christ's sacrificial death to (re)unite lost humanity with God and to establish harmony among the peoples of the world. This theological articulation is based on the scriptural interpretation of the traditional values of kinship, fellowship, sharing, caring, interdependence, respect for the others, forgiveness, peace, and reconciliation.

3.3 The Imperative of Social Justice

The Lausanne paper reads, "Reconciliation and the quest for justice go hand in hand. There cannot be reconciliation if sin is not named, judged publicly and condemned."[77] In order to analyse the relationship between justice and reconciliation in CAR, it is important to have some insight into the biblical view of justice. In Hebrew, the word *Tsedeq* refers to "the 'right' conduct of God and of humans, not within a view of an ideal norm of what is right, but rather within the perspective of the concrete life relationships of partners to each other."[78] In other words, righteousness characterizes God's conduct toward his people. It should also be the conduct of human beings toward each other. In his righteousness, God assists the needy (Psalm 40:11; 51:16; 112:9) or defends those who are deprived of their rights (Psalm 5:9; 7:9; 9:5). Since God is just, he also requires people to be just. The word *Tsedeq* has also a covenantal meaning for God's people. Thus,

> for a ruler, it means good government and the deliverance of true judgement (Isa. 32.1; Jer. 23.5); for ordinary people, it means treating one's neighbor as a covenant partner, neither oppressing nor being oppressed (Amos 5.6–7, 21–4); and for everyone it means keeping God's will as conveyed in the Torah (Deut. 6.25).[79]

---

77. Lausanne Committee for World Evangelisn, "Reconciliation as the Mission of God," 16.
78. Kertelge, "Dikaiosuné," 326.
79. Ziesler, "Righteousness," 655.

In another Hebrew word, *Mishpat*, "The biblical idea of justice can be best described as 'fidelity to the demand of a relationship,' with particular reference to the widow, the orphan and the poor."[80] In Greek, the verb *dikaioō* means to justify, to represent as just or to treat someone as just. In the writings of Paul, it means to be acquitted.[81] In contrast, the noun *dikaiosuné* is used for the "righteousness" enjoyed by believers through faith.[82] Levi Lukadi Noah highlights that "justice" means a "form of moral excellence which demands the righteous distribution of rewards and punishments, and which renders it certain under God's government that obedience will be rewarded and sin punished."[83]

In Sango, the expression *Nzapa ti mbilimbili* means "God of righteousness." The idea of *mbilimbili* also reveals the notion of honesty and perfection. To refer to God as *mbilimbili* means that there is no dishonesty, injustice, or corruption in him. God is holy and perfect in words and actions (Isaiah 6:1–6). On the other hand, the expression *Nzapa ti fangô mbanga* literally means "the God who cuts justice," referring to dispensing justice. To dispense justice is to *fa mbanga*. In the biblical sense, *fa mbanga* and *mbilimbili* complement each other: God judges (*fa mbanga*) in relation to righteousness (*mbilimbili*).[84] In other words, one cannot demand justice or righteousness from someone if one is not righteous oneself.

Justice is central to the reconciliation because, as Bruce V. Malchow points out, "Social injustice is a major problem" that affects people's lives.[85] At the centre of the reconciliation process is the restoration of the dignity of victims and the possibility of finding harmony between victims and perpetrators. As God cares about justice for the victims, applying fair justice is to satisfy the will of God. *Mbilimbili*, therefore, is indispensable for official and indigenous leaders to promote fair justice, to allow restitution when a crime or offence is committed against a person or his/her property, or to encourage

---

80. La Poorta, "Justice," 442 [The italics are from the author].

81. Kertelge, "Dikaioo," 331.

82. Douglas and Tenney (eds.), *The New International Dictionary* 863. The word *dikaiosuné* appears ninety-one times in the NT, fifty-one in Paul's writings and especially thirty-three times in Romans, as one of the "preferred words of Paul." See Kertelge, "Dikaiosuné," 326.

83. Noah, *Reconciliation and Peace in South Sudan*, 52.

84. Karan, *Kêtê Bakarî tî Sängö*, 52.

85. Malchow, *Social Justice*, xi.

mediation and restoration of broken ties. In the OT, God gave the people of Israel, through Moses, codes and ordinances to facilitate justice and maintain cohesion within the communities (Exodus 21:1–23:10).

J. J. La Poorta argues that there are three categories of justice: "*Punitive* or *retributive justice*, wherein wrongdoers are punished; *restorative* or *distributive justice*, where what has been taken from victims is given back to them; and *structural justice*, where the social structures that created injustice are dismantled and replaced with more just ones."[86] He also points out that Christians place great emphasis on restorative justice, which focuses on the redistribution of goods and promotion of the dignity of victims. While warning about "the limits of punitive justice," he indicates that Christians nevertheless recognize its necessity to end the cycle of violence.[87] In linking forgiveness and justice, Noah argues that justice helps to deter revenge and prevent victimization, while forgiveness helps to restore the broken relationships after the perpetrator has faced restorative justice.[88]

The delicate issue of blanket amnesty always arises in the reconciliation process or in transitional justice. Walter Wink argues that in every post-conflict context, people deal with reconciliation in various ways; however, amnesty is "ideally the last step in the process of reconciliation."[89] CAR has faced this situation several times in previous conflicts when perpetrators demanded amnesty as one condition for joining the government at the negotiating table.[90] The issue is whether Christians can continue to turn a blind eye and allow such a process to take place as if nothing had happened; for the sake of reconciliation.

At their synod, which coincided with the 1994 Rwandan genocide, the African bishops from the All-Africa Conferences Churches (AACC) focused focussed on the issues of violence and democracy in Africa and sounded the alarm about the commitment of Christians to justice, reconciliation, peace, democracy, and human rights. They encouraged lay Christians to get involved in politics to bring about changes based on Christian values.[91] John Mary

---

86. La Poorta, "Justice," 640.
87. La Poorta, 640.
88. Noah, *Reconciliation and Peace*, 67.
89. Wink, *When Powers Fall*, 33–34.
90. Bagayoko, *Comparative Study*, 32.
91. Katongole, *The Sacrifice of Africa*, 38; Waliggo, "'The Synod of Hope,'" 40–41.

Waliggo stressed that, "To call for peace, we are called to work for justice, for there cannot be genuine peace without justice."[92] This view also suggests that there is no reconciliation without truth and justice.

In the context of CAR, the boy's call "we must forgive the *Séléka*" puts an emphasis on forgiveness.[93] Nevertheless, in a broader sense, forgiveness calls for justice for the perpetrators of conflicts because for reconciliation to be effective, it is important to take into account the issues of truth, justice, and reparation. In *No Future Without Forgiveness*, Desmond Tutu states that transitional justice is not "a criminal court" but a body that helps "to rehabilitate the human and civil dignity of victims."[94] It is the framework in which perpetrators and victims meet to reveal their stories, express their remorse, and allow forgiveness to rebuild their harmony. Such an experience is instructive for CAR as the ongoing CVJRR is expected to carry out reconciliation.

However, in interviews, some respondents, particularly in Bouar and Bossangoa, stated that they had neither seen nor heard anything about the commission. Their demand shows the need for the CAR authorities to publicize in the towns and other areas, preferably in Sango, information on the role and function the commission will perform, as well as the contribution of each citizen to its success. The authorities can also set up local branches of the commission in prefectures or sub-prefectures in order to gather stories from the local populations.

In transitional justice, victims or families of victims require hearing the truth before forgiving perpetrators. This process is essential for restorative justice. Indeed, truth-seeking is at the heart of the transitional justice systems. Tutu stressed that those who came to the South African TRC told "their stories in their own words."[95] The commission found that there was a "forensic factual truth" that could be verified and documented, and a "social truth, the truth of experience that is established through interaction, discussion and debate."[96] He called the latter "healing truth" as formal justice "would have left many of those who came to testify" confused and even traumatized.[97] Schreiter argues

---

92. Waliggo, "'The Synod of Hope,'" 41.
93. Italics are mine.
94. Tutu, *No Future Without Forgiveness*, 26.
95. Tutu, 26.
96. Tutu, 26.
97. Tutu, 26–27.

that truth-telling is an essential process for establishing what happened and for achieving justice, because "In earlier attempts at reconciliation, efforts began with the pursuit of justice in order to bring right relations back to a society."[98] This process was part of the reconciliation initiatives in Sierra Leone. The search for truth makes it possible to determine responsibility. It even goes beyond that, as Schreiter explains that "Truth is more than getting the facts right; it involves discovering in that truth the meaning it has for the future."[99] Regarding the case of CAR, one can deduce that the success of the reconciliation process resides in the effectiveness of justice.[100]

In an interview, Kondia, a church minister, depicted the problem of justice in the country. He said,

> I think that there is a problem. Law is not fully applied in all its rigour. Political calculations influence justice. Our God is a God of justice. If justice is not applied in a society, there is anarchy. Justice maintains peace and security. Furthermore, without justice, there is no reconciliation. Nowadays, our judges have become corrupt and impunity is growing. A criminal can walk around outside without being bothered. On the other hand, the authorities can put in jail a good citizen who wants to live the virtues of society because he refuses to be part of their system. I had entitled one of my sermons: 'Justice on the way to peace.' Take the people of Israel in the Bible, when a king did not apply justice, it was a mess. When he did apply justice, there was peace and security. This pattern can be described as 'justice equals peace.' However, when there is no justice, there is disorder or anarchy. When the rich oppress the weak and the poor, the latter seek revenge, which can lead to anarchy.[101]

Kondia raised in the above statement the issues of justice, or to put it differently, the lack of justice. His view on the issue aligns with Scripture. Indeed,

---

98. Schreiter, "Peacemaking and Reconciliation," 640.

99. Schreiter, 640.

100. In chapter 1, I explained that, in addition to ICC, the Special Criminal Court (SCC) functions as a criminal justice system, while the truth commission (CVJRR) was established for truth and reconciliation.

101. Kondia, Interview, 6 May 2021 (Translation is mine).

Scripture shows that God is concerned about social justice. He condemns injustice, corruption, greed, and other practices that privilege a particular class of people, neglect and even oppress the poor. In Exodus 22:21–23, for example, mistreating foreigners (*aouandè*), widows (*aouomoua*) and orphans (*amelèngué so baba to ala ayèké pèpé*) is an injustice. Throughout Scripture, these categories of people are among the most marginalized.[102] La Poorta states that, in the OT, the books of wisdom reveal that "the just person" is the person who is concerned with maintaining peace and harmony in a community. He goes on to say that,

> Such a person strengthened the weak hands . . . 'supported those who were stumbling' (Job 4:3–4), cares for the poor the fatherless and the widow (Job 29:12–15; 31:16–19; Prov 29:7) and defends their case in court (Job 29:16; Prov 31:9). The just are portrayed as those who live in and harmony with their neighbors, their land, their employees and their animals (Job 29:16; Prov 31:9).[103]

To redress wrongs in society, the OT prophets spoked out against injustice. Megan McKenna maintains that at the time of the prophets Micah and Isaiah, "the two kingdoms of Israel . . . are prosperous and thriving lands, with a very few rich people and many, many poor."[104] For this reason, God appointed them "to speak hard word to power, to the king and the ruling class in Jerusalem."[105] He went on to say that these two prophets prophesied during the rule of kings who "have forgotten that Yahweh should be the only king in Israel."[106] Isaiah 61:8, for example, pointing out that, "salvation will be accomplished by a messiah,"[107] announces that God passionately loves justice: *Teti Mbi, L'Eternel, Mbi ndoyé fa'ngo mbanga ti mbilimbili, Mbi kè ye ti kirikiri* (For I, the Lord, love to do fair justice, I reject unrighteousness).

---

102. With regard to Exodus 22:21–23, Mae Alice Reggy-Mamo states that throughout the OT, God shows "special compassion for widow and orphans." God is their "defender" (Deut 10:18); he cares for and protects them (Ps 68:5; 146:9). See Reggy-Mamo, "Widows and Orphans," 1382.

103. La Poorta, "Justice," 442.

104. McKenna, *Prophets: Words of Fire*, 124.

105. McKenna, 126.

106. McKenna, 127.

107. Nsiku, "Isaiah," 1432.

In Isaiah 10:1–4, *mbanga ti Nzapa* (God's judgment) is firm for those who refuse to do justice to the poor, widows and orphans, those who mistreat the oppressed. On the other hand, Micah's prophecy (Mic 3:1–6) was directed against the unjust kings, *I amakounzi ti ajo ti Jacob, na i amakounzi ti ajo ti da' ti Israel; a yèké mbanga ti i ti hinga lègué ti fa'ngo mbanga mbilimbili pèpé? I so i kè ndjoni na i ndoyé sioni* (You kings of the people of Jacob, and you kings of the house of Israel; is it not for you to know how to do justice fairly? You who reject good and you love evil).

La Poorta claims that, although the theme of justice is significant in the NT, it is not "as rich or as direct as in the Old Testament."[108] According to him, even though the use of the concept of justice in the NT is not as important as it is in the OT, Valdir Raul Steuernagel sees justice as "a mark of mission" that brings about a transformation. He states, "We affirm justice as a fundamental expression of God's search for transformation, as a mark of mission and the need to integrate it into our portfolio of mission."[109] The life and earthly ministry of Jesus Christ illustrate this mission of transformation. For example, Jesus's teachings in Matthew emphasize the theme of justice. He speaks of those who thirst for justice/righteousness (5:6), those who are persecuted for justice (5:10), those who excel in justice (6:20), and those who seek the kingdom of God and righteousness (6:33). These categories describe people who understand and fulfil the mandate of justice.[110] In Luke 4:18–19, Jesus condemns the kings, the priests, and elders for mistreating *aouanzinga* (the poor), *amgba* (the captives/prisoners), *aouaziba* (the blind) and *ajo assala ngangou na ala* (the oppressed). In other words, they misuse their power and authority to do injustice.

Paul says in Romans 13:4 that a political, social, or judicial leader is *jo ti koussala ti Nzapa ti sala nzoni na mo* (the servant of God for your good). This suggests that the leaders are accountable before God whom they serve through their leadership. For this reason, they ensure that justice is equitable in the community. If someone commits a wrongdoing, the leader has the power to punish him or her according to the law. In this context, Scripture

---

108. La Poorta, "Justice," 443.
109. Steuernagel, "To Seek to Transform,"64.
110. Kapolyo, "Matthew," 1861–1869.

and law recognize the authority of traditional leaders, whether for justice or reconciliation. To deny this authority or to misuse it is to disobey God.

In light of the above analysis, when judges in CAR compromise justice and enforce impunity, it is impossible to think of a future beyond ressentiment, anger, and the spirit of vengeance in those who are unjustly marginalized. If it is true that there is no "Future without forgiveness," as Tutu points out,[111] it is also true that there is no future for victims and for the whole nation without justice. The role of indigenous leaders in this context is of great importance because they know how indigenous beliefs and practices can contribute to truth, justice, and reparation. This aspect of the issue is very important because it has led to complaints and criticisms from indigenous leaders who felt that the local and/or national authorities had suppressed them from their role related to justice and reconciliation.

In some areas of CAR, people show respect to indigenous leaders, such as chefs de quartiers (neighbourhood chiefs) or chefs de villages (village chiefs). These are the custodians of culture and tradition, and the holders of ancestral wisdom. As custodians of tradition, they know what traditional rituals mean and how they function to discover truth and deliver justice. Despite some weaknesses that people observe in their organization and functioning, traditional leaders can contribute to reconciliation as customary judges. In an interview, Maurice Dimanche Arsy spoke about a meeting in February 2021 between the head of the Bouar Court and about seventy chefs de quartiers. He stated,

> In the last two months, the head of the Court called on all the local chiefs of Bouar I, we were about 70 chiefs. This number was divided into two sections of 35 chiefs. He indicated the scope of the neighbourhood's jurisdiction by saying that civil affairs are the responsibility of the chiefs to manage. The reason is that if all criminal and civil cases were to be left to the judges to manage, they would be overwhelmed. Decisions on minor disputes are the responsibility of the chiefs. However, it is important that the chiefs take an oath, before they start.[112]

---

111. Tutu, *No Future Without Forgiveness*.
112. Dimanche Maurice Arsy, Interview, 2 April 2021, Bouar (Translation is mine).

He added that,

> The chiefs will take an oath and sign the pledge to make conciliations according to the two-day training they have received. If a case is not criminal, the chiefs are empowered to decide, but if blood is shed during a dispute, the police or the gendarmerie are responsible and can take legal action if necessary. On the other hand, marital disputes, cases of jealousy, theft and other petty offenses are the responsibility of the chiefs.[113]

Here, the head of the Bouar court of justice decided to offer the *chefs de quartiers* a legal framework for resolving minor conflicts after training them in the basic elements of informal justice, as part of capacity building. After the training, they are required to take an oath before taking up the task. This meeting endorsed Ordinance No. 88.006, article 12 of 5 February 1988 that recognized the right of the indigenous leaders to judge civil cases: "En matière de justice civile et commerciale il [chef coutumier] est investi du pouvoir pour concilier les partis. Lors de sa prise de fonction, il est tenu de prêter serment devant le Juge d'instance en présence du Conseil du village" (In matters of civil and commercial justice he [traditional chief] is vested with the power to reconcile parties. On taking office, he is required to take an oath before the magistrate in the presence of the village council).[114] The law allowed the initiative of Bouar. Unfortunately, at present, such initiatives do not exist on a national scale. This law deserves to be popularized throughout the country.

Expanding on the ancestral function in the African context, Bediako points out that, "Of the three features of our traditional heritage we are considering, ancestral function seems to be the one to which Jesus Christ least easily answers."[115] He argues that in the African culture, the notion of ancestor comes from the "lineage or family," which means from bloodline. Therefore, the question is, if an African becomes a believer, how can he or she claim that Jesus is his or her ancestor? The cult of ancestors is what determines the important place that traditional African societies give to the "transcendent realm" in which the source of authority for leadership in the community

---

113. Arsy, Interview, 2 April 2021, Bouar (Translation is mine).
114. Ordonnance No. 88.006, article 12 du 5 Février 1988 (Translation is mine).
115. Bediako, *Jesus in Africa*, 29.

originates. The myth underlying the cult of ancestors allows us to understand that the cult provides a platform for the community to develop social harmony by strengthening ties with the present, the past and the unborn. Bediako also argues that Jesus Christ has fulfilled "our aspirations in relation to ancestral function" because like our ancestors, he "lived among us" and "for having brought benefits; Jesus Christ has done infinitely more."[116] He left his divine nature, "took our flesh and blood, shared our human nature and underwent death" to free humanity from sin and death (Hebrews 2:14–15). Bediako contends that Jesus

> took on human nature without loss to his divine nature. Belonging in the eternal realm as Son of the Father (Hebrews 1:1, 48; 9:14), he has taken human nature into himself (Hebrews 10:19) and so, as God-man, he ensures an infinitely more effective ministry to human beings (Hebrews 7:25) than can be said of merely human ancestral spirits.[117]

Scripture presents Jesus as the perfect "sacrifice" and at the same time the "Kota Sacrificateur" (High Priest). Christopher T. Begg states,

> In the New Testament, particularly in Hebrews, the death of Jesus is described as a sacrifice that definitely secures for the whole of humanity the effects (atonement, fellowship with God) that older sacrifices brought about only temporarily (Heb. 9.23–28). Likewise in the New Testament, the notion of spiritual sacrifice comes to the fore (Ro. 12.1; 15.16; Phil. 2.17; 4.18; 1 Pet. 2.5). In this conception, every action of a Christian's life has the capacity, when performed in faith, to be an offering acceptable to God.[118]

By holding the position of mediator, the author of the epistle to Hebrews presents Jesus Christ as "the High Priest."[119] In light of Hebrews 5–8, the

---

116. Bediako, 30.
117. Bediako, 31.
118. Begg, "Sacrifice," 667.
119. Bediako, *Jesus in Africa*, 27.

universality of the "priestly mediation" of Jesus Christ is not derived from the Jewish priestly tradition, but from Melchizedek.[120]

Centrafricans can come to Jesus as their High Priest for mediation, redemption, and salvation by faith.[121] Only Jesus can accomplish the "eternal redemption" for them with his own blood (Hebrews 9:12). Indeed, he not only atones and stands as the High Priest to mediate for the sins of humanity, but also provides the opportunity to each believer to be "an offering acceptable to God", as Begg highlighted. One can say that being an offering to God means being like an animal offered as a sacrifice (in the old covenant or African traditions). It also means being ready to sacrifice oneself for others. In other words, Centrafricans in general and Christians in particular commit themselves for the good of others, the good of the nation. This state of being is highly valued as a guarantee for reconciliation.

With regard to the contribution of Christians in CAR to help those affected and victims of the conflict, none of the interviewees spoke of a Christian restorative justice initiative. In parallel to the public processes, churches in CAR could follow the Rwandan method of "Christian *Gacaca,*"[122] in order to establish a "Christian *Mbuki*" to promote restorative justice between blood brothers and blood sisters. This could be an effective approach to consider as the church's missional mandate for reconciliation in CAR. In this way, victims and perpetrators could talk to each other, forgive each other, and heal their wounded hearts. This is what Geoff Broughton points out about reconciliation in two Sydney communities when he says that Christians could "find restorative practices indispensable for restoring lives and relationships broken apart by injustice."[123] Since Christ is the new *Mbuki*, it is important

---

120. Tesfaye Kassa argues that, according to Hebrews 7:2, the name Melchizedek, "king of righteousness" and the title "king of Salem" or "king of peace" refer to Jesus. In Sango, "*Gbia ti mbilimbili*" means "king of righteousness", "*Gbia ti Salem*" means "king of Salem", and *Gbia ti siriri* means "king of peace." Jesus is the *Gbia ti Salem* and *Gbia ti siriri*. Jesus is the High Priest and the king of peace. See Kassa, "Hebrews," 498.

121. Again, in "*Kota Sacrificateur*" as rendered by the Sango Bible translator, the word '*Sacrificateur*' is the French version word. This can be changed to read "*Kata wa ya ngo sataga*", literally "the great one who presents sacrifice."

122. Such a perspective could offer, "a holistic approach to transitional justice." See Clark, *The Gacaca Courts*, 32. Churches in Uganda also initiated the "Christian and cultural rituals of healing and reconciliation" among the Acholi people. See Opongo, "Reconciliation in Complex Spaces," 172.

123. Broughton, "Restorative Justice," 300.

for believers in CAR to understand that, "One mark of holistic reconciliation is a commitment to pursuing justice that is primarily restorative rather than retributive, keeping open the hope for future common life between enemies and alienated peoples."[124]

3.4 Dealing With Evil Structures in Conflict

At the Forum for World Evangelization, it was clearly stated that, "Powerful historical and social forces, ujust systems, and 'spiritual forces of evil' (Ephesians 6:12) are also part of the world's brokenness."[125] It was also pointed out that, "All the agents of brokenness must be discerned and confronted – personal, spiritual, and social."[126] In line with this view, the boy's message to the churches in CAR includes the responsibility to deal with evil structures so that effective harmony, cohesion, and peace prevail. Mbaye-Bondoi said that the boy called on "the churches [to] forgive the Séléka because they were ignorant of what they had done; the devil had used them."[127] This idea evokes a call to confront evil powers. It is important that believers in CAR understand that evil structures function to oppress and marginalize people. They, therefore, provoke resentment, anger, hatred, and violence. However, The Cape Town Commitment urged believers to "forgive persecutors, while having courage to challenge injustice on behalf of others."[128]

Walter Wink argues that the notion of "powers" does not primarily imply the physical world, but rather "the confluence of both spiritual and material factors."[129] He goes on to say that in the modern context, some people disbelieve what Scripture refers to as "principalities and powers," although there are a variety of invisible demonic beings that cause demonic activities resulting in disease, lust, possession or death.[130] What Wink explains here is the Western understanding of evil or evil power, which is not the same as the African view of evil, as I will explain in this section. Despite the different

---

124. Lausanne Committee for World Evangelisn, "Reconciliation as the Mission of God," 16.
125. Lausanne Committee for World Evangelisn, 12.
126. Lausanne Committee for World Evangelisn, 12.
127. Mbaye-Bondoi, Interview, 24 July 2021, Bangui.
128. The Third Lausanne Congress, "Building the Peace of Christ," 68.
129. Wink, *Naming the Powers*, 3.
130. Wink, *Unmasking the Powers*, 4.

points of view on the subject, it is important to note that evil powers are at the origin of several disorders occurring in the physical, psychological, or social context of people.[131] Thus, they provoke killings, rape, torture, or all sorts of violence that armed men have committed.

John Howard Yoder points out that there is both clarity and ambiguity in the use of the terms such as "power" and "authority."[132] An authority holds a legitimacy but can also violate power. Sometimes, the two terms are intertwined. Yoder observes that in Paul's writings, such "confusion is present" when he speaks of "principalities and powers," "thrones and dominions," and other related political terms such as "structure."[133] For him, when theologians began to conduct critical studies on the NT, they argued that it was taken for granted that, when the apostle Paul speaks about "angels," or "demons," or "powers", he referred to "a dispensable remainder of an antique worldview, needing not even to be interpreted or translated, but simply to be dropped without discussion."[134]

It is obvious that the European Enlightenment worldview influenced the interpretation of scholars on the existence and works of evil powers.[135] Later, between 1930 and 1950, in the face of the events that shook Europe, "Protestant theology sought a more adequate theological understanding of the power of evil which has been through the crust of the most civilized societies."[136] Thus, they have begun to balance their understanding of Scripture in its original context with its meaning in their own context.

> Most of the references to the "Powers" in the New Testament consider them as fallen. It is important therefore to begin with the reminder that they were part of the good creation of God. Society and history, even nature, would be impossible without regularity, system, order- and God has provided for this need.

---

131. Wink, *Naming the Powers*, 4.
132. Yoder, *The Politics of Jesus*, 137.
133. Yoder, 137.
134. Yoder, 139.
135. Thomas Oduro explains that the Enlightenment put "humans rather than God in the centre of things and had a strong influence on the thinking and practice of Protestant mission." See Oduro, et al., *Mission in African Way*, 39. It engendered missionaries who adopted Enlightenment values in their Christianity. See Walls, *The Cross-Cultural Process*, 122.
136. Yoder, *The Politics of Jesus*, 139.

> The universe is not sustained arbitrarily, immediately, and erratically by an unbroken succession of new divine interventions. It was made in an ordered form and "it was good." The creative power worked in a mediated form, by means of the Powers that regularized all visible reality.[137]

Here, Yoder elaborates on Paul's theology concerning the evil powers in pointing out that they no longer mediate God's purposes. However, they seek to separate men from the love of God (Romans 8:38), to control the lives of those who rebel against God (Ephesians 2:2), to keep in bondage those who are under their authority (Colossians 2:20) and under their tutelage (Galatians 4:3).[138] The tutelage and servitude of the evil powers makes it difficult, if not impossible, for people to escape systems that make them vulnerable in the world.[139]

African traditional societies also had an understanding of evil or evil powers. Joseph Okello points out that, "African minds have reflected over the problem of evil just as much as every other philosopher has."[140] He points out that, in African view, evil spirits are the forces that cause evil. The following example sheds light on this reflection. In analysing Afua Kuma's prayers, Bediako argues that in the Akan worldview,

> *Mmoatia* are supposed to be mysterious creatures with superhuman powers, that dwell deep in the forest; they are believed to be tiny, with feet that point backwards; suspending themselves from trees, they wait for the unwary hunter in the pitch darkness of the night. At their head, as their head spirit, is *Sasabonsam* with bloodshot eyes. His name has found its way in Akan Christian vocabulary to designate the devil.[141]

Mbiti states that, "From the previous considerations we have seen that African people are much aware of evil in the world, and in various ways they endeavour to fight it."[142] Therefore, in traditional societies, when a conflict or

---

137. Yoder, 141.
138. Yoder, 141.
139. Gandolfo, *The Power and Vulnerability*, 168–169.
140. Okello, "Analysis of an Africa," 65.
141. Bediako, *Jesus in Africa*, 10.
142. Mbiti, *African Religions*, 204.

a calamity such as premature death, famine, disease or drought occurred in a community, people consulted the diviner or priest to understand the root cause of the problems. Usually, the diviner pointed to the violation of covenants (as in the case of *Mbuki*), an offence against the deities or a particular wrong, as the root cause of the calamity, and indicated the solution(s) to end it. Usually, this consists in performing rituals or the offering of sacrifice to appease the deities. In addition, in order to deal with problems and issues of evil, AICs re-establish the link between the primal worldview and the Christian faith through libation, use of oil, prayers, prophecy, deliverance, and other religious acts. The rituals point to Christ, the source of victory. On this point, Bediako opines that in African context,

> ... Jesus is seen above all else as the *Christus Victor* (Christ supreme over every spiritual rule and authority). This understanding of Christ arises from Africans' keen awareness of forces and powers at work in the world which threaten the interests of life and harmony. Jesus is victorious over the spiritual realm and particularly over evil forces and so answers to the need for a powerful protector against these forces and powers.[143]

It is important to note that, despite the influence of evil powers on them, human oppressors do not lose their will or sense of morality. For example, in Isaiah 10:5–34, although God used the Assyrian rulers as a rod to chastise the disobedience of his people Israel, they exceeded the limits of their power and took pride in dominating and crushing the Israelites. In this context, God held them responsible for the evil they committed against his people. Albert Nolan says that nations representing the powers of evil dominated Israel. He states that,

> the powerful empires of ancient times, like the Egyptians, Assyrians, Babylonians, Greeks and Romans, threatened them, attacked them, massacred them and enslaved them. These were the original evil powers that Israel feared. These were the nations whose sins were condemned by the prophets.[144]

---

143. Bediako, *Jesus in African Culture*, 8.
144. Nolan, *God in South Africa*, 44.

What Nolan points out here shows the reality of evil structures causing oppression, marginalization, wars, and conflicts against the people of Israel. It also shows evidence of the oppression of nations by other nations. The rulers of other nations enslaved the people of Israel because Israel sinned against God and disobeyed the covenant, which was to promote "justice, love of neighbor, concern for widows and orphans, periodic cancellation of debts, and the manumission of slaves."[145] For example, in his prophetic messages, Jeremiah advised the army of the people of Israel not to fight the Babylonian soldiers, but rather to submit to Nebuchadnezzar, for this was the will of Yahweh to make them captives (Jeremiah 27:1–22).

Moreover, the Israelites themselves enslaved their own people and oppressed widows and orphans, as I pointed out earlier. To emphasize this point, Walter Brueggemann shows that OT prophets spoke out against the exploitation and oppression of the vulnerable people of Israel. The kings prevented the people of Judah from obeying God's commands, but also enslaved them.[146] He argued that Solomon's policy of achieving "incredible well-being and affluence," according to 1 Kings 4:20–23, was an oppressive and exploitative policy that impoverished the people.[147] He contends that in "our own recent past" or to say in our context, people use violence to get rid of an oppressive and exploitative regime:

> As we know from our own recent past, such an exploitative appetite can develop insatiable momentum so that, no matter how much in the way of goods or power or security is obtained, it is never enough. The rebellion announced in 1 Kings 11:28 and the dispute of 1 Kings 12 concerning the nature of government and the role of people and leaders both show the struggle with a new self-understanding. In that new consciousness on which the regime was built but which was also created by the regime, the politics of justice and compassion has completely disappeared.[148]

It is obvious that many leaders have been responsible for the misfortune of the oppressed in their own countries or in other territories because of their

---

145. Wink, *Engaging the Powers*, 120.
146. Brueggemann, *The Prophetic Imagination*, 27.
147. Brueggemann, 27.
148. Brueggemann, *The Prophetic Imagination*, 27.

blind political or economic ambitions. Nevertheless, they have a choice to do justice and to behave in righteousness. However, while they are responsible for their choices and evil actions towards others, it is also clear that evil forces drive them or use them. In Sango, *yingo sioni* (literally, "spirit evil") has been used for the translation of the word "demon." This understanding refers to the idea that those who commit evil actions are influenced by demons.

In the spiritual realm, the kingdom of evil is opposed to the kingdom of God, and the law of the kingdom of evil is opposed to the law of God.[149] The kingdom of God describes a realm where the absolute sovereignty of God is recognized and where people proclaim the lordship of Christ with the expectation of a coming and fulfilled rule of Christ. Therefore, people under the influence of the evil kingdom are driven to commit evil and to abandon God. This was the case in Israel in OT times. The kingdom of evil characterizes what Wink calls the "Domination System."[150] To explain this term, he argues that when black South Africans fought against apartheid, they "were fully aware that they were fighting the apartheid system."[151] The spiritual forces work at manipulating people to cause violence. Thus, dealing with the ongoing conflict involves dealing with the system of evil powers that prevent peace and reconciliation from abounding. In John 7:7, the evil system hated Jesus because he testified against it that its works were evil. Wink argues that at creation there was no evil in the powers, for they were created to be good servants of God (Colossians 1:15–17), until they rebelled against God and fell.[152]

During field research, respondents, particularly in Bouar and Bangui, claimed that politicians manipulated people and implicated them in killing others. Despite this reality, it is essential that Christians maintain an exemplary attitude in this context. During his earthly ministry, Jesus led an exemplary life of love for the poor, comforting the oppressed and marginalized, and healing the sick (Matthew 4:23; 9:35; Acts 10:38). He chose the disciples to be with him and to do the work of the kingdom of God, which was to denounce

---

149. The term "Kingdom of God" or "Kingdom of Heaven" refers to the sovereign, dynamic, and eschatological dominion of God. See Giles, "Kingdom of God/Kingdom of Heaven," 417.

150. Wink, *Engaging the Powers*, 52.

151. Wink, 52.

152. Wink, 66, 69.

oppressive injustice, to identify with the poor and the marginalized, and to intervene for liberation, wholeness and peace.[153] This view describes the *missio ecclesiae* that the churches in CAR should embark on to face the powers of evil, to advocate forgiveness and justice, and care for broken communities.

In writing about the de-sacralization of power in Africa, Bediako argues that, in African traditional societies, authority and political power were sacralized but the gospel of Christ de-sacralized the authority and power in the political arena.[154] He goes on to say that during his earthly ministry, Jesus brought a new understanding of power and authority. Thus, an ultimate authority or power finds its significance in the cross of Christ, which "de-sacralises *all* the powers, institutions and structures that rule human existence and history – family, nation, social class, race, law, politics, economy, religion, culture, tradition, custom, ancestors – stripping them of any pretensions to ultimacy."[155]

Similarly, just as in the time of Jesus, political leaders "saw him as a threat and a challenge,"[156] in the CAR context, some politicians considered some church leaders as a threat and a challenge to their political regime. For example, in an interview, while giving his opinion on the interfaith leaders and their contribution to reconciliation, Kondia revealed that, "The leaders of the Platform spoke the truth. For this reason, their lives were sometimes in danger. They spoke truth that did not suit the political leaders."[157] What Kondia emphasized was the danger some religious leaders found themselves in for speaking out against evil and advocating for effective work for change to meet the needs of people for reconciliation and peace.

Bediako rightly observes that, "In the present quest for new political arrangements in Africa, the discussion is often distorted, so that it seems as if the choice is between 'Western' forms of political organisation and 'indigenous' African systems and patterns."[158] The situation Bediako points out here is even worse in many countries in French-speaking Africa and in particular in CAR, where external influences prevent local/indigenous initiatives

---

153. Steuernagel, "To Seek to Transform Unjust Structures," 67.
154. Bediako, *Jesus in Africa*, 104.
155. Bediako, 104.
156. Bediako, 103.
157. Kondia, Interview, 6 May 2021 (Translation is mine).
158. Bediako, *Jesus in Africa*, 104.

to make good choices for reconciliation and nation-building. It seems that policymakers outside the country dictate decisions and expect Centrafricans to follow. These policies are a "system" that consists in imposing agendas on CAR official authorities that do not fit the context of Centrafricans, such as holding peace meetings outside the country.

Bediako goes on to argue that power and authority find their meaning in the "way of Jesus", as "the way of non-dominating power, in the political arrangements under which members of society and nation relate to one another."[159] Indeed, authority and power belong to Jesus who gives it to leaders for the benefit of other people. Before his rapture, Jesus declared in Matthew 28:18, *A mou na Mbi ngangou na yayou na sessé* (I have been given power in heaven and on earth). Since creation, Jesus has had power and authority over all in heaven and on earth. For this reason, he was able to overcome evil spirits on the cross (Colossians 2:15).

Wink's view of the purpose of power is similar to that of Bediako. Wink argues that, in the light of Matthew 5:3–12 and Luke 6:20–23, "Jesus does not condemn ambition or aspiration [of people in power]; he merely changes the values to which they are attached."[160] In other words, he suggests that anyone who attains the status of power and authority is a servant. He or she obtains this position to ensure the good of his or her fellow human beings. Thus, being a leader is not about greed and selfishness, nor about marginalizing others. In his statement above, Kondia pointed out that in ancient Israel, if the king ruled the nation, not for his own greed and selfishness, but in accordance with the law, then the nation was at peace, people lived in harmonious reconciliation and prospered. In Deuteronomy, Moses gave the people of Israel the ordinances of God, which are part of the law of the covenant, emphasizing the blessings that came from obedience and the curses that came from disobedience (Deuteronomy 7:12–15; 28:2–12). Luciano C. Chianeque and Samuel Ngewa state that, "The specific blessings mentioned here are material, not spiritual, making it clear that God has created a good world that people can enjoy."[161] Thus, God's requirement for a peaceful nation is that the leaders

---

159. Bediako, 105.
160. Wink, *Engaging the Powers*, 111.
161. Chianeque and Ngewa, "Deuteronomy," 390–391.

and people live in accordance with his covenant. The *Mbuki* practice finds itself in the above arguments.

As in the context of the people of Israel where the violation of God's covenant brought a curse, in the *Mbuki* blood pacts also, any violation led to disastrous consequences for the individual, his/her family and clan. However, obeying and following the community or covenant rules brought blessing and harmony. The atoning work of Christ made possible his victory over the principalities and powers of evil that hold humanity in bondage. In her doctoral research on the Akan *Odwira* rituals, Ernestina Afriyie points out that sacrifice as an offering was made by a person to unite him or her with a deity, or to atone sins. She states,

> On *Odwira* Tuesday, when the team led by the *Banmuhene* and *Adumhene* go to . . . (Royal mausoleum) to bring *Nananom Nsamanfo* and *Odwira* home, a sheep is slaughtered there. Because no one is to disclose what happens there, how the sacrifice is made is not known. The only thing that has been disclosed is that the blood from the sacrifice is poured onto the graves. The carcass is then skinned and parted. Some of the meat is put on skewers and placed on the graves for *Nananom Nsamanfo*. The rest of the meat is cooked and eaten by the elders present.[162]

Afriyie explains that some Akan Christians interviewed pointed out a contrast between *Odwira* sacrifices and the sacrifice in the Christian faith. According to her respondents, "Jesus Christ has made the ultimate sacrifice beyond which no other one can be made. Any other sacrifices that are made therefore challenge that which Christ has made."[163] Referring to Koudje's argument above, one can affirm that such a reasoning did not allow Scripture to interpret the *Odwira* sacrifices. It rather treated the sacrifice of Christ in the Christian faith as a substitution for sacrifices in Akan *Odwira* tradition. As I explain below, a group of Akan Christians pointed out that the cleansing function of *Odwira* has something to do with Jesus.

The issue is how people linked together through the *Mbuki* pact can address evil powers. In fact, in *Mbuki* culture, it is forbidden for two people,

---

162. Afriyie, "The Theology of," 265.
163. Afriyie, 265.

or two groups of people linked by an *Mbuki* pact to commit evil aginst each other. Rather, they are committed to saving their allies threatened by ferocious animals, tribal conflicts, or evil powers, to preserve life. Scripture highlights that, being the new *Mbuki* for all believers, Jesus Christ saved all humanity from sin, the devil, and death when he disarmed the powers and authorities and freed people from bondage (Colossians 2:14–15).

In this context, one can understand what Paul says in Colossians 2:15, *Lo lounguela yé ti bira ti akodjo-guelé-ti-commandé na ayanga-ti-commandé, Lo fa ala na guigui, Lo hon do ti ala na lègué ti kèké-ti-croix*. I literally translate: "He tore away the weapons of all pre-existing authorities and powers, exposed them publicly and triumphed over them by the cross." From the above arguments, it is important to note that God has made provision for believers to defeat the evil powers that cause conflict in the country. Confidence in the victory of Christ is what churches in CAR need to embrace in order to defeat the evil powers of war such as those who used the Séléka to kill people during a church service. The victory of Christ, the perfect *Mbuki*, is the victory of the church, and this victory will be complete when hostilities cease, and when disarmament and the introduction of the country into the new path of reconciliation and peace becomes effective.

3.5 Embracing Victims of Trauma

At the outset of this chapter, I pointed out that the young Christian Centrafrican boy's appeal revealed four key elements that could guide a Christian approach to reconciliation. We have seen how each element has indeed helped to provide a framework for a theology of reconciliation. The boy's call centered on forgiveness and justice. The one area that is lacking relates to responding to the issue of trauma. In addition to the influence of evil structures that cause conflict, trauma is a serious consequence of conflict on human persons and requires theological responses. A study on the Sierra Leone war shows that, "talking about war atrocities can prove psychologically traumatic by invoking war memories and re-opening old war wounds."[164] If believers fail to address the issue of post-traumatic stress disorder, any effort at reconciliation will be futile. This issue forms part of a theology of reconciliation that necessitates the attention of believers.

---

164. Cilliers, Dube, and Siddiqi, "Sierra Leone," 4.

During interviews, church ministers shared their views on whether their local congregations had helped people in the communities to reconcile. This is essential to the reconciliation process because *Mbuki* promotes caring, sharing, and togetherness. On the question, one church minister, Jean Alia declared,

> Not the local church but myself as an individual, as a pastor. I have helped resolve conflicts. I told you earlier that I have conducted many workshops and seminars on trauma healing. In May 2020, I was in Alindao where I held a workshop. A Muslim man had accepted Jesus Christ but was being persecuted by his fellow Muslims. I worked to mediate between the two parties. I talked to the one who was being persecuted and the parents of the one who was being persecuted. I did this work to calm people down and help rebuild relationships that had been broken. Therefore, I did a lot of work in that sense as an individual, not as a church.[165]

In February 2016, a report on the French Sangaris operation in CAR described it as "La plus traumatisante des guerres menées par la France" (The most traumatic of the wars led by France).[166] The report also said that soldiers were traumatized when they talked about who they were allowed to kill or what bodies they were allowed to carry. It concluded by pointing out that the soldiers were not well prepared to live with death.[167]

The issue of post-traumatic stress disorder in the CAR context is obvious and serious. It requires urgent attention from the churches, and critical theological responses to address it. While forgiveness is granted and reconciliation achieved, it does not necessarily lessen the impact of trauma on victims. It is essential to address the issue of trauma and provide a theological response to help the victims and perpetrators of violence. Indeed, if *Mbuki* requires the well-being of blood brothers or blood sisters, it is therefore obvious that those who perform *Mbuki* care about others affected by trauma.

---

165. Jean Alia, Interview, 23 July 2021, Bangui (Translation is mine).
166. Denètre et Mechaï, "Centrafrique – Opération Sangaris."
167. Denètre et Mechaï, "Centrafrique – Opération Sangaris."

Shelly Rambo asserts that trauma "is an event that continues, that persists in the present. Trauma is what does not go away. It persists in symptoms that live on in communities, in layers of the past violence that constitute present ways of relating. It persists in the symptoms that fuel present wars."[168] In CAR, people who have seen all their family members massacred or their villages burned down, or those who have seen their wives, mothers or sisters raped by armed men are still traumatized. In reality, words cannot adequately describe the trauma people continue to experience. In this context, some national and international NGOs are trying to respond to the problem by assisting the victims to recover. However, stigma and community rejection remain serious challenges to the process of healing.

Rambo states that Paul Womack, a military veteran, shared his traumatic experience at a session on trauma after serving in Vietnam and Iraq. It emerged from this discussion that the church had not responded to the problem that Womack and other war veterans had experienced.[169] She, further, elaborates on the nature of trauma when she states,

> Trauma is described as an encounter with death. This encounter is not, however, a literal death but a way describing a radical event or events that shatter all that one knows about the world and all the familiar ways of operating within it. A basic disconnection occurs from what one knows to be true and safe in the world.[170]

In this context, life loses its meaning and there is no frontier between life and death. The question is what theological response the church could bring to the problem of trauma and how Christians could help victims heal from trauma. Theologians address the issue of trauma in terms of "theological discourse about suffering," which Jürgen Moltmann pioneered. Rambo points out that Moltmann "revolutionized Christian interpretations of the crucifixion by claiming that God did not stand outside of the event of the cross but, rather, experienced the suffering."[171] Other theologians have also

---

168. Rambo, *Spirit and Trauma*, Kindle, 2.
169. Rambo, 2.
170. Rambo, 4.
171. Other theological trends, such as the Womanists and Feminists, have also emphasized the notion of suffering and the cross "arguing that theologies of the cross have glorified suffering

reflected on trauma, arguing that this category goes beyond psychology and other disciplines and it "poses unique challenges, transforming the discourse about suffering, God, redemption, and theological anthropology in significant ways."[172] Nevertheless, Rambo proposes an intermediate approach, which she calls "middle," to understanding trauma from a theological perspective. She says,

> I claim that trauma returns theologians to our primary claims about death and life, particularly as they are narrated in the events of cross and resurrection. Trauma disrupts this narrative, turning our attention to a more mixed terrain of remaining, one that I will identify as the 'middle.' By reexamining the relationship between death and life as it is narrated theologically, I am seeking a picture of redemption that adequately accounts for traumatic suffering that speaks to divine presence and power in light of what we know about trauma. This picture of redemption cannot emerge by interpreting death and life in opposition to each other. Instead, theology must account for the excess, or remainder, of death in life that is central to trauma. This reconfiguration of death and life, viewed through the lens of trauma, unearths a distinctive theology that can witness the realities of the aftermath of trauma.[173]

Rambo argues that Christians generally understand trauma as an opposing state of death and life that the gospel of the redemptive death of Jesus Christ interprets and restores. She observes that traumatic experiences call into question all redemptive narratives, as asserting that, "life (resurrection) is victorious over death" is problematic. Such a portrayal runs the risk of overlooking a more mixed experience of death and life.[174] To provide theological insight to the problem of trauma, Rambo states that,

> The good news of Christianity for those who experience trauma rests in the capacity to theologize this middle. It does not rest

---

and provided sacred salvation for the perpetuation of oppressive systems for persons and communities on the margins." See Rambo, *Spirit and Trauma*, 5.

172. Rambo, 5.
173. Rambo, 5–6.
174. Rambo, 8.

in either the event of the cross or resurrection, but instead in the movements between the two—movements that I identify through the concept of witness. The good news lies in the ability of Christian theology to witness between death and life, in its ability to forge a new discourse between the two.[175]

The "middle" approach that Rambo proposes calls for a Christian theology of witness without which "theology fails to provide sufficient account of redemption."[176] In commenting on the Gospel of John about the crucifixion of Jesus, Rambo highlights that "The Johannine Gospel presents us with a testimonial landscape in which witnesses struggle to make sense of life in the aftermath of death."[177] She focuses on events described in John chapter 20 concerning the complex experiences of witnessing to the death and post-resurrection of Jesus by Mary Magdalene and the beloved disciple. She points out that witnessing, loving, and remaining are the backdrop to the witnesses of Magdalene and the beloved disciple. She also notes that, theologically, love is about staying rather than dying and that remaining "is to be one who survives Jesus and the horrifying events of the cross."[178]

In light of the above analysis, in *Mbuki* culture, any violation of social rules leads to disastrous consequences on the part of the offendor. Likewise, in Scripture, any desobdedience to God's instructions breaks covenant with God, self, others, and creation. Thus, the *Mbuki* pact does not exclude issues of trauma since covenanters, and by extension their entire families/clans, become bound until death. According to the ritual, the *Mbuki* covenanters address each other by saying that, when one partner faces any problem or danger in life and the other does not support him/her, he/she would die by the blood he/she swallows. The same idea suggests that when a blood brother or blood sister suffers from trauma, it is essential that the blood partner support him/her until recovery. Failing to do so or doing otherwise would lead to the death of the covenant breaker.

Therefore, in addressing the complex issue of trauma, it is important that Christians in CAR understand that "The challenge of theological discourse

---

175. Rambo, 6.
176. Rambo, 8.
177. Rambo, 82.
178. Rambo, 96, 102.

is to articulate a different orientation to suffering that can speak to the invisibility, gaps, and repetitions constituting trauma."[179] It is thus important for churches and religious groups in CAR to include in the elements that emerge from the boy's call, the issue of trauma, which points towards the need for a theology of reconciliation to incorporate responses to that issue.

4. Conclusion

Although many Centrafricans are disconnected from rituals and ancestral knowledge, it is essential to understand that, as mentioned earlier, theological insights emerge from the scriptural interpretation of the *Mbuki* ritual for a theology of reconciliation. These are: (1) Jesus Christ the "new *Mbuki*" (new covenant) who reconciles humanity with God, (2) his death is sufficient to forgive, save, heal, and unite divided societies, (3) the blood of Jesus has broken all barriers and made ethnic divides the new humanity in Christ, and (4) the covenant of Christ is permanent and eternal, and cares more than *Mbuki* does for the oppressed, orphans and the widows.

In conducting a Bible study in the Twi vernacular language to understand the depth of Scripture, "especially in relation to the realities of indigenous culture,"[180] a group of believers in Akropong, Ghana, critically analysed the epistle to Hebrews (1:3) and came to the following significant conclusion:

> The greater point of interest of the passage centred on the Twi verb *dwiraa*, for the time of year was *Odwira*, the traditional New Year festival which, because it marks the end of one year and the start of a new year, is above all, a festival of purification, reconciliation and renewal. As it happened, it was as we began to analyse the *Odwira* festival itself and its leading ideas that it seemed to have occurred to our group members that *Odwira* had something to do with Jesus, and that the atoning work of Jesus could be related to the traditional *Odwira* ritual and its anticipated benefits.[181]

---

179. Rambo, 169.
180. Bediako, *Christianity in Africa*, 70.
181. Bediako, 71.

In the CAR context, analysis of some passages of the Sango Bible has shown that the translation of some key verses in the *Mbéti ti Nzapa* has borrowed French words. It is possible that the translators of the Sango Bible did not integrate the understanding of the vernacular language (in this case, the Sango *lingua franca*) with the interpretation of Scripture and cultural traditions. In exploring the significance of Bible translation for biblical exegesis and Christian mission, Bediako argues that people's first encounter with Scripture was made possible through the "process of mission by translation that produced the Scriptures of the Christian Church."[182] This idea suggests that Bible translation and mother-tongue Scripture are, or should be, part of the church mission. It is, therefore, essential for theologians and Bible translators in CAR to re-examine their approach in order to produce a version of the Bible that takes into account cultural and traditional realities, thus enabling Christians to understand Scripture in their own languages and contexts.

The notion of *Mbuki* is similar to that of *Ummah* in the Muslim context, and both aim to build and maintain community ties. *Mbuki* is about sharing blood in order to ensure life, a good life for individuals and the community. In Scripture, the ultimate *Mbuki* came from Jesus Christ, who was the sacrificial victim and the High Priest, offering his blood for the eternal redemption for lost humanity. As Azandé blood brothers exchanged blood to unite their clans, Christ became the ultimate *Mbuki* "to bring unity to all things in heaven and on earth under [him]" (Ephesians 1:9). Furthermore, if in the *Mbuki* worldview, people are concerned with creating and strengthening social relationships, then so is the *Ummah* in Islam. Jesus is the "new covenant" or new *Mbuki*. In this sense, he fulfils the traditional *Mbuki* to reconcile all humanity into one people. In him, therefore, unity between Christians and Muslims is possible, for he made the divided people into one reconciled people.

As examined in this book, Christians can validly turn the *Mbuki* ritual to Christ so that Christ interprets it and reveals what he fulfils within the practice and what needs to be modified or purified. However, in exploring *Mbuki*, the notion of reparation as an aspect of reconciliation is not clear. To the best of my knowledge, sources on *Mbuki* do not make explicit reference to reparation and its process. Other cultural practices may have applied it.

---

182. Bediako, "Biblical Exegesis," 13.

CHAPTER 11

Conclusion and Recommendations

1. Introduction

This book is entititled, "The Gospel Intepreting Cultural Traditions for Reconciliation: A Theological Reflection on *Mbuki* Blood Pact in CAR." It aimed to answer the main question: "To what extent can the insights into the traditional *Mbuki* ritual bring about an emerging theology of reconciliation in CAR?" The concern was also to know what fundamental factors underlined the 2013 conflict and how parties involved in the conflict resolution approached it. Another significant issue in this book was to understand whether the characteristics of *Mbuki* are relevant to reconciliation. I addressed how the gospel could engage with these characteristics towards a Christian response to reconciliation. In order to explore this, I analysed the significant contribution of *Fambul Tok* as a background to the study of peace and reconciliation in CAR.

Analysing *Mbuki* as an alternative approach to peace and reconciliation in CAR, in comparison to the approaches applied so far was an attempt to explore how it can be a catalyst for reconciliation. The difficulty of sustaining indigenous processes and promoting traditional leadership for reconciliation has been a serious concern for this study. Although all cultural and traditional practices have not been totally lost or eradicated, those that were fundamental to preserving the CAR's primal heritage were suppressed. I showed that the practice of *Mbuki* rituals was widespread and bound many ethnic groups in CAR, prohibiting any breaking of the rules. However, during the armed conflict, several people broke the *Mbuki* pacts that bound them with others through their ancestors, injuring and killing each other.

In this study, I also analysed *Fambul Tok* as a healing process at a community-level in Sierra Leone in order to understand how it has provided, or continues to provide key insights into the reconciliation processes in that country. The purpose is to examine how it can inform the *Mbuki* ritual practice to achive peace and reconciliation in CAR. Thus, the study shows that *Fambul Tok* emphasized forgiveness as well as truth, justice, reparation, peace, and reconciliation. Although the conflict context and background in Sierra Leone are different from CAR, I have nevertheless argued that the insights brought by this indigenous process are universal and extend beyond the scope of the context. Therefore, given that indigenous processes and leadership have been sidelined in the search for reconciliation in CAR, this background study has provided helpful insights to understand and implement effective peace processes.

The book also showed that attempts to explain the factors underlying the conflict in CAR have led various groups of people and officials, both internal and external, to label it as a political, economic, or religious conflict. During field research, some respondents pointed to the power and ambition of political leaders, others pointed to the rebels' greed for mineral resources. However, the majority of interviewees emphasized that external factors fuelled the 2013 conflict by manipulating and instrumentalizing Christian and Muslim communities to promote violence. Some have even argued that the influence and control of some external powers over the conflict through regional and international organizations implied a geo-political stake. In the search for peace and reconciliation, rebel groups and government officials have signed several peace agreements that have always failed. The main reason was that initiatives under the guidance of the international community sidelined the indigenous initiatives and leadership.

Thus, I argued that if Centrafricans understood and applied the insights into *Mbuki*, it would open the way for peace and reconciliation to be achieved. Although some Christians and Muslims have tried to shelter some threatened communities and people who have fled the atrocities of gunmen since the outbreak of the 2013 conflict by providing to the needy, much remains to be done. The responsibility of Christians and Muslims in CAR consists perhaps in working beyond what has been done, to explore, understand, and explain to people how traditional values are essential for peace and reconciliation. It is also important, as part of a theology of reconciliation and Christian responsibility, to work for the healing from trauma of desperate men, widows, orphans, and the disenfranchised in order to regain their humanity and welcome them into communities. Thus, the contribution of *Mbuki* is to provide them with insights into conveying messages that encourage people to build a harmonious coexistence and reconciliation with others.

I also attempted to assess how Scripture engages with *Mbuki*. From the analysis so far, the following insights are derived from the study of *Mbuki*. These comprise (1) Christ the "new *Mbuki*" reconciles all things with God, (2) Christ's death is ultimate to forgive, save, heal, and unite divided societies, (3) his blood has broken the wall of ethnic divisions, and (4) his covenant is permanent and eternal, and cares more than *Mbuki*. These ideas could enable Christians in CAR to adequately interpret the ritual practice according to Scripture and derive more biblical/theological insights from it. Doing so will allow a better understanding of the practice to inform a Christian response to conflict transformation and reconciliation. It is, therefore, essential that Christians not only teach, but also live by the example of love, unity, tolerance, fellowship, caring and sharing, truth, justice, forgiveness, and cohesion. In this sense, these values represent the marks of mission or the call of Christians to the mission of reconciliation.

In the theological exploration of the practice, I showed how the *Mbuki* ritual would have an impact on reconciliation theology in terms of Christology and soteriology, ecclesiology and eschatology, and the ethics of reconciliation. For example, writing on forgiveness and Christian ethics, Anthony Bash argues that, although the disciplines of psychology, philosophy, politics, or law also address the notion of forgiveness, the contribution of Christian theology is more significant because it brings in Christian ethics.[1] The ethical dimension of reconciliation emerges when Centrafricans strive to value humanity, sustain life, and maintain social bonds. When Centrafricans promote the ethics of reconciliation, they promote the culture of non-violence, tolerance, and conflict transformation. In the *Mbuki* rituals, the exchange of blood between blood brothers, the sacrifice of animals and the sharing of food to seal a blood pact, as well as the exchange of small boys or girls reveal

---

1. Bash, *Forgiveness and Christian Ethics*, ix.

a soteriological dimension of reconciliation. This soteriological dimension refers to Jesus as the *Ngassambanga ti Nzapa* (lamb of God) and the *New Mbuki* that forgives, saves, and reconciles.

Mbuki also allows for the emergence of an ecclesiology of reconciliation as part of a theology of reconciliation. Danny Hunter argues that "reimagining the church as an alternative community provides the clearest way forward toward becoming ambassadors of reconciliation."[2] Rudolf Gaisie, in his analysis on St. Cyprian, points out that in a context of violence, "the local church can make considerable strides in responding to political conflict if she works in, and maintains, internal unity."[3] The analysis of *Mbuki* reveals that it promotes human fellowship, unity, harmony, togetherness, solidarity, and cohesion. If churches in CAR promote values that derive from the *Mbuki* principles, it opens the way for greater impact, as an alternative community that maintains internal unity and towards conflict transformation and reconciliation.

Indeed, reconciliation cannot be regarded as final, as there is always reconciliation to be done. Therefore, reconciliation becomes part of an eschatological event for Schreiter points out that,

> ... *reconciliation will only be complete when all things have been reconciled in Christ*. Because all of creation is interconnected, only when everything and everyone has been reconciled at the end of time (cf. Eph. 1:10; Col. 1:20–21), will God be 'all in all' (1 Cor. 15:28). God is not only the author of reconciliation. God is also the end toward which it moves. Thus that every attempt at reconciliation remains incomplete does not surprise us. But we live in hope that God will indeed bring this all about.[4]

The study on *Mbuki* contributes to the understanding that God is in the full process of restoring and reconciling creation. Thus, the appropriation and implementation of indigenous concepts provide new paradigms for a theology of reconciliation.

---

2. Hunter, "Radical Ecclesiology," 76.
3. Gaisie, "St Cyprian of Carthage and Conflict Transformation."
4. Schreiter, "Peacemaking and Reconciliation," 640 (Italics are from the author).

2. Significance of the Study

The first major point of significance in this study relates to the analysis of the reconciliation process in Sierra Leone as a background study to the CAR context. As one significant finding, the thesis showed that in reconciliation processes, there are a variety of methods or approaches. Although the processes have not been the same in each conflict context, they proved to be community-based processes of reconciliation and sustainable peace. The analysis helped to understand not only the variety of indigenous approaches relevant to peace and reconciliation processes, but also to assess how they could contribute to informing *Mbuki* in the CAR context and beyond.

Second, the study is significant because it explored the essence of an existing ritual, and its possile contribution to peace to contemporary times. As in the case of CAR, many attempts at peace and reconciliation in Africa have failed because people have sidelined their primal roots, cultural heritage, and traditional leadership. Moreover, many among the younger generation are not aware of the contribution of indigenous concepts and ritual practices to peace and reconciliation. This is partly due to the policy that has caused the loss of fundamental cultural and traditional heritage of people. This makes the study significant in relation to the search for reconciliation.

Third, the study is significant because it used action research to collect primary data through intensive field research, which is not a common research method. Assumptions and misinterpretations have distorted the truth about the conflict. Therefore, this approach helped to identify myself as a member of the researched group while remaining a researcher in order to understand the difficult conditions of people, and to assess responses with the research participants. The approach enabled the researcher and the participants to propose alternatives to remedy the inadequacy and inefficiency of reconciliation processes. Added to this, the recommendations that emerge from the analysis make the study significant because they aim to help Centrafricans and the authorities see their role in enabling indigenous initiatives to contribute to better conflict transformation and reconciliation.

3. Rationale for Key Recommendations

During the field research, nine categories of people or groups participated in interviews. Although, in this book I explored the responses provided by them, here the recommendations are limited to five categories of people: the government, traditonal leaders, armed groups, Christians and CAR Muslims. The rational for this selection is that these groups are dominant in terms of decision-making and actions, while the other groups (such as youth, women, or NGOs) are included in one or other of the groups studied here. Therefore, if these categories of people implement the recommendations I have suggested in this book, it may open the way for a more positive effect on the search for reconciliation and bringing about change in the country.

3.1 Recommendations to the Government

It is critical for the Government of CAR to involve traditional leaders in peace processes, whether at local, national, or regional/international level. This could commence with the creation of local branches of the CVJRR to accompany and facilitate the investigations that the Commission, established by the state authorities in July 2021, was charged for. It is important, in the composition of these local branches, to incorporate traditional leaders to contribute to the effectiveness of the investigations and the hearing processes. The status, function, and work of traditional leaders requires strengthening through new government legislation. The purpose of the legislation would be to upgrade and empower traditional leaders to impact their status, functions, and allowances, so that it enhances their participation in full-fledged bodies of justice, peace and reconciliation at local and national levels.

To promote sustainable peace and reconciliation, it is essential that state authorities also enact legislation on peace education. Many institutions in sub-Saharan Africa include a curriculum of peace education in their agenda. They embrace peace education as a process of acquiring "knowledge, skills, attitudes and values needed" that leads to changes in the behaviour of children, youth and adults, enabling them "to prevent conflict and violence, both overt and structural, to resolve conflict peacefully, and to create the conditions conducive to peace, whether at intrapersonal, intergroup, national or international level."[5] Peace education is therefore relevant in a post-conflict context because, as Olowatoyin Olusegun Olowo suggested about Nigeria, its

---

5. Alimba, "Peace Education," 340.

agenda includes respect of life, non-violence, sharing, tolerance and solidarity, equality and democracy.[6]

In CAR, it is important to include teaching on traditional moral concepts and practices that emphasize respect for elders, human dignity, community spirit, mutual assistance, interdependence, tolerance, forgiveness, and many other values that bind people in traditional societies. It could include the study of initiation rites, blood pacts and non-violent insurgencies to promote knowledge of CAR history. These educational activities will require the writing, editing, and printing of new textbooks that assist in explaining the primal worldviews that existed in every ethnic group. This has important implications for the use CAR languages as well as French.

The organizing cultural festivals that occur throughout the academic calendar is a way to encourage students to learn and participate in songs, dances and folklores related to their cultures and ethnic groups. These could be organized through the Ministry of Art and Culture and the Ministry of Education. This will be an effective way for students from primary, secondary, and tertiary levels to learn and gain practical understanding of their roots, culture, and tradition and to apply the values they have learned to build their future and their relations with others. This form of education will also help them acquire knowledge and skills and have a positive effect on their understanding of the imperative of cohesion, conflict resolution, reconciliation and peace in communities and the country as a whole.

Another key area to bring to the attention of government authorities relates to the importance of research and the collection of indigenous knowledge. This implies that officials from the Ministry of National Education can contribute to the organization of training for students and young people using educational manuals that they would design for this purpose. In addition, indigenous researchers could also participate in this process by collecting stories from elders about tribes and ethnic groups and their traditional practices in their own languages, which could then be recorded in books to facilitate their use in teaching programmes. It would then require translation into other CAR languages and French. The researchers will also collect and document the stories of tribal wars, methods of conflict resolution, and reconciliation

---

6. Olowo, "Effects of Integrating," 10.

rites of each ethnic group which will be used to produce documents that will provide a wealth of research and knowledge for the younger generation.

As noted in the study, enacted laws and bodies dealing with disarmament programmes or with reparation for victims related to previous conflicts have failed due to lack of follow-up, mismanagement and other shortcomings. In addition to establishing official bodies to investigate truth and apply justice, it is important that the government ensure that expectations of people are met regarding reparation, in particular. Furthermore, it is the responsibility of the government to monitor peacekeepers and other force troops operating in the country. Most often, their misconduct has led to violations of human rights and other forms of crimes that deserve prosecution; violations which peacekeeping officials deny. It is important that CAR authorities draw the attention of peacekeeping member states to the issues of misconduct by some peacekeeper soldiers – those that merit prosecution – and the need for law enforcement.

Apart from the "Journée Internationale de la Paix" (International Peace Day) that is celebrated every year in CAR, it is essential that the government establish a "Journée Nationale pour la Réconciliation" (National Day of Reconciliation) in memory of the victims of the conflict. This will give every Centrafrican the opportunity to reflect on how to move forward and build peaceful relations with others, as blood brothers or blood sisters. Furthermore, in its efforts towards national cohesion and reconciliation, it is important for the government to prioritize reparation for victims as one of the fundamental aspects of effective reconciliation. However, national, hybrid and international courts continue to prosecute perpetrators of crimes and human rights violations, in particular leaders of armed groups and perpetrators of crimes, in order to bring justice to victims.

3.2 Recommendations to Traditional Leaders

I explained how respondents claimed that the role of traditional leaders in CAR was not recognized. It is important that those who hold positions of community leadership carry out their duties with honour and consideration so that people respect their authority and value their work. Despite the government's neglect of traditional leaders and the tight control of public administration over the judicial system at local level, traditional leaders are the custodians of culture and tradition. They know the customs, ritual practices, and the mother tongues of the local population. Thus, they are the best placed to contribute to mediation, justice, forgiveness, and reconciliation in their communities.

Some traditional leaders were accused of being morally corrupt and others of being involved in armed groups. Being involved in armed groups is risky for themselves, their family members, and their local population. Moreover, such a practice is against the law. It is, therefore, essential that indigenous leaders demonstrate moral fairness not by being involved, but by reporting criminal acts in their areas to security forces. It is also essential that they reject corruption while managing conflict issues for which they have legitimacy.

The loss of appreciation for the role of traditional leaders is a result of a lack of their being organized into an active council. Indigenous leaders themselves have a critical role to play by putting into place an active council that would include neighbourhood chiefs, village chiefs, sultans and lamido. This will help them to hold regular, if not annual, summit meetings to discuss issues related to their functions and challenges vis-à-vis their local populations and the government, as well as issues concerning the nation. These initiatives would have the potential to enable their functions to be recognized widely by citizens and state representatives, as their voices are heard.

3.3 Recommendations to Armed Groups

In CAR, the armed conflict was fuelled by the support of political leaders desperate for power. Evidence has shown that external hands have helped some political leaders to foment the rebellion, which has resulted in thousands of casualties, half the population living in IDP camps or in refugee camps in neighbouring countries, child soldiers, and many other humanitarian consequences. It is, therefore, crucial that these leaders align themselves with the democratic principle that the country can only be ruled through elections and not through violence. Since their criminal actions have caused distress and desolation in the country, they need to face justice, whether national or international, and to repair the damage their actions have caused or continue to cause.

In the conflict, there were also people who often have been forcefully involved in armed groups. It is important that they stop committing atrocities and engage in dialogue with their comrades-in-arms to opt for peaceful solutions. This would require those who take advantage of insecurity and violence to extort people or loot the herds of transhumant Fulani to cease such activities, as their actions have only fuelled more violence. The best option for them to emerge from a life of violence is to join the disarmament programme (DDRR) that has already started. However, as their actions during the fighting resulted in rape, murder, torture, abduction of young girls and boys, burning of villages, looting and the like, they will be held accountable and face justice for their crimes.

There are foreign mercenaries who have committed serious crimes during the conflict. Since 2013, they have signed agreements with government representatives, yet often violated them. It is vital that they respect the ceasefire agreements and peace recommendations for the sake of forgiveness, reconciliation, and peace. It is also imperative that they face justice, as the national, the SCC and the ICC are working on prosecution cases, and repair the crimes they have committed.

3.4 Recommendations to Christians

Past colonial and missionary proclamation have resulted in the loss of traditional heritage in CAR because it has led the majority of Christians to consider, for example, the practice of libation, sacrifice, and ancestor worship as idol-worshipping. Western colonialists and missionaries regarded the stories, tales, riddles, and proverbs as outdated and not modern practices. Thomas Christensen argues that African proverbs contain words that "always have the potential for becoming 'good-new-words' when brought into the service of the word of God, Christ Jesus."[7] Church leaders have a profound primal heritage to explore of the CAR songs, proverbs, or rituals. They have a lot to explore in *Mbuki*. Within this indigenous knowledge, there are definitive "sparks of truth,"[8] which the gospel and Christ affirm and which they can in their sermons demonstrate the truths of Scripture and of their cultural heritage. This would involve looking closely at songs, dance, and rituals, as performed

---

7. Christensen, "A Meeting of Biblical," 221.

8. Christaller, *Three Thousand*, ix. In his preface to the Christaller's book, Peter Kwasi Sarpong states that, "Proverbs deal with every aspect of human life, religious, moral, spiritual, political, economic, corporal, cultural, pragmatic, utilitarian, psychological and social. They contain deep theology about the nature, attributes, and activities of God. They also contain significant truths about human nature and how we ought to comport ourselves in life." See Peter Kwasi Sarpong, "Forward" in Christaller, *Three Thousand*, ii.

within ethnic groups, as well as proverbs, tales, and riddles to understand their insights and relevant contribution to achieving peace and reconciliation.

As I explained above, Christians have much to learn from culture and tradition. It is essential that they be open to learning about the affinities between some practices in CAR tradition and in Christian tradition. Christian leaders can provide avenues for learning through teaching, seminar workshops, youth camps, women's meetings, and similar gatherings during which they address the contribution of some traditional practices to the Christian faith and how the gospel interprets the *Mbuki* cultural practice. For example, respect for the elders was an essential moral rule in traditional societies. Such a rule is found among the moral laws in the Scripture. For instance, Leviticus 19:32 reads, *A lingbi mo loundou, mo louti na gbè lé jo so kouali ti lo avoulou, na mo yè kia lè ti mbakoro jo, na mo kpè mbito ti Nzapa ti mo – Mbi yèké l'Eternel!* (You have to get up, to stand there in the presence of the one with white hair, and you honour the elderly, and you fear your God - I am the Lord!).

The 2013 conflict affected the relations between Christians and Muslims in several parts of the country. The interfaith platform, including the leaders of Roman Catholics, Evangelicals and Muslims, has been at the forefront of the search for reconciliation. Thus, to strengthen further relations between the two communities, it is essential that the platform organize interfaith gatherings that enable Christians and Muslims to address various issues that undermine their relationships. In doing so, they will be able to understand the values of religious tolerance/freedom, coexistence, acceptance of the other, and mutual respect, which are key elements for peace and reconciliation. All this is ecompassed in *Mbuki* as described earlier in this book. Moreover, the thesis argued that it is possible to achieve an effective reconciliation on what unites the two communities. Therefore, it is important for Christians and church leaders to take the initiative to organize such meetings and involve their Muslim fellow-citizens. *Fambul Tok* succeeds in contributing to healing individuals and communities in Sierra Leone thanks to this approach.

In an interview, Mbaye-Bondoi revealed that many young Christians from evangelical churches have been involved in the violence. As a pastor and member of the "Commission Nationale des Droits de l'Homme et des Libertés Fondamentales" (National Commission on Human Rights and Fundamental Freedoms), he and his team visited prisons throughout the country. He noticed that some of those who were in youth ministries in the evangelical churches were in prison for participating in the conflict. It is possible that many other young Christians are in this condition and have not been arrested. Church leaders and all Christians have an important role to play in setting up a transitional justice process in parallel with the official judicial system. As this study showed, *Fambul Tok* emphasizes restorative justice in which victims and their perpetrators come face-to-face before the community for justice. This common approach will enable church members who have been involved in violence in CAR to take responsibility for the consequences of their actions, to ask for forgiveness and to commit themselves to reparation.

I have outlined above the necessity for the churches in CAR to provide a theological and spiritual response to the issue of trauma. As the study of trauma is recent, having started in the aftermath of the Vietnam War, African scholars are not yet fully involved in trauma research. Further studies are needed to help churches respond to victims of trauma in different contexts of conflict.

3.5 Recommendations to CAR Muslims

Relations between Christians and Muslims have become more affected and the resolution of the conflict has become complex because of foreign Muslims who have infiltrated CAR's Muslims and become involved in conflict. The former urged the latter not to give up, but to continue the violence.[9] In other words, the presence of Muslims and Fulani foreigners among the Séléka fighters fuelled the conflict.[10] In Bangui, in some Muslim areas such as the Km 5 neighbourhood, groups of bandits have taken Muslim civilians hostage by extorting them and imposing taxes on their goods. It is critical that CAR Muslims distance themselves from the criminals and report their plans and actions to the security forces in order to apprehend them.

Abdul Moumi Hussein argues that the Qur'an "is the truth" and teaches that Allah rewards a person who forgives a wrong committed against him or her.[11] It is clear from principles such as this that Imams have a basis to encourage faithful Muslims to follow such an Islamic principle so as not to resort to violence or revenge. In 2021, when a group of criminals entered

---

9. Mbaye-Bondoi, Interview, 24 July 2021.
10. Soudess Mouktar, Interview, 7 April 2021, Bouar.
11. Abdul Moumi Hussein, Interview, 8 April 2021 (Translation is mine).

Bouar, the senior Imam and his assistants went to meet the leader of the group and tell them to leave the locality. Bako Mamadou reported that, as they refused to do so,

> The imam appealed to other imams to have Muslims read a verse from the Qur'an every day that talks about protection. We had read it day and night, asking God to send the bandits away. Finally, they were gone and the Russians and the FACA came to Bouar. In this way, we understood the effectiveness of the Qur'an and we saw the greatness of God.[12]

Such an initiative and spiritual response gives hope for expelling armed groups from each community without violence. Furthermore, every Imam has the responsibility to exhort and involve Muslims in every mosque to prayer for the cessation of gunshots and violence. They could emphasize the importance of people engaging in rebuilding cohesion with others for effective peace and reconciliation to come, as learned from the lessons on *Mbuki* and the practice of *Fambul Tok*.

4. Implications for Christian Mission and Scholarship

As shown in this study, the Forum for World Evangelization reads that God is the first concerned with reconciliation. Emmanuel Katongole and Chris Rice also argue that reconciliation is "the mission of God."[13] They develop "ten theses" as guidelines for "recovering reconciliation as the mission of God."[14] This argument underlines the notion of *missio Dei*. It suggests that God is the initiator of the saving and reconciling mission for the benefit of humanity. It was (and still is) God's mission that Christ mandated the church to accomplish. This mandate makes the mission of reconciliation the *missio ecclesiae*. This understanding provides Christians with theological insights for evangelism and discipleship. In 2 Corinthians 5:18–21, Paul describes that mandate as follows:

---

12. Bako Mamadou, Interview, 9 April 2021, Bouar (Translation is mine).
13. Katongole and Rice, *Reconciling All Things*, Kindle, 142.
14. Katongole and Rice, 142–150.

¹⁸Mais yé kouè ayèké ti Nzapa, Lo so assala si ani ga songo na Lo na lègué ti Christ, na Lo mou na ani koussala ti sala si ani ga songo; ¹⁹so atèné, Nzapa ayèké na ya Christ ti sala si sessé so aga songo na Lo, Lo diko kèngo-ndia ti ala pèpé, na Lo mou na ani tèné ti sala songo. ²⁰Tonga so ani yèké abazènguèlé ti Christ, tèti Nzapa avoro i na yanga ti ani; ani hounda i mingui na iri ti Christ, i lèké songo na Nzapa. ²¹Lo so ahinga siokpari oko pèpé, Nzapa assala Lo ti ga siokpari tèti ani, si ani lingbi ga mbilimbili na Nzapa na ya Lo.

¹⁸But all this is from God, he who made us to reconcile to himself through Christ, and has given us the work of reconciliation; ¹⁹that means, God was in Christ to reconcile the world to himself, he did not take account of their rebellion, but gave us the message of reconciliation. ²⁰Therefore, we are the ambassadors for Christ, for God pleads with you by our mouths; we plead with you in the name of Christ, be reconciled to God. ²¹The one who never knew sin, God made him to become sin for us, so that we become righteous in God through him.

The question here is what it means for the Church to be entrusted with the mission of reconciliation or to be the "ambassadors for Christ." The spread and growth of Christianity in a context of violence and conflict that continues to tear apart CAR society and many societies of the world have important implications to interrogate in Christian mission studies. People and societies that experience armed conflict can learn from violence that occurs and divides communities, and ask themselves why such things happen. Christians in other African contexts have learned from the violence they have endured in recent years; although not all have learned, at least some have realized the horror of sin in human beings and the destructive evil that is conflict.

Another implication for Christian mission stems from the fact that dealing with trauma is part of the *missio Dei*. Therefore, the work of the Christian mission consists in integrating the issue of trauma as part of their mission work. This perspective enables researchers to conduct research in order to propose effective methods and responses for the redemption of the victims of trauma.

Profound implications for scholarship have also emerged from this reflection. Researchers are needed to investigate aspects of cultural traditions that are relevant to contribute to peacebuilding and reconstruction. These aspects will include further exploration of the insights of songs, proverbs, dances, proverbs, tales, riddles, and life stories of people who stood for non-violence. It is, therefore, essential for scholars in countries torn apart by violence and conflict in Africa and beyond, to develop approaches to peace education for people at academic level. Peace education can also benefit people at non-academic level. These approaches would build on the sources of cultural traditions and methods of conflict resolution and reconciliation to include peace analysis, reconciliation, truth, forgiveness, justice, tolerance, and nation-building.

5. Conclusion

This book contributed to reconciliation efforts and aimed to help augment the initiatives undertaken so far for successful results in CAR. It has shown that the *Mbuki* ritual practice explored so far has the potential to address issues of conflict and to provide responses to reconciliation efforts in the country. It can also provide new paradigms for a theology of reconciliation, as the lessons learned from it form the basis of Christian faith.

It also argued that the analysis of *Mbuki* allows understanding that the ritual contains and conveys values of humanity, respect for others, fellowship, truth, justice, forgiveness, peace, protection, and well-being; which transcend cultural and geographical barriers. These values are essential to initiate and maintain a harmonious and sustainable reconciliation. To this end, efforts to settle conflicts and promote reconciliation at the local or national level can draw on the *Mbuki* pre-Christian heritage from which the concepts above and values derive. Furthermore, the ritual takes on a deeper meaning when interpreted through Scripture. It is, therefore, in a way, God's witness, as it can positively contribute to building harmony and cohesion.

Bediako points out that, "If the God of African pre-Christian tradition has turned out to be the God of the Christians, then it is to be expected that He has not left Himself without testimony in the past."[15] This statement shows that every good thing that comes out of African pre-Christian past and cultural traditions testifies to God. This is the case for the *Mbuki*. This

---

15. Bediako, *Christianity in Africa*, 225.

understanding is essential to help churches in CAR fulfil their prophetic call and the work of reconciliation.

To conclude, on the question whether it is possible to continue to use cultural traditions (such as the *Mbuki* tradition) in the present context, Tychique Nzouketia replied in an interview that people in villages could apply cultural traditions without problem; however, "Those in cities cannot. The youth and city urbans are uprooted. They are familiar with the modern civilisation not with tradition: books, television, internet, and so on."[16] According to Nzouketia, the younger generation has lost their culture and tradition because of modern education and lifestyle. However, although the younger generation is disconnected from cultural traditions, it is possible to educate them on how to reconnect with their own past.

---

16. Tychique Reggy Reo-Olar Nzouketia, Interview, 17 July 2021, Bangui.

APPENDIX 1

Interview Questions

(Translated from Sango into English).

1.1 Common questions to all groups

Nzorôko ti hounda _____ Lango ti hounda tèné _____
Interview No. _____ Date _____

Ndo _____ Iri ti zo so a hounda tèné _____
Location _____ Name of Interviewer _____

Nzorôko ti mo: Kôli _____ Wâli _____
Gender: Male _____ Female _____

Ngou ti mo: 15–24 ___ 25–34 ___ 35–44 ___ 45–54 ___ 55 wala a hôn so ___
Age: 15–24 ___ 25–34 ___ 35–44 ___ 45–54 ___ 55 or above ___

Séwa ti mo: Kumbämbä ___ Mariyazi ___ Kangbi tèlé ___ Kangbi séwa ___ Wa mouwa ___
Marital Status: Single ___ Married ___ Separated ___ Divorced ___ Widow/er ___

Dä mbéti: pèpé ___ Kêtê dä mbéti ___ Kota dä mbéti ___ Dä sénda guigui ___ Tènè nï ___
Education: None ___ Primary ___ Secondary ___ University ___ Others, Specify ___

Nzapa ti gnê mo sala? Wamabé ___ Musilimi ___ Nzapa ti a kotara ___ Oko apë ___

What is your Religion? / Christian ___ Muslim ___ Traditional Religion ___ None ___

Mo yéké wamabé? Ti da Nzapa wa?
If you are a Christian, which church do you attend?

Mo yéké Musilimi? Mo sambéla na ndo wa?
If you are a Muslim, where is your area of worship?

Mo sambéla nzapa ti a kotare wa?
If you are from the Traditional Religion what shrines are in your family house or do you go.

Conflict, peace, and reconciliation questions to all groups

1. (a) Na bibé ti mo, a gnê la a yéké na gonda ti a bira Kwê na Bê-Afrika?
   (b) Gnê la a fä tonga so?
   (a) According to you, what are the root causes of conflicts in the CAR? Please, explain:
   (b) What justifies your arguments?

2. (a) A yé gnê a yéké na göndä ti a bira so a fouti ködörö ti Bê-Afrika? Na guigui ___ Na ya kodro ___ Hinga apê ___ Mbéni yé ndé ___
   (b) A yé ni yéké gnê, nga na légué wa?
   (a) What factors foster or aggravate armed conflicts in CAR? External ___ Internal ___ Don't know ___ Other ___
   (b) What are the factors and how?

3. (a) Sôngô na pöpö ti a wamabé na a Musilimi kozo ni si bira ti ngou 2013 a tonda ni a yéké tonga na gnê? Nzoni ___ Nzoni apê ___ Hinga apê ___
   (b) Mo tèné sôngô ni a yéké tonga na gnê?
   (a) How was the coexistence between Christians and Muslims before the 2013 conflict? Good ___ Not good ___ Don't know ___
   (b) If 'Yes' or 'No', please explain what the coexistence was like.

4. (a) Bira so a fouti sôngô na pöpö ti a Wamabé na a Musilimi? Ta tèné/Ta tèné apê.
   (b) Tonga na a yéké ta tèné, na légué gnê?
   (c) Tonga na a yéké ta tèné apê, ndali ti gnê ala tèné tonga so?

Interview Questions

199

(d) Mo lingbi fa na guigui mbéni yé oko so a bian sôngô na pöpö ti a Wamabé na a Musilimi?

(a) Has the conflict affected the relationship between Christians and Muslims? Yes/No.

(b) If Yes, in what ways has it affected the relationship?

(c) If No, what leads you to think this way?

(d) What example can you give of a broken relationship between Christians and Muslims?

5 (a) Na lé ti mo, ndali ti gnê a tourougou toumba ti Séléka a ngba ti sala sioni na azo?

(b) Ndali ti gnê ala ngba ti tiri bira?

(a) What do you think are the motives for the Séléka rebels to continue the abuses?

(b) Why do you think the rebels keep fighting?

6 (a) Na lé ti mo, ndali ti gnê a Anti-Balaka a ngba ti sala sioni na azo?

(b) Ndali ti gnê ala ngba ti tiri bira?

(a) What do you think are the motives for the Anti-Balaka militias to continue the abuses?

(b) Why do you think the rebels keep fighting?

7 (a) A yé ti kpalé wa si mo wara na ya bira so?

(b) Yé gnê mo sala ti sigui na ya ti a kpalé ni?

(a) What specific problems have you encountered since the outbreak of this conflict?

(b) How did you handle them?

8 Na lé ti mo, na légué gnê si lèkére ngo tèné ti sîrîri na légué ti a mbaïé na tango ti a kotara a lingbi ti mou mabôko na sîrîri na Bê-Africa? Na légué gnê?

In your opinion, what insights from songs, proverbs, stories, and traditional wisdom can a person use to convey the message of peace and reconciliation.

9 (a) Fa mbéni tèné ti ndara ti a kotara so a sala tèné ti bira, sîrîri wala léngo sôngô so ala hinga.

(b) Ndä ni a yéké gnê?

(a) Cite a proverb or a saying related to conflict, reconciliation, or peace that you know.
(b) What does it mean?

10 (a) Yé gnê si mo hinga na ndo mbèlé ti mênë so a boumbi a mara na ngoï ti a kotara?
(b) Ndara ti gnê si mbèlé ti mênë a lingbi èdé ti kpingba sîrîri na Bê-Afrika?
(a) Do you know anything about the practices of *Mbuki* in the history of the CAR? Yes/No.
(b) If Yes, what insights could be drawn from the practice of blood-brotherhood to help consolidate peace in the CAR today?

11 (a) Na légué gnê a zo a sala yé ti âkötarä sö?
(b) Zo gnê si a lingbi boungbî na salangö Mbuki tî mênê?
(c) Yé tî nzönî ti gnê a lingbi ti na tönga na azo so a yéda na ndia ti Mbuki? Yé ti sioni gnê a lingbi si na zo so a ke ndiä ti Mbuki?
(d) Yé tî âkötarä na légué ti Mbuki a a yéké lêgëöko töngana na so mbéti ti Nzapa a fa?
(a) How did people perform it in your culture?
(b) Who participated in the *Mbuki* ritual?
(c) What were the benefits of *Mbuki*? What were the consequences of breaking the pact?
(d) Is there continuity or discontinuity between blood pacts in African societies and the covenant of God in the Christian tradition?

12 (a) Na lé ti mo, gövöröma a mou mabôko na koussala ti fangô ngbanga ti a kotara na Bê-Africa? Ta tèné/Ta téné apê.
(b) Nda ni a yéké gnê?
(c) Tonga na gnê a mokonzi a lingbi èdé ti kiri na sôngô na sîrîri?
(a) Do CAR people recognize and value the role of traditional leaders in the search for reconciliation? Yes/No.
(b) What could be the reasons?
(c) How could the customary/traditional chiefs contribute to peace and reconciliation?

13 (a) Na lé ti mo, a mokonzi na lingbi ti mou mabôko na sîrîri na Bê-Afrika? Ala lingbi/ala lingbi apê.
(b) Tonga na mo lingbi, na légué gnê?

(c) Tèné ti gnê mo lingbi apê?
(a) According to you, can the indigenous leaders contribute to the effective resolution of the ongoing conflict? Yes/No.
(b) If Yes, how can they contribute?
(c) If No, why not?

14 (a) Na bibé ti mo, ndä ti embargo so Nations Unies a bi na ndô FACA a yéké gnê?
(b) Tèné ti embargo so a yéké na légué ni? Ta tèné/Ta tèné apê.
(c) Ndäli ti gnê?
(a) In your opinion, what are the reasons for the embargo imposed on the armed forced (FACA)?
(b) Are the reasons for this embargo legal and justified?
(c) Why do you think so?

15 (a) Yé gnê si a sala si lèkére ngo tèné ti sîrîri na Bê-Afrika a ga nzoni pèpé?
(b) Tèné ti gnê mo tèné tonga so?
(a) What were the main reasons for the failure of peace processes?
(b) Why do you say so?

16 (a) Mo ba tèné ti kota pätärä na sûngo mbéti ti Khartoum na popo ti a tourougou kpalé na gövöröma tonga na gnê?
(b) A wa soungo mabôko na gbélè kota mbéti so a kpé ndia ni? Ta tèné/Ta tèné ape
(c) Na légué gnê ala kpé ndia ni apê?
(a) What do you understand from the Khartoum political agreement signed in February 2019 between the fourteen armed groups and the government?
(b) Do the parties comply with the agreement? Yes/No.
(c) In what ways did the parties comply or not comply with it?

17 (a) Bibé ti mo na ndö koussala ti Plateforme ti gâ na siriri a yéké tonga na gnê? Nzoni ___ Nzoni apê ___ Wala mbéni ye ndé ___ Hinga apê ___
(b) Ndali ti gnê mo tèné tonga sö?
(a) What is your opinion of the Inter-Religious Platform's search for peace and reconciliation? Effective ___ Useless ___ Other ___ Don't know ___
(b) What is the reason for your answer?

18 Yé gnê mo lîngbi tèné na ndö koussala ti ngbanga tèné ti a zo so a bâa passi na ya bira so?
  (a) Tèné ti dä ngbanga na Bê-Afrika;
  (b) Tèné ti kota dä fa ngo ngbanga;
  (c) Tèné ti kota dä ngbanga ti dünia mobimba.
  What do you think about the efficacy and reliability of the three jurisdictions and the request for justice for the victims?
  (a) The national jurisdictions
  (b) The Special Criminal Court
  (c) The International Criminal Court.

19 (a) Fangô ngbanga ti âkötarä a lingbi èdé ti kiri na sîrîri nga na sôngô na Bê-Afrika? A lingbi/a lingbi ape.
  (b) Ndali ti gnê?
  (c) Na légué gnê fangô ngbanga ti âkötarä a lingbi èdé ti kiri na sîrîri?
  (a) Is indigenous justice essential for restoration of peace in the CAR? Yes/No.
  (b) Why do you think so?
  (c) To what extent can indigenous justice contribute to peace?

20 (a) Dä ti fangô ngbanga (Commission Vérité Justice Réconciliation et Rapatriement) a yéké nzoni ti lèkére tèné ti bira na ti kiri na siriri na Bê-Afrika? Ta tèné/Ta tèné apê.
  (b) Yé gnê si ala kou na mbégué ti kota ndö ti ngbanga so?
  (a) Do you think that the Truth Justice Reparation and Reconciliation Commission is essential to resolve the conflict issues that the country has experienced? Yes/No.
  (b) What are your expectations of that commission?

21 (a) Bibé ti mo na ndô koussala ti a turûgu ti Minusca a yéké gnê?
  (b) Koussala ti Minusca ti kiri na sîrîri a nzërë na bé ti a zo? Ta tèné/Ta tèné apê.
  (c) Fa bibé ti ala:
  (a) What do you think is the role of the United Nations Mission in the CAR (Minusca)?
  (b) Does the mission satisfy the population in terms of peacekeeping? Yes/No.
  (c) Please, explain:

22. (a) Koussala ti béndo ti guigui na a ködörö so mou mabôko ti kiri tènè ti sîrîri na Bê-Afrika a yéké nzoni na lé ti ala? Ta tèné/Ta tèné apê.
    (b) Mo fa ndä ni.
    (c) Yé gnê si mo kou na mbégué ti béndo ti guigui na a ködörö so?
    (a) Do you support the peace process that the United Nations and other institutions and countries are carrying out in the CAR? Yes/No.
    (b) Could you please explain the reason(s)?
    (c) What are your expectations vis-à-vis these countries and institutions?

23. Ye gnê mo yé ti tènè a bian na légué ti léngo sôngô na Bê-Afrika?
    What are your expectations for changes in the process of the peace and reconciliation in the CAR?

1.2 Questions to Specific Groups

Church Members

1. (a) Mbéti ti Nzapa a lingbi ti kiri tènè na a bira to Bê-Afrika? A lingbi/A Lingbi apê.
   (b) Tonga na a lingbi, na légué gnê?
   (c) Tonga na a lingbi apê, ndali ti gnê?
   (a) Is the Bible, the word of God, effective to address the problems of conflict that the CAR faces? Yes/No.
   (b) If Yes, how can it address the problem?
   (c) If No, why not?

2. (a) A kotä mamâ tènè wa si a gbôtô na ya fangô tènè ti Nzapa na ndo tènè ti léngo sôngô na ya da Nzapa ti mo?
   (b) Mo lingbi ti fa tènè kété na ndô a fangô tènè so?
   (a) What are the most important themes in relation to reconciliation that emerge from Bible sermons in your church?
   (b) Can you give a brief description of these sermons?

3. (a) A boï ti Nzapa a lingbi fa tènè ti Nzapa na légué ti mbaïe na ndara ti a kotara si a zo lingbi ti hinga léngo sôngô? Ta tèné /Ta tèné apê.
   (b) Tonga na ala sala ape, a yéké nzoni a boï ti Nzapa a sala tonga so? Ta tèné /Ta tèné apê.
   (c) Tonga na gnê si ala lingbi ti sala ni?

(a) Do your church leaders often use stories, proverbs, and African wisdom to illustrate and convey the message of peace and reconciliation? Yes/No.
(b) If No, do you think that they can do it? Yes/No.
(c) How can they do it?

4 (a) Dä Nzapa ti mo a yéké èdé a zo so kpé akpé bira?
Gnê la si dä Nzapa ti mo a sala ti èdé a zo so kpé akpé bira?
(b) Tonga dä Nzapa ti mo a sala apê, nda ni a yéké gnê?
(c) Tonga na dä Nzapa ti mo a mou mabôko, na légué gnê ala sala ni?
(a) Does your local church assist the internally displaced people? Yes/No.
(b) If it does provide assistance, what does it do?
(c) If No, why?

Church ministers

1 (a) A kota mama tèné ti Nzapa so ala fa a yéké gnê?
(b) Ala fa tèné ti Nzapa na do tèné ti léngo songo?
(c) Tonga na ala sala ni, na ya mbéti ti gnê?
(d) Tonga na ala sala apê, ndali ti gnê?
(a) What are some of the themes of sermons you preach?
(b) Do you ever preach about peace and reconciliation? Yes/No.
(c) If yes, what Bible passages do you use or emphasize?
(d) If no, why not?

2 (a) Tonga na boï ti Nzapa, na ya fangô tèné, ala mou tèné ti mbaïé na ti a ndara ti a kotara ti èdé a wamabé si ala ma ya ti tèné ti sôngô na siriri? Ta tèné /Ta tèné apê.
(b) Tonga na ala sala ape, ala ba a yéké nzoni ti sala tonga so? Ta tèné/Ta tèné apê.
(c) Na légué gnê?
(a) As church leader, do you often use stories, proverbs, and African wisdom to illustrate and convey the message of peace and reconciliation? Yes/No.
(b) If No, do you think that you can do it? Yes/No.
(c) How can you do it?

3 (a) Dä Nzapa ti ala a êdë a zo so akpé bira?
(b) Tonga na ala sala, yé gnê si ala sala?

(c) Tèné ti gnê ala sala apê?
(a) Does your local church assist IDPs? Yes/No.
(b) In case it assists displaced people, what does it do?
(c) If No, why?

4 (a) Dä Nzapa ti ala a sala koussala ti kiri na sôngô na pöpö ti a membre?
(b) Tonga na ala sala, ye gnê ala sala?
(c) Tonga na ala sala apê, tèné ti gnê?
(d) Dä Nzapa ti ala a sala koussala ti kiri na sôngô na ya väkä/ködörö? E sala/E sala apê.
(e) Tonga na ala sala, yé gnê ala sala?
(f) Tonga ala sala apê, tèné ti gnê?
(g) Tonga na boï ti Nzapa, yé gnê ala lingbi sala si dä Nzapa ti ala a èdé na légué ti kiringo na sôngô na pöpö ti a zo?
(a) Is your church involved in resolving conflicts among the church members? Yes/No.
(b) If Yes, what does it do?
(c) If No, why not?
(d) Does your church play a social cohesion role in the community? Yes/No.
(e) If Yes, what does it do?
(f) If No, why not?
(g) As a church minister, what can you do to involve your church in the search for peace in your community?

The Youth

1 (a) Ala hinga a yé ti a kotara so a lingbi mou sîrîri, a yé so a masséka a glissa la so?
(b) A yé so a yéké gnê?
(c) Na lé ti ala, na légué gnê si a yé ti a kotara a lingbi èdé si siriri na sôngô na kiri na Bê-Afrika?
(a) Do you know any cultural or traditional values essential for addressing issues related to peace and reconciliation that young people lost today? Yes/No.
(b) If Yes, which ones?

(c) In your opinion, how can these values help contribute to peace and reconciliation in CAR?

2. (a) A masséka a yéké mou mabôko na kiringo na sôngô na Bê-Afrika?
   (b) Na légué gnê?
   (a) Are the youth helping to restore peace in CAR? Yes/No.
   (b) If Yes, how do they contribute?

Women

1. (a) A wali a yéké tiri bira tèné ti a masséka wali so a sala lissolo ti koubou na ala na ngangou, nga na a wali a hou pönö ndali ti bira so?
   (b) Yé gnê a yéké sala?
   (c) Tonga na ala sala ape, tonga na gnê si ala lingbi èdé a masséka wali na ya väkä/ködörö ti ala?
   (a) Are women taking action to solve the problem of rape against girls and women and the trauma they have suffered in your community? Yes/No.
   (b) If Yes, what are they actually doing?
   (c) If Not, how can they do to solve these problems and initiate social cohesion within the community?

2. Yé gnê si a wali a lingbi sala ti kiri na sôngô na ya väkä/ködörö ti ala? How can women contribute to restoration of peace in CAR?

CAR Muslim Citizens

1. (a) Coran a sala tèné ti kaï bira na ya ködörö? A sala/A sala apê.
   (b) Tonga na a sala, na légué gnê ?
   (c) Tonga a sala apê, ndali ti gnê?
   (a) Is the Qur'an effective in addressing the problems of conflict that the CAR faces? Yes/No.
   (b) If Yes, how can it address them?
   (c) If No, why not?

2. (a) Mbéti ti Coran a fa légué ti siriri na ngoi ti bira ? A fa/A fa apê.
   (b) Tonga na ape, ala lingbi sala kété na ndo ni ?
   (c) Fango tèné na ya Mosquée a sala tènê ti sîrîri? A sala/A sala apê.

(d) A kotä mamâ tènê wa si a gbôtô na ya Coran na ndo tènê ti léngo sôngô na ya Mosquée?
(e) Tonga na a sala apê, nda ni a yéké gnê?
(a) Does the Qur'an teach how to seek peace in the context of conflict? Yes/No.
(b) If Yes, can you give a brief description?
(c) Do the Qur'anic teachings at the mosque address the question? Yes/No.
(d) If Yes, what are the most important themes that emerge from these teachings?
(e) If No, why not?

3 (a) Ala hinga azo so akpé bira na ya väkä/ködörö ti ala?
(b) Ala sala gnê ti mou mabôko na azo so apê bira?
(a) Do you know internally displaced peoples or those who have lost everything due to the conflict? Yes/No.
(b) What did your mosque do to assist them?

4 (a) Tonga na Musilimi ti na Bê-Afrika, ala mou mabôko ti kiri na sîrîri na ködörö?
(b) Tonga na ala sala ni, na légué gnê?
(c) Tonga na ala sala apê, nda ni a yéké gnê?
(a) As a CAR Muslim, are you contributing to the restoration of peace in the CAR? Yes/No.
(b) If Yes, how?
(c) If No, why not?

5 Yé gnê si ala kou:
(a) Na mbégué ti gövöröma?
(b) Na mbégué ti a wamabé?
What are your expectations?
(a) Vis-à-vis the government
(b) Vis-à-vis the Christian population.

Government Employees

1 (a) Na lé ti ala, a yé ti a kotara wa si a mara ti Bê-Afrika a lingbi ti mou na ti lèkére na ködörö si léngo sôngô a ga? A lingbi/A lingbi apê.
(b) Ala lingbi di iri ti a yé ti a kotara so ala hinga?

(c) Tonga na a lingbi ape, tèné ndani a yéké gnê?

(a) In your opinion, are there cultural or traditional values capable of promoting or strengthening patriotism, social cohesion, and reconciliation in CAR? Yes/No.

(b) If Yes, name some values you know.

(c) If No, please explain.

2   (a) Ndö koussala ti ala (parlement, police, armée, éducation, justice, etc.) a èdé ti kiri na sîrîri na Bê-Afrika?

(b) Na légué gnê?

(c) Ala ba so légué ti koussala ni a lingbi kiri na siriri?

(d) Ala sala tèné Kêtê na ndö ni.

(a) Does your sector of activity (parliament, police, army, education, justice, etc.) help restore peace? Yes/No.

(b) If Yes, how does it do it?

(c) Do you think that such a contribution is effective and sufficient? Yes/No

(d) Please give further detail.

NGOs and UN Employees

1   (a) A yé a bian na légué ti sîrîri na ngoi so a tourougou ti bendo ti guigui a tonda ti koussala na Bê-Afrika?

(b) Yé gnê a bian?

(c) Tonga na a yé a bian ape, nda ni a yéké gnê?

(a) Have there been changes in the security situation in the CAR since Minusca became involved in stabilizing peace? Yes/No.

(b) If Yes, please state what has changed?

(c) If Not, please explain why.

2   (a) A molengué ti Bê-Afrika a yéké na nguia na koussala ti Minusca?

(b) Ye gnê a fa so ala yéké na nguia?

(c) Tinga na ala yéké na nguia ape, nda ni a yéké gnê?

(a) Are the civilian population satisfied with the results of Minusca in terms of security? Yes/No.

(b) If Yes, please state what justifies it.

(c) If Not, why not?

The Inter-Religious Platform

1 Ala yéké membre ti Plateforeme, ye gnê ala lingbi tèné na ndo koussala ti Plateforme ti kiri na sîrîri na Bê-Afrika?
   As a member of the platform, what is the outcome of your efforts for restoring peace and reconciliation in the CAR?

2 Maï ngo ti gnê si ala ba na légué ti koussala ti Plateforme?
   What progress has been made in this process?

3 Kpalé ti gnê si ala wara na ya koussala ti Plateforme ti ga na sîrîri na Bê-Afrika?
   Can you briefly describe the difficulties you have encountered in the ongoing conflict resolution process?

Traditional Leaders

1 (a) Ala mou télé ti ala na koussala ti kiri ngo na sîrîri na ya ködörö?
   (b) Na légué gnê?
   (c) Tonga na ala sala apê, nda ni a yéké gnê?
   (a) As a traditional leader, are you involved in the process of conflict resolution at local or national level? Yes/No.
   (b) If Yes, how do you proceed?
   (c) If No, why not?

2 (a) Ngöbö ti gövöröma na bendo ti guigui ti kiri na sîrîri a yéké nzoni na lé ti ala?
   (b) Fa bibé ti ala.
   (c) Yé gnê ala lingbi sala?
   (a) Do you think the peace process put in place by the government, the UN and the CAR partners is effective? Yes/No.
   (b) Please, explain further.
   (c) What reform do you think they can bring to this process?

APPENDIX 2

Focus Group Discussions

(Translated from Sango into English)

Tènè ti hounda na ya boumbi
(Questions for group discussions)

1) Yé gnê a yéké sôngô na sîrîri a yéké gnê?
What do you understand by reconciliation and by peace?

2) Ti a zo na ya ködörö/väkä ti ala, sôngô na sîrîri a yéké gnê? Bibé ti ala na ndo tènè ti sîrîri a yéké ndé na ti a mbéni a zo?
How do people in your community understand it? Does their understanding of peace and reconciliation differ from other people's understanding?

3) Bira ti Bê-Afrika a yéké tènè ti a wamabé na a Musilimi? Fa bibé ti ala:
Is the current conflict a war between Christians and Muslims? Please, explain:

4) A yé gnê si a kânga légué na kîrî ngo na sîrîri nga na léngo sôngô na ya ködörö/väkä ti ala?
What are the shortcomings in the process of peace and reconciliation in your community?

5) Na légué gnê si a kpale so a fouti douti ti ala nga na ti a zo na ya ködörö/väkä to ala?
How do these shortcomings affect your life and your community?

6) Ala hinga mbéni mamâ tènè ti âkötarä wala tènè ti ndara so a lingbi bian bangö ndo ti a zo na tènè ti sôngô na ya ködörö/väkä ti ala?

Mention a traditional concept capable of shaping people's perception on reconciliation in your context.

7) Yé gnê ala hinga na a Mbuki ti mèné ti âkötarä to lëkërë tènè ti bira na ti kpingba siriri?
What do you know about the practice of blood-brotherhood in the traditional era to resolve conflicts and consolidate peace?

8) Ala wala a zo ti ködrö/väkä ti ala a yéké mou mabôko na a zo so a zia da ti ala ti kpé bira so?
Do you or your community assist internally displaced people from other communities?

9) Ala lingbi sala gnê ti kiri na tâ sôngô na ya ködrö/väkä ti ala?
What would you do to achieve lasting reconciliation?

10) A kota ndo kwa ti ködrörö a lingbi sala gnê ti kiri na sîrîri na Bê-Afrika?
What should the public institutions do to achieve sustainable peace?

11) A wamabé na a Musilimi a lingbi sala gnê ti yé tërë na popo ti ala na ti lëkërë sôngô?
What should Christians and Muslims do to accept each other and to be reconciled?

12) Fadé ala sala gnê si a tourougou toumba so a sala sioni na ya ködörö nga na a zo a lingbi ga nzoni?
What should you do to re-integrate rebels so they become good citizens in spite of the wrongs they committed?

Bibliography

Adrake, K. D. "Mission and Reconciliation from a Christian-Muslim Relations Perspective: The Case of PROCMURA in Africa." *International Review of Mission*, Vol. 110, no. 1. (2021): 145–155. doi: 10.1111/irom.12360.
Partie 2/2. 12 December 2020. https://www.youtube.com/watch?v=t7Kx5uIyuB0.
Afriyie, E. "The Theology of the *Okuapehene*'s *Odwira*: An Illustration of the Engagement of the Gospel and Culture Among the Akan of Akropong-Akuapem." PhD Diss., Akrofi-Christaller Institute of Theology, 2010.
Ajiambo, D. "In Central Africa, a Cathedral Shelters Muslims Amid Sectarian Violence." 24 April 2020. https://www.ncronline.org/news/world/central-africa-cathedral-shelters-muslims-amid-sectarian-violence.
Al Jazeera News. "CAR Government Signs Deal with Rebel Groups." 28 April 2020. https://www.aljazeera.com/news/2017/06/car-government-signs-peace-deal-rebel-groups-170619175516668.html.
Alie, J. A. D. "Reconciliation and Traditional Justice: Tradition-Based Practices of the *Kpaa Mende* in Sierra Leone." In *Traditional Justice and Reconciliation after Violent Conflict: Learning from African Experiences*, edited by Luc Haye and Mark Salter, 122–146. Stockholm: IDEA, 2008.
Alimba, C. N. "Peace Education, Transformation of Higher Education and Youth Empowerment for Peace in Africa." *International Journal of Scientific and Technology Research*. Vol. 2, Issue 12 (2013): 338–347.
Amnesty International. 2021. "République Centrafricaine. Arrestation et Transfert à la CPI d'un Ancien Leader du Groupe Armé de la Séléka: Un Espoir de Justice pour les Victimes." 24 March 2022. https://www.amnesty.org/fr/latest/news/2021/01/central-african-republic-arrest-and-transfer-of-former-seleka-armed-group-leader/.
ANOM. "GGAEF 4(3) D 16. Le Petit Temps, No. 2710 (16 Mai 1909).", 4 March 2022.
———. "GGAEF 4(3) D 16. Politique à l'égard des Sultans du M'Bomou (1909–1917)." 4 March 2022.

———. "GGAEF 5 D 87d (1928–1959), Les Missions Catholiques en Afrique Equatoriale Française." 25 February 2022.

———. "GGAEF 5 D 47, Oubangui-Chari: Situation Politique en Haute-Sangha, Lobaye, Bouar, Bambari (1931–1932) – Operations de Police dans la Région d'Amada Gaza, No. 70/CMS." 1 March 2022.

———. "GGAEF 5D 95–96, Confidentielle, No. 3861/430 (19 Mai 1932)." 8 March 2022.

———. "Direction des Affaires Politiques, Kimbanguisme No. 575/c (21 Juillet 1932)." 8 March 2022.

———. "Affaires Politiques No. 831. Note sur la Mise en Valeur des Territoires de l'Oubangui-Chari (14 Décembre 1934)." 3 March 2022.

———. "GGAEF 5 D 95–96, Esclavage: Rapport de la Commission Consultative d'experts – Société des Nations, n° Official C. 189 M 145." Vol. VI (1936): 1–99. 8 March 2022.

———. "GGAEF 5 D 87d, Dossier en Communication, No. 1645/APA (3 Juillet 1952)." 25 February 2022.

Arendt, H. *The Human Condition*. Chicago: University of Chicago Press, 1958.

Asante, M. K. "Azande." In *Encyclopedia of African Religion*, edited by Molefi Kete Asante and Ama Mazama, 84. London: Sage Publications Ltd, 2009.

Autesserre, S. *Peaceland: Conflict Resolution and Everyday Politics of International Intervention*. Cambridge: Cambridge University Press, 2014.

Azumah, J. "Fault Lines in African Christian Responses to Islam." In *The African Christian and Islam*, edited by John Azumah and Lamin Sanneh, 125–146. Carlisle: Langham Academic, 2013.

Bagayoko, N. *Comparative Study of Transitional Justice in Africa: Central African Republic*. Johannesburg: The Centre for the Study of Violence and Reconciliation, 2018.

Baker, G. *Central African Republic: Violence and Genocide – Ethnic Conflict Political Unrest, and Religious Crises*. N. P.: Sonit Education Academy, 2016.

Balcomb, A. "Primal or Indigenous: A Critical Assessment of an Ongoing Debate on African Religion." *Brill: Religion and Theology*. Vol. 28. (2021): 1–19. doi:10.1163/15743012-bja10015.

Bambi, J. "Protesters in Bangui Call for Expulsion of MINUSCA Staff." *Africa News*. 25 April 2020. https://www.africanews.com/2020/02/18/protesters-in-bangui-call-for-expulsion-of-minusca-staff-morning-call/.

Bash, A. *Forgiveness and Christian Ethics*. Cambridge: Cambridge University Press, 2007.

Battle, M. A "Theology of Community: The Ubuntu Theology of Desmond Tutu." *Interpretation: A Journal of Bible and Theology*. Vol. 54, No. 2 (2000):173–182.

Bediako, K. "Biblical Exegesis in Africa: The Significance of the Translated Scriptures." In *African Theology on the Way: Current Conversations,* edited by Diane B. Stinton, 12–20. London: SPCK, 2010.

———. *Christianity in Africa: The Renewal of a Non-Western Religion.* Akropong-Akuapem: Regnum Africa, 2014.

———. *Jesus in African Culture: A Ghanaian Perspective.* Accra: Asempa Publishers, 1990.

———. "Scripture as the Hermeneutic of Culture and Tradition." *Journal of African Christian Thought.* Vol. 4, no. 1 (2001): 2–11.

———. "Gospel and Culture: Some Insights for our Time from the Experience of the Earliest Church." *Journal of African Christian Thought.* Vol. 2, no. 2 (1999): 8–17.

Beevor, E. "How Rebels Became Kingmakers in the Central African Republic." *Analysis.* 21 April 2020. https://www.iiss.org/blogs/analysis/2019/04/central-african-republic-armed-groups.

Begg, C. T. "Sacrifice." In *The Oxford Companion to the Bible,* edited by Bruce M. Metzger and Michael D. Coogan, 666–67. Oxford: Oxford University Press, 1993.

Beidelman, T. O. "The Blood Covenant and the Concept of Blood in Ukaguru." *Africa: Journal of the International African Institute* 33, no. 4 (1963): 321–342.

Berg, P. "The Dynamics of Conflict in the Tri-Border Region of the Sudan, Chad, and the Central African Republic." *County Conflict-Analysis Studies,* 1–50 (8 April 2020). https://library.fes.de/pdf-files/iez/05423.pdf.

———. "A Crisis-Complex, Not Complex Crises: Conflict Dynamics in the Sudan, Chad, and Central African Republic Tri-Border Area," 72–86 (8 April 2020). https://library.fes.de/pdf-files/ipg/ipg-2008-4/08_a_berg_gb.pdf.

Bissengue, V. *Les Maux de la République Centrafricaine: Infantilisation, Arrogance, Nihilisme, Kôbetîyângâ.* Paris: L'Harmattan, 2021.

Bissengué, V. and P. Indo, *Barthélemy Boganda: Héritage et Vision.* Paris: L'Harmattan, 2018.

Bjørn, M. "Africa's Sub-Regional Organisations: Seamless Web or Patchwork?" *Crisis States Research Centre Working Paper,* no. 56. 13, 1–31 (April 2020). http://www.lse.ac.uk/international-development/Assets/Documents/PDFs/csrc-working-papers-phase-two/wp56.2-africa-sub-regional-organisations.pdf.

Bloomfield, D. "Reconciliation: An Introduction." In *Reconciliation After Violent Conflict: A Handbook,* edited by David Bloomfield, Theresa Barnes and Luc Huyse, 10–18. Stockholm: IDEA, 2003.

Bongoyok, M. "The African Christian and Muslim Militancy." In *The African Christian and Islam,* edited by John Azumah and Lamin Sanneh, 193–217. Carlisle: Langham Academic, 2013.

Bonsu, N. O. "African Traditional Religion: An Examination of Terminologies Used for Describing the Indigenous Faith of African People, Using an Afrocentric Paradigm." *Africology: The Journal of Pan African Studies* 9, no. 9 (2016): 108–121.

Bouessel, C. "Central Africans Still Waiting for Truth Commission." *Justice Info*, 7 May 2020. https://www.justiceinfo.net/en/truth-commissions/41344-central-africans-still-waiting-for-truth-commission.html.

Bouwknegt, T. B. "Between Truth, Justice and Tradition: Transitional Justice in Africa – A Case Study on the Truth Reconciliation Commission for Sierra Leone, the Special Court for Sierra Leone and Fambul Tok." *Peace Palace Library*, 7 May 2020. https://www.peacepalacelibrary.nl/ebooks/files/338446338.pdf.

Bozanga, S. S. "Dialogue National centrafricain." 11 April 2020. http://dialogue.national.free.fr/.

Bradshaw, R., and J. Fandos-Rius. *Historical Dictionary of the Central African Republic*. New Edition. London: Rowman & Littlefield, 2016.

Bridger, J. S. *Christian Exegesis of the Qur'an: A Critical Analysis of the Apologetic Use of the Qur'an in Select Medieval and Contemporary Arabic Texts*. Cambridge: James Clarke & Co, 2016.

Brosig, M., and N. Sempijja. "Does Peacekeeping Reduce Violence? Assessing Comprehensive Security of Contemporary Peace Operations in Africa. *Stability: International Journal of Security and Development* 7, no 1 (2018): 1–23. doi:10.5334/sta.576.

Broughton, G. "Restorative Justice: Opportunities for Christian Engagement." *International Journal of Public Theology*. Vol. 3 (2009): A–B. doi: 10.1163/156973209X438265.

Broodryk, A., and H. Solomon. "From War Economies to Peace Economies in Africa." *Scientia Militaria, South African Journal of Military Studies* 38, no 1 (2010): 1–24. doi:10.5787/38-1-77.

Brown, M. J., and M. J. Zahar. "Social Cohesion as Peacebuilding in the Central African Republic and Beyond." *Journal of Peacebuilding and Development* 10, no 1 (2015): 10–24. doi: 10.1080/15423166.2015.1008349.

Brueggemann, W. *The Prophetic Imagination*. Minneapolis: Fortress Press, 2001.

The Third Lausanne Congress. "Building the Peace of Christ in our Divided and Broken World." *The Cape Town Commitment: A Confession of Faith and a Call to Action*. Forward by Doug Birdsall and Lindsay Brown. 21 April 2024. https://lausanne.org/wp-content/uploads/2021/10/The-Cape-Town-Commitment---Pages-20-09-2021.pdf.

Burchard, S. "The Central African Conflict is About Far More than Religion." *Think Africa Press*, 24 April 2020. https://thinkafricapress.com/identity-politics-coding-religion/.

Campo, J. E. *Encyclopedia of Islam*. New York: Facts On File, 2009.
Clár, N. C. "Central African Republic Still a Powder Keg, Warn Clerics Awarded Peace Prize." *The Guardian,* 21 August 2015. https://www.theguardian.com/global-development/2015/aug/21/central-african-republic-powder-keg-sergio-vieira-de-mello-prize-interfaith-peace-platform.
Carayannis, T., and L. Lombard. "Making Sense of CAR: Introduction." In *Making Sense of the Central African Republic,* edited by Tatiana Carayannis and Louisa Lombard, 53–75. London: Zed Books, 2015.
Castle, B. *Reconciling One and All: God's Gift to the World*. London: Society for Promoting Christian Knowledge, 2002.
Castelino, N. "Central African Republic: Another Episode in a History of Pillage." *Economic and Political Weekly* 14, no. 45 (1979): 1835–1836.
Caulker, J. "Introducing Fambul Tok: Community Healing in Sierra Leone." YouTube video, 11 February 2020. https://www.youtube.com/watch?v=YllEnuPMe2g.
Chauvin, E. *La Guerre en Centrafrique à l'ombre du Tchad: Une Escalade Conflictuelle Régionale ?* Paris:Agence Française de Développement, 2018.
Chauvin, E. et al. 2015 "Le contrôle des ressources dans une guerre civile régionalisée (Centrafrique). Une dynamique de décentralisation par les armes," *Cahiers d'outre-Mer,* Octobre-Décembre 2015, 1–124; https://journals.openedition.org/com/7617#tocto1n2.
Chianeque, L. C., and S. Ngewa. "Deuteronomy." In *Africa Bible Commentary,* edited by Tokunboh Adeyemo, 369–442. Nairobi: WorldAlive Publishers, 2006.
Chilisa, B. *Indigenous Research Methodologies*. London: SAGE Publications, 2012.
Christaller, J. G. *Three Thousand Six Hundred Ghanaian Proverbs. From the Asante and Fante Language*. Translated by Kofi Ron Lange; Lewiston: The Edwin Mellen Press, 2000.
Christensen, T. "Rites of Reconciliation in Traditional Gbaya Society." In *Grafting Old Rootstock: Studies in Culture and Religion of the Chamba, Duru, Fula, and Gbaya of Cameroun,* edited by Philip A. Noss, 369–442. Dallas: International Museum of Cultures, 1982.
———. "Karnu: Witchdoctor or Prophet?" In *Grafting Old Rootstock: Studies in Culture and Religion of the Chamba, Duru, Fula, and Gbaya of Cameroon,* edited by Philip A. Noss. Dallas: International Meseum of Cultures, 1982.
———. "A Meeting of Biblical Wisdom with Gbaya Wisdom." In *Grafting the Old Rootstock: Studies in Culture and Religion of the Chamba, Duru, Fula, and Gbaya of Cameroun,* edited by Philip A. Noss, 221–31 Dallas: International Museum of Cultures, 1982.
———. *An African Tree of Life*. Maryknoll: Orbis Books, 1990.

Cilliers, J. et al. "Sierra Leone: Does Reconciliation Heal the Wounds of War?" *Innovations for Poverty Action*, 22 April 2024. https://poverty-action.org/sites/default/files/publications/Sierra%20Leone%20Reconciliation_Policy%20Memo_IPA.pdf

Clark, P. *The Gacaca Courts, Post-Genocide Justice and Reconciliation in Rwanda: Justice Without Lawyers*. Cambridge: Cambridge University Press, 2010.

Coppi, G. 2016 "Focus on Central African Republic." *L'Osservatorio*, 4 May 2020. http://www.losservatorio.org/images/CP/FocusOnCentral_African_Republic.pdf.

Council on Foreign Relations. "Violence in the Central African Republic." *Global Conflict Tracker*, 12 April 2020. https://www.cfr.org/interactive/global-conflict-tracker/conflict/violence-central-african-republic.

Courtney E. C. "All in the 'Fambul': A Case Study of Local/Global Approaches to Peacebuilding and Transitional Justice in Sierra Leone." *United States Institute of Peace,* 17 June 2022. https://www.usip.org/sites/default/files/files/case-study-competition/20130322-All-in-the-Fambul.pdf.

Cruvellier, T. 2018 "CAR Special Court Will Not Prosecute Child Soldiers." *Justice Info,* 30 April 2020. https://www.justiceinfo.net/en/tribunals/mixed-tribunals/39073-car-special-court-will-not-prosecute-child-soldiers.html.

Degras, A. *Tengbi ti Abakoro Zo: L'histoire officieuse du Nord-Ouest Oubanguien des Origines Préhistoriques à l'indépendance*. 3ᵉ Partie. Vice-Province Tchad-RCA: Frères Mineurs Capuciens, n.d.

Deiros, T. 2014 "Central African Republic: The Invention of a Religious Conflict." *IEEE,* 10 March 2020. http://www.ieee.es/en/Galerias/fichero/docs_opinion/2014/DIEEEO67-2014_RCA_InvencionConflictoReligioso_T.Deiros_ENGLISH.pdf.

Denètre, E. et H. Mechaï 2016. "Centrafrique – Opération Sangaris : Quand le Stress Post-traumatique s'en Mêne." *Le Point*, 15 August 2022. https://www.lepoint.fr/afrique/centrafrique-operation-sangaris-quand-le-stress-post-traumatique-s-en-mele-page-3-05-02-2016-2015667_3826.php#xtatc=INT-500.

Denov, M. *Child Soldiers: Sierra Leone's Revolutionary United Front*. Cambridge: Cambridge University Press, 2010.

Diatta, P. N. "Le concept de la réconciliation à la lumière du pacte de sang en Centrafrique et dans le christianisme." *Annales*. Année II, no. 2 (2010). Bangui: Paroisse Notre Dame d'Afrique.

Dick, B. "Postgraduate Program Using Action Research." *The Learning Organization*. Vol. 9, no. 3–4. (2002): 159–170. doi:10.1108/09696470210428886.

Dickson, K. A. *Theology in Africa*. Maryknoll: Orbis Books, 1984.

Dimanche, R. 2019 "Les méthodes traditionnelles de résolution des conflits à Obo." *Radio Ndeke Luka,* 25 January 2021. https://www.radiondekeluka.org/debats/e-le-songo/34096-les-methodes-traditionnelles-de-resolution-des-conflits-a-obo.html.

Documentary Educational Resources, "Fambul Tok – PREVIEW." YouTube video, 10 February 2020. https://www.youtube.com/watch?v=irLB6AXY_jw.

Dongombe, C. D. *L'Oubangui-Chari et son évangélisation dans le contexte de la politique colonial française en Afrique centrale: 1889–1960.* Paris: L'Harmattan, 2012.

Donovan, J. "A Timeless Way to Forge Bonds Between Men." In *Blood Brotherhood and Other Rites of Male Alliance,* edited by Nathan F. Miller and Jack Donovan, 5–10. Portland: Dissonant Hum, 2009.

Douba, H. "L'importance du jugement coutumier dans la résolution des conflits." *Radio Ndeke Luka,* 10 October 2019. https://www.radiondekeluka.org/debats/e-le-songo/33457-l-importance-du-jugement-coutumier-dans-la-resolution-des-conflits.html.

Douglas, J. D. and M. C. Tenney (eds.). *The New International Dictionary of the Bible.* Grand Rapids: Zondervan Publishing House, 1987.

Douglas-Bowers, D. "Colonialism, Coup and Conflict: The Violence in the Central African Republic." *Foreign Policy Journal,* 24 April 2020. http://www.foreignpolicyjournal.com.

El Gantri, R. "Pourquoi, en Centrafrique, les réparations doivent passer avant tout." *Justice Info,* 5 August 2021. https://www.justiceinfo.net/fr/75942-pourquoi-en-centrafrique-les-reparations-doivent-passer-avant-tout.html.

Endjito, F. "La guerre du pétrole en République centrafricaine." *Ecole de Guerre Economique,* 20 April 2020. https://infoguerre.fr/2018/12/guerre-petrole-republique-centrafricaine/.

Epaye, B. "Les conflits centrafricains et leurs règlements : de 1996 à 2003." In *Dialogue interlocuteur et culture de la paix en Afrique centrale et dans les Grands Lacs : le rôle des chefs traditionnels et spirituels dans les mécanismes de prévention et de résolution des conflits,* edited by Makhily Gassama, 114–155. Libreville:UNESCO, 2005.

Evans-Pritchard, E. E. "Zande Blood-Brotherhood." *Africa: Journal of the International African Institute,* Vol. 6, No. 4 (1933):369–401.

Fambul Tok Project. "Fambul Tok Filmmaker Interview - Complete." YouTube video, 12 February 2020. https://www.youtube.com/watch?v=vlDrIq78E9U.

Fancello, S. and A. Mary. "Institutions du pardon et politiques de la délivrance en Afrique de l'Ouest." *Journal des Africanistes.* Vol. 88, no. 2 (2018): 1–17.

Fanny P. "Reforme du franc CFA: les députés français mal informés par leurs techniciens." *Media Part,* 18 May 2020. https://blogs.mediapart.fr/fanny-pigeaud/blog/220220/reforme-du-franc-cfa-les-deputes-francais-mal-

informes-par-leurs-techniciens-0?fbclid=IwAR2w13HViyU3a_ajOFeIFNJay-6tgaNGRK7jO8dShwSM9j2ZbQ-epBhA8VE.
FIDH. "Central African Republic: A Country in the Hands of Seleka War Criminals." *FIDH*, 18 March 2020. https://www.fidh.org/IMG/pdf/rca616a2013basdef.pdf.
FIDH/LCDH. "Central African Republic: 'They Must All Leave or Die'- Answering War Crimes Against Humanity." *FIDH Investigative Report*, No. 636a, 13 April 2020. https://www.fidh.org/IMG/pdf/rapport_rca_2014-uk-04.pdf.
Fiedler, R. *The Contribution of the Interfaith Platform to the Reconciliation Process in the Central African Republic*. Geneva: Geneva Liaison of the World Evangelical Alliance, 2014.
———. *Making Peace a Reality – the Impact of the Interfaith Peace Platform on the Peace Process in the Central African Republic*. Geneva: Geneva Liaison of the World Evangelical Alliance, n.d.
Foster, K. "From War to Peace in the Central African Republic." *Harvard Politics*, 25 April 2020. https://harvardpolitics.com/world/car-peace/.
Fukuyama, F. *Identity: The Demand for Dignity and the Politics of Resentment*. New York: Farrar, Straus and Giroux, n.d.
Gaisie, R. K. "St Cyprian of Carthage and Conflict Transformation: Some Reflections from a West African perspective." *INFEMIT*, 15 August 2022. https://infemit.org/st-cyprian-carthage-conflict-transformation/.
Gandolfo, E. O. *The Power and Vulnerability of Love: A Theological Anthropology*. Minneapolis: Fortress Press, 2015.
Geneva Centre for Security Sector Governance. "Central African Republic Background Note." *ISSAT*, 29 April 2020. https://issat.dcaf.ch/Learn/Resource-Library/Country-Profiles/Central-African-Republic-Background-Note.
Genta, A. et al. "What Went Wrong in the Central African Republic? International Engagement and the Failure to Think Conflict Prevention." *Geneva Graduate Institute*, 16 March 2020. https://www.gpplatform.ch/sites/default/files/PP%2012%20-%20What%20went%20wrong%20in%20the%20Central%20African%20Republic%20-%20Mar%202015.pdf.
Giles, K. "Kingdom of God/Kingdom of Heaven." In *Dictionary of Jesus and the Gospels*, edited by Joel B. Green and Scot McKnight, 417–32. Downers Grove: InterVarsity Press, 1992.
Goins, S. *Forgiveness and Reintegration: How the Transformative Process of Forgiveness Impacts Child Soldier Reintegration*. Oxford: Regnum Books International, 2015.
Goyémidé, E. *Le dernier survivant de la caravane*. Paris: Hatier, 1985.
Harrison, A. *Blood Timber: How Europe Helped Fund War in the Central African Republic*. London: Global Witness, 2015.

Herbert, S. et al. *State Fragility in the Central African Republic: What Prompted the 2013 Coup? Rapid Literature Review*. Birmingham: University of Birmingham, 2013.

Herlehy, T. J. "Ties that Bind: Palm Wine and Blood-Brotherhood at the Kenya Coast During the 19th Century." *The International Journal of African Historical Studies* 17, no. 2 (1984): 285–308.

Hoffman, E. "Reconciliation in Sierra Leone: Local Processes Yield Global Lessons." *The Fletcher Forum of World Affairs* 32, no. 2 (2008): 129–141.

Hoffman, L. "Community Healing, from the Inside Out - Systems Lessons from Fambul Tok in Sierra Leone." *Catalyst For Peace,* 11 February 2020. http://www.catalystforpeace.org/catalyst/wp-content/uploads/2019/07/Community-Healing-From-the-Inside-Out-LH-chapter-2.pdf.

Howell, A. M. "Researching Gospel and Culture Issues: Tools of Research." *Journal of African Christian Thought*. Vol. 2, no. 2 (1999): 22–28.

———. *The Religious Itinerary of a Ghanaian People: The Kasena and the Christian Gospel*. Achimota: Africa Christian Press, 2001.

———. "Researching Gospel and Culture Issue: Process of Engagement and Tools of Research." Unpublished manuscript. ACI, 2022.

Human Rights Watch. *State of Anarchy: Rebellion and Abuses Against Civilians*. Vol. 19, no. 14. Human Rights Watch, 2007

———. "Background: The Varied Causes of Conflicts in CAR." *Human Rights Watch,* 18 March 2018. https://www.hrw.org/reports/2007/car0907/4.htm.

Humphreys, M., and J. M. Weinstein. "Who Fight? The Determinants Participation in Civil War." *American Journal of Political Science*. Vol. 52, no. 2 (2008): 436–455.

Hunter, D. "Radical Ecclesiology: The Church as an Arena for Reconciliation through Cultivating Alternative Community." *Missiology: An International Review*. Vol. 48, no. 1 (2019): 75–82. doi:10.1177/0091829619887391.

ICC. "Situation in Central African Republic II: Maxime Jeoffroy Eli Mokom Gawaka Surrendered to the ICC for Crimes against Humanity and War Crimes." *International Criminal Court,* 24 March 2022. https://www.icc-cpi.int/Pages/item.aspx?name=pr1646.

———. "Questions and Answers: Situation in the Central African Republic II – The Procurator v. Alfred Yekatom and Patrice-Edouard Ngaïssona." *International Crimncal Court,* 30 April 2020. https://www.icc-cpi.int/itemsDocuments/201912110-coc-hearing-carII-eng.pdf.

Idris, I. "Supporting Reconciliation in Post-Conflict Situations." *GSDRC Helpdesk Research*, No. 1343. Birmingham: University of Birmingham. (2016):1–14 (12 September 2019), http://www.gsdrc.org/wp-content/uploads/2016/04/HDQ1343-.pdf.

Ilham Nasser, M. A. "Forgiveness in the Arab and Islamic Contexts: Between Theology and Practice." *Journal of Religious Ethics*. Vol. 41, no. 3 (2013): 474–94.

International Crisis Group. "Central African Republic: Anatomy of a Phantom State." *Africa Report*, No. 136, 21 September 2019. https://d2071andvip0wj.cloudfront.net/central-african-republic-anatomy-of-a-phantom-state.pdf.

International Peace Information Service. *Central African Republic: A Conflict Mapping* Antwerp: Danish Institute for International Studies, 2018.

Isaacs-Martin, W. "The Motivations of Warlords and the Role of Militias in the Central African Republic." *Accord*, 6 April 2020. https://www.accord.org.za/conflict-trends/the-motivations-of-warlords-and-the-role-of-militias-in-the-central-african-republic/.

Jang, S. Y. "The Causes of the Sierra Leone Civil War: Underlying Grievances and the Role of the Revolutionary United Front." *International Relations*, 9 February 2020. https://www.e-ir.info/pdf/29018.

Kääriäinen, J. A. "The Gospel of Reconciliation and the Promise of a New Identity." *International Review of Mission*. Vol. 110, no. 2 (2021): 217–30.

Käihkö, I., and M. Utas. "The Crisis in the CAR: Navigating Myths and Interests." *Africa Spectrum*. Vol. 49, no. 1 (2014): 69–77.

Kaldor, M., and J. Vincent. "Evaluation of UNDP Assistance to Conflict-Affected Countries: Case Study Sierra Leone." *UNDP*, 9 February 2020. http://web.undp.org/evaluation/documents/thematic/conflict/SierraLeone.pdf.

Kaldor, M. *New and Old Wars: Organised Violence in a Global Era*. Third Edition. Malden: Polity Press, 2012.

Kappel, R. "Future Prospects for the CFA Franc Zone." *Intereconomics*, Vol. 28, no. 6 (1993): 268–84. doi:10.1007/BF02926213.

Kapolyo, J. "Matthew." In *Africa Bible Commentary*, edited by Tokunboh Adeyemo. Nairobi: WorldAlive Publishers, 2006.

Karan, E. *Kêtê bakarî tî Sängö: Farânzi, Angelëe na Yângâ tî Zâmani*. Bangui: SIL International, 1995.

Kassa, T. "Hebrews." In *Africa Bible Commentary*, edited by Tokunboh Adeyemo. Nairobi: WorldAlive Publishers, 2006.

Katongole, E. *The Sacrifice of Africa: A Political Theology for Africa*. Nairobi: African Theological Network Press, 2020.

———. *Born from Lament: The Theology and Politics of Hope in Africa*. Grand Rapids: Wm. B. Eerdmans Publishing Company, 2017.

Katongole, E., and C. Rice. *Reconciling All Things: A Christian Vision for Justice, Peace and Healing*. Downer Groves: InterVarsity Press, 2009.

Kertelge, K. "Dikaiosuné." In *Exegetical Dictionary of the New Testament*, Vol. 1, 326–330. Edited by Horst Balz and Gerhard Schneider. Edinburgh: T & T Clark, 1990.

King, J. C. "Demystifying Field Research." In *Surviving Field Research: Working in Violent and Difficult Situations,* edited by Chandra Lekha Sriram, John C. King, Julie Mertus, Olga Martin-Ortega, and Johanna Herman, 8–18. London & New York: Routledge, 2009.

Kirby, J. *Jesus of the Deep Forest: Prayers and Praises of Afua Kuma.* Accra: Asempa Publishers, 1981.

Klosowicz, R. "Central African Republic: Portrait of a Collapsed State after the Last Rebellion." *Politeja,* Vol. 3, no. 42 (2016):33-51. doi:10.12797/Politeja.13.2016.42.04.

Kossi, K. "La passation des valeurs ancestrales en perte de vitesse en RCA." *Radio Ndeke Luka,* 20 December 2019. https://www.radiondekeluka.org/debats/e-le-songo/34291-la-passation-des-valeurs-ancestrales-en-perte-de-vitesse-en-rca-htlm.

Kpamo, D. *La christianisation et les débuts du nationalisme en Oubangui-Chari de 1920 à 1960.* Paris: Publibook, 2013.

Kpatindé, F. "Pourquoi Bozizé a-t-il été lâché par ses frères?" *Radio France Internationale.* https://www.rfi.fr/fr/afrique/20130412-rca-bozize-deby-itno-sassou-nguesso-franc-macon-seleka.

La Poorta, J. J. "Justice." In *Global Dictionary of Theology,* edited by William A. Dyrness and Veli-Matti Kärkkäinen. Downer Groves: InterVarsity Press, 2008.

Langa, M. F. "The Role of Religion in the 21st Century Democracy: The Case of the Central African Republic." *ACADEMIA,* 24 April 2020; 1–16. http://www.academia.edu/243884.

Lasor, W. S. et al. *Old Testament Survey: The Message, Form, and Background of the Old Testament.* Second Edition. Grand Rapids: William B. Eerdmans Publishing Company, 1996.

Le Roux, E., Y. and Sandoua. "Leadership Responses during Armed Conflict." In *African Christian Leadership: Realities, Opportunities, and Impact,* edited by Robert J. Priest and Kirimi Barime, 85–101. Maryknoll: Orbis Books, 2017.

Locke, B. "The CFA Franc: A Stabilizing Franc or Neocolonial Relic in West Africa?" *Policy Brief: Brussels International Center for Research and Human Rights,* 8 May 2020. https://www.bic-rhr.com/sites/default/files/inline-files/Final%20Report-%20CFA%20Franc.pdf.

Lombard, L. *State of Rebellion: Violence and Intervention in the Central African Republic.* London: Zed Books, 2016.

———. "Central African Republic: Peacebuilding Without Peace." *SWP Comments,* no. 15. 20 December 2020.

Lovejoy, P. E., and S. Schwarz. "Sierra Leone in the Eighteenth and Nineteenth Centuries." In *Slavery, Abolition and the Transition to Colonialism in Sierra Leone,* edited by Paul E. Lovejoy and Suzanne Schwarz, 1–28. Trenton: Africa World Press, 2015.

Magesa, L. *African Religion: The Moral Traditions of Abundant Life*. Nairobi: Paulines Publications Africa, 1997.

Malchow, B. V. *Social Justice in the Hebrew Bible: What Is New and What Is Old*. Collegeville: The Liturgical Press, 1996.

Mangan, F. et al. "The 'Green Diamond': Coffee and Conflicts in the Central African Republic." *Special Report – United States Institute of Peace*, No. 464, 2020.

Marchant, B. "'Fambul Tok' Reveals the Power of Forgiveness - A Film Review by Brent Marchant." https://vividlife.me/ultimate/22325/fambul-tok-reveals-the-power-of-forgiveness/.

Marshall, R. "Being Rich, Being Poor: Wealth and Fear in the Central African Republic." In *Making Sense of the Central African Republic*, edited by Tatiana Carayannis and Louisa Lombard, 53–75. London: Zed Books, 2015.

Mayneri, A. C. *Sorcellerie et prophétisme en Centrafrique: L'imaginaire de la dépossession en pays banda*. Paris: Karthala, 2014.

Mbiti, J. S. 1970 "Christianity and Traditional Religions in Africa. *International Review of Mission*. Vol. LIX. Geneva: World Council of Churches, 1970.

———. *African Religions and Philosophy*. Nairobi: East African Educational Publishers, 1994.

———. "Relating Peace in African Religion to Theologies of Liberation and Reconstruction." In *Religion and Social Reconstruction in Africa*, edited by Elias Kifon Bongmba, 108–123. London and New York: Routledge, 2018.

McGregor, A. "South African Military Disaster in the Central African Republic: Part One – The Rebel Offensive." *Terrorism Monitor: In-Depth Analysis of War on Terror*. Vol. XI, no. 7 (2013).

McKenna, M. *Prophets: Words of Fire*. Maryknoll: Orbis Books, 2002.

Mehler, A. "Rebels and Parties: The Impact of Armed Insurgency on Representation in the Central African Republic." *Journal of Modern African Studies*. Vol. 49, no. 1 (2011):115–139. doi:10.1017/S0022278X10000674.

Ministère de la Réconciliation Nationale, du Dialogue Politique et de la Promotion de la Culture Civique. "Rapport des consultations populaires à la base en République centrafricaine." https://jfaki.blog/wp-content/uploads/2016/05/rapport-consultations-populaires.pdf.

Moenga, M. O. "A Response to the Biblical Question 'How Many Times Shall I Forgive My Brother?' (Matt 18:21–22)." In *Forgiveness, Peacemaking, and Reconciliation*, edited by David K. Ngaruiya and Rodney L. Reed, 3–29. Carlisle: Langham Global Library, 2020.

Monger, T. J., M. and Methuselah 2020. "God's Masterpiece: Ephesians 2:11–22 as Inspiration for Church's Involvement in Peacemaking and Reconciliation with People with Albinism in Tanzania." In *Forgiveness, Peacemaking, and*

Reconciliation, edited by David K. Ngaruiya and Rodney L. Reed, 103–26. Carlisle: Langham Global Library, 2020.

Muck, T. C. "Religion." In *Evangelical Dictionary of World Missions,* edited by A. Scott Moreau, 818–19. Grand Rapids: Baker Books, 2000.

Mulago, V. "Le pacte du sang et la communion alimentaire, pierres d'attente de la communion eucharistique." In *Des prêtres noirs s'interrogent: cinquante ans après* . . . 171–187. Edited by Léonard Santedi Kinkupu, Gérard Bissainthe et Meinrad Hebga. Paris: Karthala, 2006.

Murphy, C. *The Conceptual Foundations of Transitional Justice.* Cambridge: Cambridge University Press, 2017.

Mutwol, J. *Peace Agreements and Civil Wars in Africa: Insurgent Motivations, State Responses, and Third-Party Peacemaking in Liberia, Rwanda, and Sierra Leone.* New York: Cambria Press, 2009.

Mwaura, P. N. "Reconstructing Mission: The Church in Africa in the Service of Justice, Peace, and Reconciliation." In *Religion and Social Reconstruction in Africa*, edited by Elias Kifon Bongmba, 183–96. London & New York: Routledge, 2018.

Nash, K. "Political Unsettlement and Continuing Conflict in Central African Republic." *Peace Rep.* https://www.politicalsettlements.org/2018/11/18/political-unsettlement-and-continuing-conflict-in-central-african-republic/.

Neill, H. U. "What Hope for an Extended Ceasefire in the CAR?" *African Arguments.* https://africanarguments.org/2014/08/14/what-hope-for-an-extended-ceasefire-in-the-car-by-hanna-ucko-neill/.

Ngoupandé, J. P. *Chronique de la crise centrafricaine 1996–1997 : le syndrome Barracuda*. Paris: Harmattan, 1997.

Niebuhr, R. H. *Christ and Culture.* New York: Harper Collins, 2001.

Noah, L. L. *Reconciliation and Peace in South Sudan: A Christian Perspective.* Carlisle: Langham Global Library, 2012.

Nolan, A. *God in South Africa: The Challenge of the Gospel.* Grand Rapids: Wm. B. Eerdmans Publishing Company, 1988.

Nolte-Schamm, C. M. 2006. "A Comparison Between Christian and African Paradigms of Reconciliation and How They Could Dialogue for the benefit of South African Society." https://researchspace.ukzn.ac.za/items/2e295235-e44a-49b9-8087-21f6a3436e6c

Nsiku, E. K. "Isaiah." *Africa Bible Commentary*, edited by Tokunboh Adeyemo, 1363–469. Nairobi: WorldAlive Publishers, 2006.

O'Brien, P. T. "Fellowship, Communion, Sharing." In *Dictionary of Paul and His Letters*, edited by Gerald F. Hawthorne and Ralph P. Martin, 293–295. Downers Grove: InterVarsity Press, 1993.

Ochab, E. U. "The Religious War in the Central African Republic Continues." *Forbes.* https://www.forbes.com/sites/ewelinaochab/2018/05/09/the-religious-war-in-central-african-republic-continues/#45cab03f3c0d.

Oduro, T. 2015. "Contributions and Challenges of the African Instituted Churches in Developing African Theology." In *African Theology on the Way: Current Conversations*, edited by Diane B. Sinton, 46–55. Minneapolis: Fortress Press.

Oduro, T. et al. *Mission in African Way: A Practical Introduction to African Instituted Churches and their Sense of Mission.* Wellington: Christian Literature Fund, 2008.

Okello, J. B. O. "Analysis of an Africa Reflections on Evil." *Africa Journal of Evangelical Theology* 22, no. 2 (2006): 63–84.

Olowo, O. O. "Effects of Integrating Peace Education in the Nigeria Education System." *Journal of Education and Practice* 7, no. 18 (2016): 9–14.

Opongo, E. O. "Reconciliation in Complex Spaces: Christian-Cultural Approaches to Reconciliation in Post-Conflict Northern Uganda." *International Bulletin of Mission Research* 46, no. 2 (2022): 169–177. doi:10.1177/2396393211013674.

Ordonnance No. 88.006, article 12 du 5 Février 1988. https://uclgafrica-alga.org/wp-content/uploads/2019/05/Centrafrique-MDB-Ordonnance-88.006.pdf.

Oyètádé, B. A., and V. Fashole-Luke. "Sierra Leone: Krio and the Quest for National Integration." In *Language and National Identity in Africa*, edited by Andrew Simpson, 122–140. Oxford: Oxford University Press, 2008.

Pastoor, D. "Vulnerability Assessment of the Christians in the Central African Republic." *World Watch.* https://www.worldwatchmonitor.org/old-site-imgs-pdfs/2914097.pdf.

Père G. et C. Zondé. *De l'esclavage à la liberté : l'œuvre de libération de la mission Sainte-Famille 1894 à 1929.* Bangui: Foyer de Charité, 1987.

Pettersson, T. "UCDP Non-State Conflict Codebook Version 19.1." *Uppsala Conflict Data Program.* https://ucdp.uu.se/downloads/nsos/ucdp-nonstate-191.pdf.

Picco, E. "Can the Central African Truth Commission Do Better Than Its Predecessor?" *Justice Info.* https://www.justiceinfo.net/en/justiceinfo-comment-and-debate/opinion/43905-can-the-central-african-truth-commission-do-better-than-its-predecessor.html.

Prince, R. "Is the Central African Republic on the Verge of Genocide?" *Foreign Policy In Focus.* https://fpif.org/central-african-republic-verge-genocide/.

Radio Ndeke Luka. "Ali Darassa paraphant l'accord de réconciliation entre les groupes armés à Bria le 18 mars 2020." *Radio Ndeke Luka.* https://www.radiondekeluka.org/actualites/securite/35299-bria-un-nouvel-accord-de-reconciliation-entre-groupes-armes-sur-fond-de-tension-ethnique.html.

———. "Centrafrique: les communautés Goula et Rounga se réconcilient à Ndélé." *Radio Ndeke Luka.* https://www.radiondekeluka.org/actualites/securite/35887-

centrafrique-les-communautes-goula-et-rounga-se-reconcilient-a-ndele. html?fbclid=IwAR3yhr1kpPU0LE0Q6R255LF73BlUGGfifBMwxM-zgiEGrVoav4JceWDlX7M.

———. "Dialogue républicain: plus de 600 recommandations formulées par les participants." *Radio Ndeke Luka*. https://www.radiondekeluka.org/actualites/politique/38395-dialogue-republicain-plus-de-600-recommandations-formulees-par-les-participants.html.

Raghu, P. "From Retribution to Restoration in Sierra Leone: Fambul Tok's Drive to Heal Post-Civil Communities." *Inquiries: Social Sciences, Arts and Humanities*. Vol. 7, No. 7 (2015), http://www.inquiriesjournal.com/articles/1055/from-retribution-to-restoration-in-sierra-leone-fambul-toks-drive-to-heal-post-civil-communities.

Ramadan, T. "Tariq Ramadan (1962–): Texts." In *Tradition and Modernity: Christian and Muslim Perspectives*, Edited by David Marshall, 201–7. Washington, DC: Georgetown University Press, 2013.

Rambo, S. *Spirit and Trauma: A Theology of Remaining*. Louisville: Presbyterian Publishing Corporation, 2010.

Reconciliation as the Mission of God: Faithful Christians Witness in a World of Destructive Conflicts and Divisions. Pattaya, Thailand: Lausanne Occasional Paper No. 51, October 2004. https://lausanne.org/wp-content/uploads/2007/06/LOP51_IG22.pdf.

Reggy-Mamo, M. A. "Widows and Orphans." In *Africa Bible Commentary*, edited by Tokunboh Adeyemo, 1363–1439. Nairobi: WorldAlive Publishers, 2006.

Schreiter, R. "Peacemaking and Reconciliation." In *Global Dictionary of Theology*, edited by William A. Dyrness and Veli-Matti Kärkkäinen, 637–641. Downers Grove: InterVarsity Press, 2008.

Security Council Report. "Chronology of Events: Central African Republic." *Security Council Report*. https://www.securitycouncilreport.org/chronology/central-african-republic.php.

Sesay, S. M. "Sierra Leone: Government and Society." *Encyclopaedia Britannica Online*. https://www.britannica.com/place/Sierra-Leone/Government-and-society.

Shenk, D. W. *Justice, Reconciliation and Peace in Africa*. Nairobi: Uzima Press, 1983.

———. *Journeys of the Muslim Nation and the Christian Church: Exploring the Mission of Two Communities*. Waterloo: Herald Press, 2003.

Shepler, S. "The Rites of the Child: Global Discourse of Youth and Reintegrating Child Soldiers in Sierra Leone." *Journal of Human Rights*. Vol. 4. (2005):197–211, doi:10.1080/14754830590952143.

———. "Sierra Leone, Child Soldiers and Global Flows of Child Protection Expertise." In *The Upper Guinea Coast in Global Perspective*, edited by

Jacqueline Knörr and Christoph Kohl, 241–251. New York/Oxford: Berghahn Books, 2016.

Sichler, J. 2020 Transcribed from Ch 10 Clip Fambul Tok. Accessed 11 February 2020. https://www.youtube.com/watch?v=KbEiv42M2r4.

Smith, L. T. *Decolonizing Methodologies: Research and Indigenous Peoples*. London & New York: Zed Books, 2012.

Songo, N. "Le LaBi, 'rite d'initiation' des Gbaya." In *Peuples et culture de l'Adamawa (Cameroun)*, 181–186. Edited by Adala H. and Boutrais Jean. Paris: ORSTOM, 1993.

Stamm, J. J. "To Forgive." In *Theological Lexicon of the Old Testament*, Vol. 2, edited by Ernst Jenni and Claus Westermann. Translated by Mark E. Biddle; Peabody: Hendrickson Publishers, 1997.

Steuernagel, V. R. "To Seek to Transform Unjust Structures of Society." In *Mission in the Twenty-First Century: Exploring the Five Marks of Global Mission*, edited by Andrew F. Walls and Cathy Ross, 62–76. Maryknoll: Orbis Books, 2008.

Tako-Ali, P. A. "Les méthodes traditionnelles de résolution des conflits à Obo." *Radio Ndeke Luka*. https://www.radiondekeluka.org/debats/e-le-songo/34096-les-methodes-traditionnelles-de-resolution-des-conflits-a-obo.html.

Taylor, Charles, *A Secular Age*. Cambridge: Harvard University Press, 2007.

Taylor, J. B. *Primal World-Views: Christian Involvement in Dialogue with Traditional Thought Forms*. Ibadan: Daystar Press, 1976.

Taylor, J. V. *The Primal Vision: Christian Presence Amid African Religion*. London: SCM Press, 1963.

The New Humanitarian. "A Tentative Ceasefire in CAR." *Relief Web*. https://reliefweb.int/report/central-african-republic/tentative-ceasefire-car.

Thomas, Y. *Centrafrique: un destin volé – Histoire d'une domination française*. Marseille: Agone, 2016.

TRC. "Truth and Reconciliation Commission Act 2000." http://www.sierra-leone.org/Laws/2000-4.pdf.

Turner, H. "The Primal Religions of the World and Their Study." In *Australian Essays in World Religions*, edited by Victor C. Hayes, 27–37. Bedford Park: Australian Association for the Study of Religions, 19777.

Tutu, D. M. *No Future Without Forgiveness*. New York: Doubleday, 1999.

TV5 Monde. "Centrafrique: l'ex-président François Bozizé demande 'pardon' depuis son retour à Bangui." Youtube Video. https://www.youtube.com/watch?v=BVi5o2aU5Fg.

United Nations. *Rapport du Projet Mapping documentant les violations graves du droit international des droits de l'homme et du droit international humanitaire commises sur le territoire de la République centrafricaine de janvier 2033 à décembre 2015*. Bangui: UNHR, 2017.

Villarreal, J. E. M., and D. A. J Montalvo. "Sexual Violence in Post-Conflict Zones: Reflections on the Case of the Central African Republic." *Colombian Journal of Military and Strategic Studies*. Vol. 17, no. 27 (2019): 505-523. doi:10.21830/19006586.436.

Virculon, T. "A la recherche de la paix en Centrafrique. Médiations communautaires, religieuses et politiques." *IFRI*. https://www.ifri.org/sites/default/files/atoms/files/vircoulon_recherche_paix_centrafrique_2017.pdf.

Vlavonou, G. "Understanding the 'Failure' of the Seleka Rebellion." *African Security Review*. Vol. 23, no. 3 (2014): 318–326. doi:10.108010246029.931624.

Voice of America. "'Détérioration' de la sécurité et montée en puissance des groupes 'd'auto-défense' en Centrafrique, prévient l'ONU." *Voice of America*. https://www.voaafrique.com/a/deterioration-de-la-securite-et-montee-en-puissance-des-groupes-d-auto-defense-en-centrafrique-previent-l-onu/4176365.html.

Volf, M. *Exclusion and Embrace: A Theological Exploration of Identity, Otherness, and Reconciliation*. Nashville: Abingdon Press, 1989.

———. "Forgiveness, Reconciliation, and Justice: A Christian Contribution to a More Peaceful Social Environment." In *Forgiveness and Reconciliation: Religion, Public Policy, and Conflict Transformation*, edited by Raymond G. Helmick and Rodney L. Peterson, 27–49. Philadelphia and London: Templeton Foundation Press, 2002.

Vreÿ, F., and A. Esterhuyse. "South Africa and the Search for Strategic Effect in the Central African Republic." *Scientia Militaria, South African Journal of Military Studies* 44, no. 2 (2016): 1–27. doi:10.5787/44-2-1174.

Waliggo, J. M. "'The Synod of Hope' at a Time of Crisis in Africa." In *African Theology on the Way: Current Conversations*, edited by Diane B. Stinton, 35–45. Minneapolis: Fortress Press, 2015.

Walls, A. F. "The Background to the Project and the Term 'Primal.'" *Journal of African Christian Thought* 12, no. 1 (2009): 1–2.

———. *The Missionary Movement in Christian History: Studies in the Transmission of Faith*. New York: Orbis Books, 2017.

———. *The Cross-Cultural Process in Christian History: Studies in the Transmission and Appropriation of Faith*. Maryknoll: Orbis Books, 2002.

Wan Muhammad, R. "Forgiveness and Restorative Justice in Islam and the West: A Comparative Analysis." *Islam and Civilisational Renewal: A Journal Devoted to Contemporary Issues and Policy Research* 11, no. 2 (2020): 177–297.

Wendy, I. M. "The Motivations of Warlords and the Role of Militias in the Central African Republic." *Accord*. https://www.accord.org.za/conflict-trends/the-motivations-of-warlords-and-the-role-of-militias-in-the-central-african-republic/.

Weinstein, J. M. *Inside Rebellion: The Politics of the Insurgent Violence*. Cambridge: Cambridge University Press, 2007.

Welz, M. "Briefing: Crisis in the Central African Republic and the International Response." *African Affairs*. Vol. 113, no. 453 (2014): 601-610. DOI:10.1093/afraf/adu048.

Welz, M., and A. Meyer. "Empty Acronyms: Why the Central African Republic Has Many Peacekeepers (sic), But No Peace." *Foreign Affairs*. https://www.foreignaffairs.com/articles/2014-07-24/empty-acronyms.

Weys, Y. et al. *Mapping Conflict Motives: The Central African Republic*. Antwerp: International Peace Information Service, 2014.

White, L. "Blood Brotherhood Revisited: Kinship, Relationship, and the Body in East and Central Africa." *Africa* 64, no. 3 (1994): 359–372.

Wink, W. *Jesus and Nonviolence: A Third Way*. Minneapolis: Fortress Press, 2003.

———. *When Powers Fall: Reconciliation in the Healing of Nations* Minneapolis: Fortress Press, 1998.

———. *Engaging the Powers: Discernment and Resistance in a World of Domination*. Minneapolis: Fortress Press, 1989.

———. *Naming the Powers: The Language of Power in the New Testament*. Philadelphia: Fortress Press, 1984.

———. *Unmasking the Powers: The Invisible Forces that Determine Human Existence*. Philadelphia: Fortress Press, 1984.

Woodfork, J. *Culture and Customs of the Central African Republic*. Westport: Greenwood Press, 2006.

Yarafa, T. I. "La refonte des forces de défense et de sécurité, condition d'une paix et d'un développement durable en République centrafricaine." PhD diss., Université Clermont Auvergne, France, 2017. https://tel.archives-ouvertes.fr/tel-02091042/document.

Yoder, J. H. *The Politics of Jesus: Vicit Agnus Noster*, 2nd ed. Grand Rapids: William B. Eerdmans Publishing Company, 1994.

Yogo, E. E. *L'Etat et les groupes politico-militaires en Afrique centrale*. Paris: Publibook, 2017.

Zahar, M. J., and D. Mechoulan. "Peace by Pieces? Local Mediation and Sustainable Peace in the Central African Republic." *International Peace Institute*. https://www.ipinst.org/wp-content/uploads/2017/11/1701_Peace-by-Pieces.pdf.

Ziesler, J. "Righteousness." In *The Oxford Companion to the Bible*, edited by Bruce M. Metzger and Michael D. Coogan, 655–56. Oxford: Oxford University Press, 1993.

Langham Literature, with its publishing work, is a ministry of Langham Partnership.

Langham Partnership is a global fellowship working in pursuit of the vision God entrusted to its founder John Stott –

> *to facilitate the growth of the church in maturity and Christ-likeness through raising the standards of biblical preaching and teaching.*

Our vision is to see churches in the Majority World equipped for mission and growing to maturity in Christ through the ministry of pastors and leaders who believe, teach and live by the word of God.

Our mission is to strengthen the ministry of the word of God through:
- nurturing national movements for biblical preaching
- fostering the creation and distribution of evangelical literature
- enhancing evangelical theological education

especially in countries where churches are under-resourced.

Our ministry

Langham Preaching partners with national leaders to nurture indigenous biblical preaching movements for pastors and lay preachers all around the world. With the support of a team of trainers from many countries, a multi-level programme of seminars provides practical training, and is followed by a programme for training local facilitators. Local preachers' groups and national and regional networks ensure continuity and ongoing development, seeking to build vigorous movements committed to Bible exposition.

Langham Literature provides Majority World preachers, scholars and seminary libraries with evangelical books and electronic resources through publishing and distribution, grants and discounts. The programme also fosters the creation of indigenous evangelical books in many languages, through writer's grants, strengthening local evangelical publishing houses, and investment in major regional literature projects, such as one volume Bible commentaries like the *Africa Bible Commentary* and the *South Asia Bible Commentary*.

Langham Scholars provides financial support for evangelical doctoral students from the Majority World so that, when they return home, they may train pastors and other Christian leaders with sound, biblical and theological teaching. This programme equips those who equip others. Langham Scholars also works in partnership with Majority World seminaries in strengthening evangelical theological education. A growing number of Langham Scholars study in high quality doctoral programmes in the Majority World itself. As well as teaching the next generation of pastors, graduated Langham Scholars exercise significant influence through their writing and leadership.

To learn more about Langham Partnership and the work we do visit **langham.org**

www.ingramcontent.com/pod-product-compliance
Lightning Source LLC
Chambersburg PA
CBHW051540230426
43669CB00015B/2671